Public Service and Good Governance for the Twenty-First Century

PUBLIC SERVICE AND GOOD GOVERNANCE FOR THE TWENTY-FIRST CENTURY

Edited by James L. Perry

Foreword by Paul A. Volcker

PENN

UNIVERSITY OF PENNSYLVANIA PRESS

PHILADELPHIA

Published by
University of Pennsylvania Press
Philadelphia, Pennsylvania 19104-4112
www.upenn.edu/pennpress

Printed in the United States of America on acid-free paper
10 9 8 7 6 5 4 3 2 1

Library of Congress Cataloging-in-Publication Data
Names: Perry, James L., editor. | Volcker, Paul A., writer
    of foreword.
Title: Public service and good governance for the twenty-first
    century / edited by James L. Perry ; foreword by Paul A. Volcker.
Description: 1st edition. | Philadelphia : University of Pennsylvania
    Press, [2020] | Includes bibliographical references and index.
Identifiers: LCCN 2019044995 | ISBN 978-0-8122-5204-0 (hardcover)
Subjects: LCSH: Public administration—United States. | Civil
    service—United States. | United States—Politics and
    government—2017–
Classification: LCC JK421 .P825 2020 | DDC 351.73—dc23
LC record available at https://lccn.loc.gov/2019044995

To the millions of public servants across America who make our democracy special. Without their commitment, good judgment, and sacrifice, our democracy could not function effectively. It is our hope that the ideas in this book will help transform their public spirit, on which we depend, into real differences for the lives of all Americans.

CONTENTS

FOREWORD

Paul A. Volcker

I recently had the rare good fortune of celebrating my ninety-first birthday, which afforded an opportunity to reflect on the changes that have occurred over these past nine decades.

They have been enormous, and our approach to governance has not been exempted. The powers and expenditures of the federal government have been extended to vast new retirement, health, and welfare programs. National security still accounts for 16 percent of the federal budget, with enormous technological changes. State and local governments are hard pressed to maintain the educational systems and infrastructure on which we are all dependent. Electronics are rapidly damaging how we communicate with each other.

Amid all the change, our governments have grown in size, in complexity, in responsibility. The strains and lapses in effective government are evident. Our ability to maintain healthy democratic practices is at risk.

Can our great republic maintain the sense of responsiveness, of efficiency, of integrity essential to maintaining trust and confidence in our government processes? Whether in the small towns like that in which I was born; in our national capital, where I spent most of my professional life; or in great urban centers like the one in which I now live, the challenge is enormous.

Are we paying enough attention to the need for educated, dedicated public servants who are committed, able, and willing to devote the energy and intelligence required? Do we have the right support systems and protections in place?

The Volcker Alliance stands for one central theme. A successful American democracy at home, equipped to continue the effort to establish a peaceful and prosperous global society, rests on the faithful and effective execution of government at every level.

The volume before you suggests the nature and breadth of what must be done in our schools and universities, in efforts to rethink organizational needs, by well-educated civil servants, and in order to bring forward the full potential of new technologies. It probes for intelligent answers. It deserves attention.

Introduction

James L. Perry

Two big ideas are at the core of this book. The first is that Americans variously perceive the state of governance in America as broken, frustrating, and unresponsive. A common expression may summarize public sentiment: "The wheels are coming off!" This sentiment is rooted in at least three simultaneous developments: government's failure to do basic work that once was taken for granted, an accelerating pace of change that quickly makes past standards of performance antiquated, and a dearth of the intellectual capital that generates the know-how to fix the gulfs between expectations and performance.

The second big idea is how to respond to the dissatisfaction and distrust surrounding the state of governance in the United States. In the early 1990s, Camille Cates Barnett, then city manager of Austin, Texas, observed that a core value—perhaps *the* core value within American public administration since its inception in the 1880s—was reform (Barnett, 1993). Since the beginning of the Progressive Era, Americans have been committed to better administration of their government at all levels, federal, state, and local. The spirit of reform is the second big idea at the core of this book.

These two big ideas—that the capacity for effective governance is diminishing and that it must be reformed to meet the aspirations of the American people—are veering in opposite directions. These ideas are reminiscent of those that animated two commissions headed by Paul A. Volcker.

Critical Questions

In seeking to illuminate these ideas, the contributors to this book address five critical questions. The first question—the benchmark that begins the conversation—is, What is the state of government today? Regardless of how favorably some among us may construe government's current performance, a clear majority of Americans view its performance as weak and getting weaker—and their trust in its operations is declining as a result. How can we characterize government's performance today, and how does it measure up to past performance?

A second critical question involves new sources of jeopardy—and opportunity—for governments, ranging from regulatory challenges, to technological change, to fiscal and political stresses: What are the coming disruptions to government, governance, and public service? Knowing the changing context of governance and government permits us to understand contemporary challenges to government's performance and prospects for closing gaps between aspirations and achievements.

Recent and long-standing trends, what government is capable of delivering now, and changes and disruptions experienced in the near term will forcefully shape the future, which leads to a third critical question: What government will emerge as a result of our past practices and the coming disruptions? This question is fraught with uncertainty, but answers to it are vital to society's well-being.

The fourth critical question envisions what should emerge: What institutions and structures will ready us to meet the coming changes? Given the enormous challenges we face, the complexity of our problems, and the impediments to planned change, specifying the architecture and rules for institutions and structures is daunting. How should the new institutions and structures differ from those that preceded them? Who should initiate change? These and other questions confront those who are seriously focused on proactive change.

Although much about the future architecture of and demands on government is unknown, we must begin now to ask the fifth critical question, which involves talent: What knowledge, skills, and abilities will be needed to contend with emerging government and governance realities? Tomorrow's government will be shaped by people who are developing today, so we have no time to waste. How will tomorrow's talent be developed? Where will we turn for leadership? Questions about future talent deserve widespread attention across our society, from governments, think tanks, universities, political and civic leaders, and citizens.

The State of Government

The self-critical nature of American society and the continuous attention to reform routinely force us to ask, What is the state of government today? Although the response occasionally veers toward the self-satisfied—as in the answer given in the president's annual State of the Union address to Congress, "The state of our union is strong"—the usual response is filled with lists of things that need to be improved, suggesting that the cup is at least half-empty. A viewpoint expressed frequently throughout this book is that our legislators and leaders have much to do to put America's government and governing institutions on a course that inspires more confidence as midcentury approaches.

Paul C. Light's essay conveys the spirit of stocktaking, assessment, and self-critical reflection that is prominent in the book. He codifies government's greatest achievements of the latter half of the twentieth century (Light, 2002). The list includes many achievements that most Americans would agree are significant, among them rebuilding Europe after World War II, ensuring safe food and drinking water, and promoting financial security in retirement. Similar achievements are more difficult to identify today. Light concludes that decades of disinvestment in administrative capacity have forced many agencies to pursue their missions with minimal capacity, and, absent reforms, faithful execution of the laws is more a hope than a guarantee. His trenchant analysis echoes across the contributions in this volume.

Disruptive Influences

If the performance gaps documented by Light in Chapter 1 were fixed targets, then the task of remedying them might be reducible to a series of manageable and known challenges. But fixed targets are a rarity, especially in a rapidly changing world. The contributors to Part I of the book, "Disruptive Influences," explore unpredictability, threat, and opportunity in several well-known domains. They focus largely on the second of the five critical questions introduced at the beginning of this essay: What are the coming disruptions to government, governance, and public service?

Although each contribution in Part I focuses on distinct disruptive influences, they all share a unified perspective. The relative stability of the late twentieth century is being displaced by extensive technological and social innovations and broad-based populist political movements. Technological innovations such as artificial intelligence (AI) carry with them great uncertainty and represent a significant threat because they could alter work, the transparency of operations, and privacy more radically than any other innovations we have experienced in our lifetimes. Social media appeared to alter power relationships when they were used to great effect during the Arab Spring, but their subsequent use as a tool for Russian intervention in American elections has cast them in a new light. Donald Trump's style of populism burst on the stage, surprising his opponents and delighting his supporters, who saw a new reality dawning. Not only has the Trump brand of populism been replicated elsewhere—in Hungary and Brazil, for example—but it has also helped to call into question globalization and the world order established in the aftermath of World War II.

Such contemporary disruptive influences have many implications for governance, government performance, and the capacity to "right the ship." Financial technology and its regulation, for example, simultaneously create prospects for positive innovation, regulatory capture by the most powerful players, and the use of technology to undermine the public interest. Recent experiences with social media reinforce the view that this innovation can promote democratic movements but simultaneously create opportunities for control by interests at odds with democracy and democratic institutions.

Another consequence is the magnification of uncertainty. This theme is ever present in the media's coverage of Trump, who attained the presidency with promises to "drain the swamp" and challenged what has been taken for granted in the way the American political system has historically worked. Although AI has been welcomed for its potential to improve efficiency and effectiveness across many domains of society, Ramayya Krishnan illustrates many ways in which it magnifies uncertainty, ranging from hidden bias associated with policies derived from machine learning to unknowns embedded in the flow of news from the internet.

A by-product of the current disruptive influences is declining trust in institutions and declining confidence in their efficacy. Declining trust in institutions is the result of many factors, not just the present disruptions, but these disruptions may be disproportionately significant because of the uncertainties they create in efforts to reestablish public trust. To the extent that the disruptions undermine confidence in the efficacy of governance, they are significant factors in the big idea that governance is failing. The declining trust in institutions is a central focus in Part II, which looks at adaptations required of our institutions in light of the state of government and the changes occurring across society that are addressed in the first four chapters of the book.

Emerging Government and Governance

If you were a legislator, political appointee, or civil servant, the picture I have just painted might give you pause before you crossed the threshold of your office. The federal government's current performance is sobering, perhaps less encouraging than at any time in the last half century. Ordinary changes, such as mounting federal debt, may cause society to reach a tipping point. Technological, regulatory, and political disruption is upon us. Do we have the institutional capacity to weather the storm? What resides in our institutional bag of resources that might rescue us from seemingly dire straits?

Part II, "Emerging Government and Governance," offers some answers to these questions. It focuses on two of the critical questions that are logical extensions of the first four chapters: What government will emerge as a result of our past practices and the coming disruptions? What institutions and structures will ready us to meet the coming challenges? Much like the phenomena the contributors describe, the answers to these questions are tentative, accompanied by uncertainties.

The first essay in Part II, by Francis Fukuyama, is firmly rooted in the Constitution, the most resilient and valued of American institutions. Fukuyama poses the question, What is the intrinsic function of government that cannot or should not be surrendered to nongovernmental actors? Fukuyama, like many of the contributors to this volume, is concerned by the scale of outsourcing and the propensity to do so. He explores the question of what the intrinsic functions of government are in order to identify which functions can legitimately be delegated to bodies outside government.

At least two aspects of Fukuyama's analysis reverberate across Part II. The first is his assertion that American institutions have evolved over time to accommodate public demands that may now put them at odds with more encompassing public values. Fukuyama refers to the accommodations as "workarounds," which is a term useful for describing how actors work creatively to achieve the goals of government when confronted with conflicting choices. In the case of outsourcing, we have crossed the boundaries of decisions that can appropriately be made in the public interest by private agents.

Donald F. Kettl's analysis of the mismatch between institutions and policy parallels Fukuyama's workaround argument. Kettl contends that we do not focus our electoral debates on what we are really doing or how we are doing it. Citizens are thereby becoming ever more distant and disconnected from the government they elect, the services they pay for, and the institutions designed to serve them. Many of government's most important problems flow directly from this mismatch of institutions and policy. In fact, it is even responsible for at least some of the hyperpartisanship that is fueling discontent with our democracy.

The second aspect of Fukuyama's analysis that surfaces in the other chapters of Part II is his argument that the "fixes"—that is, reforms—that would enable our institutions to operate in accordance with their original design will be difficult, if not impossible, to enact. Fukuyama concludes, for instance, that the civil service reforms necessary to restore the intrinsic functions of government that have been surrendered to nongovernmental actors are just not feasible in today's political climate. John J. DiIulio Jr. argues that several developments have made improving government performance and achieving public service reform not only more difficult but seemingly impossible. He sees three obstacles to reform: the growth in mass public disaffection toward—and ignorance about—government, the ever-widening gap between our limited government constitutional system and our actual "Leviathan by Proxy" state, and the present and potential pitfalls and prospects of paving a path to better performance and real reform via technological fixes.

Government performance is at the core of the first big idea I refer to earlier, and it is a bright spot in the government emerging from recent challenges. We have gradually become more attentive to and better at integrating performance measurement and management into the way government works, as argued by Shelley Metzenbaum. The transformation may have begun with the Government Performance and Results Act of 1993, and the commitment has withstood several presidential transitions, indicating bipartisan consensus. Metzenbaum suggests a path forward for outcome-emphasizing, goal-focused, data-rich government.

Public Service and Public Leaders

The primary focus of Part II is America's governance institutions, their fidelity to their historical functions, and the institutional rules that may need to be modified to keep pace with expectations and accelerating change. Part III, "Public Service and Public Leaders," looks at the human capital needed to shape our future. It is devoted to the last of the five critical questions I refer to in the introduction to this essay: What knowledge, skills, and abilities will be needed to contend with emerging government and governance realities? How will this talent be developed?

The contributors to this volume show that the human capital equation is more complex and nuanced than we typically acknowledge. William W. Bradley's essay calls attention to an often overlooked component of human capital, the public service ethic, what has come to be called public service motivation (Perry and Wise, 1990). The ethos that Bradley describes, and that motivated people before him like Paul Volcker and so many others, is integral to building a government and public service for the twenty-first century. Good government depends on people who are committed to the missions of their respective agencies and to the public interest.

The human capital equation also depends on specific knowledge, skills, and abilities that will be necessary to serve the public interest in the future. Paul R. Verkuil identifies important competencies but is also attentive to the systems that connect people to the work of government. What systems are in place to meet today's human capital challenges? Verkuil is aware that although we may know what competencies must be marshaled to meet demands on the federal government, the present systems for responding often do not work. He warns of the use of contractors, which garner attention throughout the book, and how they can simultaneously undermine the civil service system and ensure the highly qualified workforce it needs.

Angela Evans focuses on the diminishing relevance of schools of public affairs and public policy and how they can reclaim their place in emerging government challenges. She contends that these schools must reexamine their unique role in public affairs, the programs they offer, the curriculum they deliver, the partners with whom they collaborate, and the students they recruit. She builds a case for what schools of public policy can offer to ensure that their graduates engage constructively in policy deliberation and execution and how the schools instill skills to address the demands and expectations of people affected by public decisions.

Developing synergy among human capital assets and smoothing fissures in the fragmented American political system often depend on effective leadership. Leadership in turbulent times is not just about doing things right; it is about doing the right things. This is a shared process whereby leaders work with others in the development and implementation of public policies. Norma M. Riccucci envisions the emerging public leader in this context, focusing on the skill set and values needed to steer public processes.

An Agenda for the Future

The answers to the critical questions posed in this book inform an agenda surrounding the big ideas. I highlight this agenda in this section.

Big Idea 1: The Governance Deficit

The governance deficit in America is complex and multitiered, rooted in simultaneous developments: government's failure to do basic work that we once took for granted, an accelerating pace of change that quickly makes past standards of performance antiquated, and a dearth of intellectual capital to fix the gulfs between expectations and performance. Let me summarize what we now know about these developments.

THE DECLINE OF ADMINISTRATIVE AND GOVERNANCE CAPACITY

Government's capacity has declined in recent decades. The decline begins in the core administrative capacity to tend reliably and effectively to both the big and the small of the daily operations of governmental services. Many of the basic systems on which the U.S. federal government relies— procurement, information technology, program management, and hiring and compensation, among others— either are performing well below past levels or are broken altogether. Many factors account for the decline in administrative capacity, but disinvestment—deferring investments that keep pace with demands and accelerating change—is the major reason. Declines at the federal level do not necessarily affect state and local capacity, but the spillovers are likely substantial and consequential for many programs and services.

Governance capacity has also declined, and it may be harder to fix than administrative capacity. The decline in governance capacity is an outgrowth of changes in the "instruments" or "tools" used by government (Salamon,

1981) during the past four decades. As policy makers have progressively shifted from direct government provision of services to indirect, private instruments (for example, contracting, outsourcing, tax expenditures, intergovernmental grants, and public-private partnerships), government has shifted from maintaining its own expertise and human capital to assuming responsibility for monitoring and managing third parties. Some of the asset transfers in this evolution have been direct—for example, substitution of private human capital for public—but others have been indirect, involving transfers of political power and decision making to different spheres of American society (Perry, 2007). One of the starkest examples of the evolution involves the creation, rise, and demise of Fannie Mae and Freddie Mac, two government-sponsored enterprises whose actions helped spark the Great Recession (Stanton, 2009). The story of these two corporations is a lesson in the larger problem of the devolution of governance capacity.

ACCELERATING PACE OF CHANGE THAT OUTSTRIPS PERFORMANCE STANDARDS

The shift from direct to indirect provision of public services is the result of a political system seeking to respond to public demands. We turn to outsourcing, for example, to overcome talent shortages and transparency-rule inertia. The workarounds that routinely embody creative attempts to meet public demands, however, have consequences, intended and unintended. We have reached the juncture at which the unintended consequences are no longer tolerable because they threaten the foundations of the very legitimacy of government.

The mismatches between institutions, policies, and structures are in urgent need of reconciliation to stem both the decline in governance capacity and the erosion of political accountability. Failure to act creates the potential for a loss of sovereignty, the alienation of citizens from democratic government, and a loss of control in the creation of public value as outgrowths of the evolution toward indirect and private delivery of public services. The unhealthy consequences eventually extend to the pinnacle of our governance institutions, the functioning and legitimacy of democracy itself.

The difficulties in enforcing accountability take a toll on citizens. The inability to effect change, or at least hold the appropriate parties responsible, diminishes citizens' confidence in the legitimacy of governance institutions. The decline of legitimacy feeds a corresponding decline in citizen confidence and engagement.

DEARTH OF INTELLECTUAL CAPITAL

Although it may be difficult to know what information we are lacking, I conclude that the deficits in the intellectual capital necessary to fix the gulfs between expectations and performance are substantial. The essays in this volume show that we have large gaps in knowledge about what courses of action to pursue to address an array of important questions concerning technology, institutions, competencies, and more.

For example, our intellectual capital surrounding technology poses several quandaries about appropriate courses of action. Waves of new technologies, physical and social, are resetting the ways governments do business. The essays in this volume describe a multidirectional future in which what we fear or are incapable of controlling today turns out to be the thing that rescues us. It is possible that blockchain and AI could solve many existing issues in how we view government and governance, concerning everything from the accuracy and intrusiveness of regulation to the efficiency and effectiveness of public service delivery. Putting our faith in magic-bullet solutions like new technology, however, often results in unmet expectations and sometimes in outright and miserable failure. This is not to reject rosy scenarios, but simply to suggest that we should not rely on them. Good results are more likely to flow from assuming individual and collective agency, knowing the context of and opportunities in our environment, and expending the intellectual and other forms of capital necessary to change the direction we are headed.

Two aspects of the intellectual capital needed to guide change deserve mention here. One is experimentation, which has become increasingly common in our search for solutions to public problems. The United Kingdom's Behavioural Insights Team and former president Barack Obama's Social and Behavioral Sciences Team are two examples. The second aspect is knowledge about the processes of change themselves. We need to better understand how to effect change within the multiple layers of the modern American governance system. This is a tall order, but one that is merited because of what is at stake.

Big Idea 2: The Reform Imperative

The contributors to this book came together to share their considerable talent, experience, and wisdom regarding key governance challenges facing the nation and how our institutions and public servants might respond. They propose many ideas for building a government and public service for the mid-twenty-first century. In concluding, I would like to highlight some prospects for reform.

REMEDYING ADMINISTRATIVE DISINVESTMENT

Early in the book's first chapter, Paul Light proposes one avenue that I want to highlight because it represents a worst-case scenario. He writes, "Federal employees still make miracles every day, but many do so against the odds created by poorly designed policy, antiquated administrative systems, uncertain funding, widening skill gaps, and uncertain political leadership." Light's observation is complimentary to federal employees, but his point is that we do not want to have to rely on miracles to get the work of our government done satisfactorily. The American public deserves something better—and more dependable—to solve the extraordinary problems we collectively face.

GROWING INTELLECTUAL CAPITAL

Angela Evans identifies a host of ways our universities and their students can better contribute to public service. American universities are among our most effective and highly regarded institutions. They can and should help lead the way in increasing the capacity and performance of our government and public service. Similarly, as Norma Riccucci argues, universities and governments at all levels can play prominent roles in developing talent needed for the emerging demands of public leadership.

Beyond what leaders and managers in government can do at their initiative, creating the good government America needs will require solutions that are broad and confirmed in the political realm. The deficiencies of policy design, antiquated administrative systems, and underfunding can be resolved neither by heroism nor by individual leaders and managers acting within their assigned offices. Collective action by political leaders and citizens in the political sphere is necessary.

CREATING A CIVIL SERVICE FOR THE
TWENTY-FIRST CENTURY

One common conclusion among many of the contributors to this book was that comprehensive personnel or civil service reform is necessary. The calls for comprehensive civil service reform reflect judgments about both the deficiencies of current federal systems in providing adequate human capital for federal missions and the perceived importance of having the right people to execute those missions. Despite a consensus about the need for civil service reform, some contributors were pessimistic about the possibility of achieving such a reform.

In the absence of comprehensive civil service reform, I can envision an alternative that is more piecemeal but strategic, targeting improvements in talent and pay, like recent proposals from the National Academy of Public Administration (2017, 2018) and the Partnership for Public Service and the Volcker Alliance (2018). The growing evidence from research on prosocial and public service motivation represents important intellectual capital (Christensen, Paarlberg, and Perry, 2017) that has been largely unused to reform federal civil service. Although some changes, such as pay reform, would require legislative action and therefore political consensus, others could be executed by administrative action, thereby preserving time-honored merit system principles.

CLOSING THE GAP BETWEEN INSTITUTIONAL CAPACITY AND GOVERNANCE DEMANDS

One path for reducing mismatches between institutions and public demands eschews comprehensiveness and instead pursues a disaggregated approach to reform. It depends on changing dynamics within different policy domains rather than administrative systems, creating effective policy through multiple coherent legislative decisions. This may be the political equivalent of well-matched institutions and policy. Thus, a disaggregated approach to reform in the policy realm may complement reforms in different administrative domains.

It is worth noting, however, that the contributors repeatedly use the word *bipartisan* to describe successful reform. Bipartisanship is associated with government's biggest successes over the course of the past seventy years. In contrast, the contributors use the terms *political polarization* and *hyperpartisan* either to describe past policy failures or to explain why progress on any manner of reform is so difficult. We should seek to rebuild bipartisanship so that the broad changes needed to restore good government become possible in the political realm. This will be a heavy burden, but one worth bearing.

This brings me to my final point. No matter how many smart and thoughtful civil servants are dedicated to the faithful and effective execution of public policy, political actors need to come together to create broad solutions in the political realm. In the absence of actions to change laws for the better, there is a real ceiling on government's performance. The voices of the outstanding scholars, opinion leaders, and public servants gathered together in this volume are unified in their assertion that we have reached a juncture at which both effective political and administrative actions are needed to elevate government's performance. It is now time for politicians, public servants, and citizens to begin this task.

Bibliography

Barnett, Camille Cates. 1993. "A Call to Action: A Marshall Plan for America: Renew Our Core Value of Reform." *Public Management* 75 (1): 6.

Christensen, Robert K., Laurie Paarlberg, and James L. Perry. 2017. "Public Service Motivation Research: Lessons for Practice." *Public Administration Review* 77 (4): 529–42.

Light, Paul C. 2002. *Government's Greatest Achievements: From Civil Rights to Homeland Defense.* Washington, DC: Brookings Institution.

National Academy of Public Administration. 2017. *No Time to Wait: Building a Public Service for the 21st Century.* Washington, DC: National Academy of Public Administration. https://www.napawash.org/uploads/Academy_Studies/No-Time-to-Wait_Building-a -Public-Service-for-the-21st-Century.pdf.

———. 2018. *No Time to Wait, Part 2: Building a Public Service for the 21st Century.* Washington, DC: National Academy of Public Administration. https://www.napawash.org /uploads/Academy_Studies/NTTW2_09192018_WebVersion.pdf.

Partnership for Public Service and the Volcker Alliance. 2018. "Recommendations from Renewing America's Civil Service." https://www.volckeralliance.org/recommenda-tions-renewing-americas-civil-service.

Perry, James L. 2007. "Democracy and the New Public Service." *American Review of Public Administration* 37 (1): 3–16.

Perry, James L., and Lois R. Wise. 1990. "The Motivational Bases of Public Service." *Public Administration Review* 50 (3): 367–73.

Salamon, Lester M. 1981. "Rethinking Public Management: Third-Party Government and the Changing Forms of Government Action." *Public Policy* 29:255–75.

Stanton, Thomas H. 2009. "Government-Sponsored Enterprises: Reality Catches Up to Public Administration Theory." *Public Administration Review* 69 (4): 632–39.

CHAPTER 1

Catch-22 Government

Federal Performance in Peril

Paul C. Light

The federal government is caught in a catch-22 that promises to frustrate faithful execution of the law far into the future. Asked to do more with less every year, many departments and agencies are caught in a cascade of highly visible breakdowns that increases public demand for major repairs in how government works even as the cascade undermines confidence that such repairs are worth the investment. Absent comprehensive action to improve performance, public anger will continue rising, while the odds of improvement will remain doubtful.

Federal employees still make miracles every day, but many do so against the odds created by poorly designed policy, antiquated administrative systems, uncertain funding, widening skill gaps, and uncertain political leadership. Although the federal government continues to make progress on long-standing endeavors such as establishing financial security for older Americans and combatting more recent threats such as terrorism, too many national priorities are only an accident away from a breakdown.

Along the way, many Americans have come to believe the worst about the federal government. Some of these doubts are rooted in partisan conflict and a drumbeat of antigovernment rhetoric, but some reflect the escalation of government failures. Americans pay close attention to federal performance in the news and can find plenty of cause for concern. Exaggerated though the stories about federal failure might be in this era of intense polarization and fake news, Americans may be quite right to believe that the federal government cannot be trusted to do the right thing. As this chapter suggests, the pressure to do more with less is unlikely to relent until Congress and presidents realize that it is impossible to deliver twenty-first-century performance in twentieth-century organizations that still use variations of nineteenth-century systems.

The federal government's peril affects all elements of the intergovernmental system as states and localities struggle to absorb resource shortages and growing responsibilities. One level's failures and frustration become another level's challenge. Much as state and local governments have tried to fill the gaps created by federal neglect, the intergovernmental system relies on all levels to do their jobs well. Catch-22 government in Washington, DC, produces a wave of secondary and tertiary pressure that undermines performance in every corner of the nation, not to mention the international community.

Performance in Peril

The emergence of catch-22 government can be tracked with every data point I have been monitoring since I worked with the National Commission on the Public Service in 1989 (National Commission, 1989). Despite repeated calls for urgent action issued by dozens of blue-ribbon commissions, study groups, congressional hearings, and presidential promises over the decades, most of the trends I follow have worsened as government faces increased pressure to do more with less.

The pressure can be found at all three levels of the federal delivery process. At the workforce level, the personnel system undermines faithful execution with a sluggish hiring process, failure to address workforce aging, and lack of access to resources and training. At the production level, the federal bureaucracy weakens execution with skill gaps in hard-to-recruit occupations, an ever-thicker leadership hierarchy, and a blended workforce driven more by catch-22 pressure than by careful sorting. At the outcome level, the pressure to do more with less can be tracked by employee frustrations with their leaders and organizations, public demands for more of almost everything government delivers mixed with distrust toward the institutions in charge of the delivery, and a recent rise in the number of government breakdowns.

The three trends and their components amplify each other through constant feedback loops—for example, the sluggish hiring system amplifies the impact of employee aging, which widens government-wide skill gaps in hard-to-recruit occupations, which increases the dependence on contract and grant employees, which may lead to government breakdowns, which may increase public demands for smaller government, which may increase the catch-22 effect. Tempting though it might be to look for a single domino that might reverse decades of neglect and tinkering, the interactions suggest the need for comprehensive reforms that tackle the federal performance crisis more broadly. However, as this chapter will conclude, it is not at all clear that Congress and the president have the capacity to design and pursue comprehensive action given recent changes in the tides of federal management reform.

A Public Service Under Stress

The federal workforce is essential to the faithful execution of the law. Although often criticized as overpaid and underworked, the clear majority of federal employees work hard to deliver on the promises Congress and presidents make. At the same time, my trend lines show continued problems in the federal hiring process, an aging workforce, high promotion speeds, and an inflated performance appraisal process.

Waiting for Arrival

There are many ways to measure hiring effectiveness, not the least of which is the quality of the workforce it produces. Quality being infinitely subjective, however, the easiest way to track effectiveness is time to hire, shorter being generally better than longer. In theory, applicants should move from application to "onboarding" without delay. In reality, the federal government continues to impose time penalties at every step of the process. Hiring speed increased during the Obama administration, but its simplistic eighty-day post-to-process goal was more than twice as long as the goals of its private and nonprofit competitors in industries such as accounting, aerospace, biotechnology, energy, health, higher education, logistics, telecommunications, and transportation (Chamberlain, 2017).

The Senate Committee on Homeland Security and Governmental Affairs focused on time to hire when it pressed the new Obama administration to fill most federal vacancies in eighty days or less: "Those seeking federal employment have long faced an opaque, lengthy, and unnecessarily complex process that serves the interests of neither federal agencies nor those seeking to work for them. . . . Weak recruiting, unintelligible job announcements, onerous application requirements, an overly long hiring process, and poor communications with applicants deter potential candidates from applying and cause many of those who do apply to abandon the effort before a hiring decision is made" (Committee on Homeland Security and Government Affairs, 2010).

The Obama administration deflected the legislation by launching the first of three hiring reforms in May 2010. "I understand the frustration of every applicant who previously has had to wade through the arcane Federal hiring process," the director of the Office of Personnel Management (OPM) said of the president's decision to create a plain-language application for most jobs and allow résumés and cover letters in lieu of essay questions. "If qualified applicants want to serve our country through the Federal service, then our application process should facilitate that" (Davidson, 2010). The commitment was strong enough to convince Congress to shelve the Senate's bill, but not strong enough to move the federal hiring model from its "post and pray" motto to "post and pursue."

Despite reports on recent congressional hearings with hopeful goals such as *Jobs, Jobs, Jobs: Transforming Federal Hiring* (2010) and *Uncle Sam Wants You! Recruitment in the Federal Government* (2009), comprehensive reform remains a distant goal. Even the federal government's ongoing overhaul of its sluggish one-stop-shopping USAJobs hiring platform is unlikely to have an impact if its "human-centered design" does not lead to good jobs.

At least for now, USAJobs is more a disappointment than a source of pride. As one expert told a Senate roundtable in 2016, "USAJobs has become home to a seething group of confused and angry job seekers and fulfills a main purpose for a limited set of people desperately seeking any kind of employment or those who don't really know what job they seek" (Davidson, 2016). Other witnesses at the roundtable showed more confidence in the job seekers, but all agreed on the need for significant reform.

Aging Upward

The federal workforce is aging ever closer to a demographic crisis created by a steady rise in its number of older employees. As of September 2017, there were about five federal employees over 50 years of age for every one employee under 30. Translated from ratios into headcounts, the number of federal employees under 30 held steady between 2001 and 2017 at about 115,000, the number over 55 also held steady at about 850,000, average age crept past 47.5, and eligibility for retirement across the workforce passed the 30 percent mark (Light, 2018a).

The aging confirms a potential "retirement tsunami" as federal employees move closer to exit. "The rapid shift of the workforce profile is significant and a bit shocking," federal personnel expert Jeffrey Neal writes. "This rapid demographic shift is unlike what we have seen in the past and it is safe to say no one knows when current employees will retire. Societal trends are moving in the direction of longer careers, both for lifestyle and economic reasons. If this continues, we are likely to see a retirement bubble at some point in the future" (Neal, 2014).

The timing of the retirement wave may be uncertain, but its effects are predictable. First, it will create a "brain drain" as the government's intellectual capital and institutional memory decline. These assets are not easily gained through the federal government's weak career development systems. Moreover, much of the nation's intellectual capital has been shaped by repeated budget and hiring freezes that teach younger employees how government does not work. The best way to secure these assets has been through contract and grant employees who acquired their skills inside the corridors of government.

Second, the retirement wave will create employee shortages at the middle levels of government, where so many contract and grant employees work. Service contract employees rarely reach the top of the federal hierarchy, but they often perform tasks that would have been reserved for federal employees in the past. Absent a steady pipeline of civil service employees, federal managers and supervisors have little choice but to call for outside help. The contract and grant employees who fill the gaps are often highly qualified for the work, but they cannot take the higher-level posts without crossing the dividing line. They also create dependency that managers and supervisors cannot easily break.

These retirements could provide the opportunity to strengthen the career paths and development opportunities that are essential for recruiting the next generation of federal employees. According to the federal government's own personnel surveys, younger and older federal employees share the same desire for constructive performance conversations, career development and training, work-life balance, an inclusive work environment, involvement in decisions, and open communication, but younger employees are less likely to believe their talents are well used in the workplace, know how their work relates to their organization's goals and priorities, say their work gives them a sense of accomplishment, or know what is excepted of them (U.S. Government Accountability Office [GAO], 2015a).

Speeding Toward Promotion

Time on the job drives advancement for most federal employees through nearly automatic promotions up the formal career ladder. Departments and agencies can reduce promotion speed during funding crises, but the career ladder guarantees promotions across the federal government's ten-step pay system and presumes steady movement up its fifteen-grade classification ladder. Federal employees can also rise through reclassification into higher-level jobs or promotions into vacancies created as other employees move up ahead of them.

Promotions also depend on performance. Much as federal employees themselves question the relationship, there is at least some evidence to suggest a link between annual performance appraisals and advancement. According to a recent study of federal personnel records from the 1988–2003 period, white-collar employees who received an "outstanding" performance rating during the period were 50 percent more likely to receive promotions than employees who received a "fully successful" rating. Because employees tend to receive the same ratings from year to year, outstanding performers advance faster than their fully successful peers over the long term (Oh and Lewis, 2013).

Education and the experience that goes with it also matter for promotion speed—educational advancement appears to be closely linked to upward movement. Indeed, many higher-level jobs require a college degree or more. Age and federal support give current employees the opportunity to gain more education, as does the ongoing recruitment of new employees (Bolton et al., 2015).

Promotion speed often increases during employment caps, cuts, and freezes. It also increases in retention wars with contract firms and grant-funded agencies, think tanks, research universities, and highly specialized nonprofits such as the RAND Corporation. As a former OPM senior officer recently recalled, the movement of talented employees to contract and grant posts increased promotion speed, largely as a result of supervisors using pro-motions as a retention strategy and backdoor bonus system:

> This pressure comes not only from employees but from management as well. Supervisors use constant upgrades as a retention strategy, es-pecially for employees in technical and hard-to-fill positions. Three years of pay freezes, increased oversight of awards programs and elim-ination of promotion opportunities due to senior people who have delayed retirement, means that the only avenue for getting a raise (other than a periodic step increase) is to get your position reclassi-fied to a higher grade, regardless of whether the job has changed and thus deserves a higher grade. (Romero, 2014)

Faster promotions may be the logical response to hiring cuts, caps, and freezes, but they contribute to the erosion of accountability and the confus-ing chain of command that has resulted in so many government breakdowns since 2000. It also gives managers and supervisors a reason to favor contract and grant employees as a lower-cost, fast-to-deploy, easier-to-manage alter-native to federal employees.

All Above Average

The federal government's performance appraisal system also affects work-force performance. First, it determines the promotion speed that moves fed-eral employees ever upward. Second, it contributes to the antigovernment portrait of federal employees as overpaid, poorly monitored, and immune to discipline.

In theory, an accurate employee appraisal system should create a mea-surable "line of sight" between individual performance and organizational performance. In reality, the federal government's line of sight has been distorted by years of grade inflation. Between 1986 and 2013, for example, the percentage of employees who were rated as "outstanding" rose from just 21 percent to 52 percent, while the percentage of employees who were rated as "fully exceeds satisfactory" and "satisfactory" dropped from 50 percent to 36 percent and 20 percent to 12 percent, respectively (GAO, 2015b).

This appraisal inflation eventually led GAO to warn federal managers to remind employees that a "fully successful" rating is not average or ordinary but rather a "high bar" whose achievement should be rewarded and valued as a significant level of accomplishment (GAO, 2015b). It is always possible that federal employees are almost all above average, but even the employees have their doubts about the system. In 2016, for example, just 41 percent said awards depended on how well employees performed their jobs, 34 percent said differences in performance in their work units were recognized in a meaningful way, and 29 percent said steps were taken to deal with a poor performer who could not or would not improve (OPM, 2017).

Contrary to the myth of the unaccountable civil servant, the federal government laid off or discharged about 6 percent of its employees in 2017. Although the private sector laid off or discharged more than 15 percent of its employees the same year, the rate varied from a high of 47 percent in arts and entertainment to a low of 8 percent in education and health services. The question is not whether federal employees are impossible to fire—after all, almost sixteen thousand lost their jobs in 2017—but whether they are essential in good economic times and bad (U.S. Bureau of Labor Statistics, 2018).

This is not to suggest that the process should favor speed over fairness. Federal employees must be protected from the kind of political and sexual harassment documented in early 2018. At the same time, they must also face sure consequences for poor performance. "The civil service needs to find a way to do an honorable discharge," one federal human capital officer told the Partnership for Public Service in 2014. "More than hiring reform, we need firing reform. In that reform you need to one, address poor performers and two, address skills that become outdated from otherwise good performers. There are just simply way too many hoops" (Partnership for Public Service, 2014, 15).

Bureaucratic Reality

The federal bureaucracy is a central agent in converting inputs into public goods. Although it is often criticized as an unmanageable force, it has an impressive record in pursuing what Alexander Hamilton called "extensive and arduous enterprises for the public benefit" in *Federalist No. 72*. At the same time, my trend lines show increasing gaps in hard-to-recruit skills, a dense leadership hierarchy, and a hidden hierarchy composed of two contract and grant employees for every one federal employee (Light, 2018a).

Hollowing Out

The federal government currently faces significant shortages in hard-to-recruit fields such as cybersecurity, telecommunications, acquisitions, information management, and the traditional science, technology, engineering, and mathematics. The resulting skill gap reflects not only a shortage of incoming talent and the failure to hold current strength in an overheated job market but also a mismatch between current federal skills and a more demanding mission that includes constant cyber threats. Bluntly put, not enough talented employees are entering the federal workforce, while too many current employees may be standing still (GAO, 2015c). This hollowing-out creates intense pressure to fill the gaps with contract and grant employees. The mission must come first.

Having tracked the hollowing-out for more than a decade, GAO finally acknowledged the skill gap in its report on high-risk troubled federal programs in 2001. According to GAO, the cascade of agency-by-agency personnel problems finally crossed the threshold from one-off instances to government-wide crisis: "The combined effect of these challenges serves to place at risk the ability of agencies to efficiently, economically, and effectively accomplish their missions, manage critical programs, and adequately serve the American people both now and in the future" (GAO, 2001, 8).

GAO's decision to list the skill gap as a government-wide high-risk issue finally confirmed what public administration scholars Charles H. Levine and Rosslyn S. Kleeman described as a "quiet crisis" in federal personnel management in 1986 (Levine and Kleeman, 1986) and Federal Reserve Board chairman Paul A. Volcker referenced in his introduction to the final report of the National Commission on Public Service in 1989: "Simply put, too many of the best of the nation's senior executives are ready to leave government, and not enough of its most talented young people are willing to join. This erosion in the attractiveness of public service at all levels—most specifically in the federal civil service—undermines the ability of government to respond effectively to the needs and aspirations of the American people, and ultimately damages the democratic process itself" (National Commission on Public Service, 1989, 1).

Even under persistent pressure from the second Volcker Commission in 2003 and rising congressional concerns, most departments and agencies barely passed the planning stage by 2017 (National Commission on Public Service, 2003). Although GAO acknowledged OPM's commitment to action, it also noted that skill gaps were contributing causes to fifteen of the thirty-three other items on its high-risk list: "Regardless of whether the shortfalls are in such government-wide occupations as cybersecurity and acquisitions, or in agency-specific occupations such as nurses at the Veterans Health Administration (VHA), skills gaps impede the federal government from cost-effectively serving the public and achieving results" (GAO, 2017, 1). The collateral damage is almost certain to increase as federal retirements increase in coming years.

Thickening Government

Even as the federal government struggles to address its skill gaps, it continues to labor under a daunting leadership hierarchy that weakens accountability and direction. It may be struggling to hire the next generation of civil servants, but it seems to have an inexhaustible supply of high-level political and career executives. Whereas John F. Kennedy entered office in charge of seven cabinet departments in 1961, Donald Trump entered in charge of fifteen. Whereas Kennedy's cabinet departments had seventeen layers open for new leaders, Trump's departments had seventy-one. Finally, whereas Kennedy's hierarchy contained 451 political or career occupants, Trump's contained 3,265 (Light, 2018a). From 1961 to 2017, the number of layers grew 318 percent, while the number of leaders per layers grew 624 percent. (See Table 1.1 for the March 2016 title list and Table 1.2 for the long-term trend.)

This thickening starts at the very top of government in the five leadership compartments headed by Senate-confirmed presidential appointees: (I) secretaries, (II) deputy secretaries, (III) undersecretaries, (IV) assistant secretaries, and (V) administrators. Some of these positions are subject to Senate confirmation, while others are selected by the president as nonconfirmed appointees or advanced upward into the five compartments as senior career

Table 1.1. Layers and Leaders, 2016

I
1. Secretary
2. Chief of staff to the secretary
3. Deputy chief of staff to the secretary
II
4. Deputy secretary (or FBI director, Federal Emergency Management Agency administrator, etc.)
5. Deputy secretary with portfolio
6. Chief of staff to the deputy secretary
7. Deputy chief of staff
8. Principal associate deputy secretary
9. Associate deputy secretary
10. Deputy associate deputy secretary
11. Assistant deputy secretary
12. Associate assistant deputy secretary
III
13. Undersecretary
14. Chief of staff to the undersecretary
15. Deputy chief of staff to the undersecretary
16. Principal deputy undersecretary
17. Deputy undersecretary
18. Chief of staff to the deputy undersecretary
19. Principal associate deputy undersecretary
20. Associate deputy undersecretary

21. Principal assistant deputy undersecretary
22. Assistant deputy undersecretary
23. Deputy assistant deputy undersecretary
24. Associate undersecretary
25. Assistant undersecretary
IV
26. Assistant secretary (or inspector general, general counsel, etc.)
27. Chief of staff to the assistant secretary
28. Deputy chief of staff to the assistant secretary
29. Principal deputy assistant secretary
30. Associate principal deputy assistant secretary
31. Deputy assistant secretary
32. Chief of staff to the deputy assistant secretary
33. Principal deputy to the deputy assistant secretary
34. Deputy to the deputy assistant secretary
35. Associate deputy assistant secretary
36. Deputy associate deputy assistant secretary
37. Chief of staff to the associate deputy assistant secretary

38. Deputy associate assistant secretary
39. Assistant deputy assistant secretary
40. Principal associate assistant secretary
41. Associate assistant secretary
42. Chief of staff to the associate assistant secretary
43. Deputy associate assistant secretary
44. Principal assistant assistant secretary
45. Assistant assistant secretary
46. Chief of staff to the assistant assistant secretary
47. Deputy assistant assistant secretary
V
48. Administrator
49. Chief of staff to the administrator
50. Assistant chief of staff to the administrator
51. Principal deputy administrator
52. Deputy administrator
53. Chief of staff to the deputy administrator
54. Associate deputy administrator
55. Deputy associate deputy administrator
56. Assistant deputy administrator
57. Deputy assistant deputy administrator

Table 1.1. (*Continued*)

58. Principal assistant deputy administrator	63. Deputy chief of staff to the associate administrator	68. Chief of staff to the assistant administrator
59. Associate assistant deputy administrator	64. Deputy executive associate administrator	69. Deputy assistant administrator
60. Senior associate administrator	65. Deputy associate administrator	70. Associate assistant administrator
61. Associate administrator	66. Senior associate deputy administrator	71. Associate deputy assistant administrator
62. Chief of staff to the associate administrator	67. Assistant administrator	

Source: Light, 2018a.

Table 1.2. Layers and Leaders, 1961–2017

	Layers of leaders						*Number of leaders*					
	1960	*1992*	*1998*	*2004*	*2010*	*2016*	*1960*	*1992*	*1998*	*2004*	*2010*	*2016*
Total	17	33	51	64	61	71	451	2,409	2,385	2,592	3,123	3,265
Absolute increase	—	16	18	13	−3	10	—	1,958	−24	207	531	142
Percentage increase	—	94%	55%	26%	−5%	16%	—	434%	−1%	9%	21%	3%

Source: Light, 2018a.

executives and lower-level civil servants. Congress exempted two hundred positions from Senate confirmation under the Presidential Appointment Efficiency and Streamlining Act of 2011. This statute was designed in part to reduce what the Senate Homeland Security Committee called an inexorable increase in the number of high-level vacancies that undermine presidential authority, but the old positions were left standing subject to presidential approval, while three hundred executive positions remained under Senate review.

The evidence of increased thickening comes from my inventories of the number of layers (titles) and leaders (titleholders) collected every six years between 1960 and 2016. The inventories are based on a careful coding of the federal telephone books at six-year intervals. The directories contain the titles, names, addresses, and phone numbers of all senior appointees in the federal government's departments and agencies, but the thickening is particularly troublesome at the very top of the fifteen cabinet departments.

Some of the titles may challenge credulity, but the March 2016 federal phonebook included tongue twisters such as the associate principal deputy assistant secretary for regulatory and policy affairs in the Department of Energy, the associate assistant deputy secretary for innovation and improvement in the Department of Education, a principal deputy associate attorney general and a principal deputy assistant attorney general in the Department of Justice, and associate deputy assistant secretaries for logistics and supply chain management, human resource systems and analytics, and acquisition and logistics in the Department of Veterans Affairs. Past patterns suggest that these new titles will spread to other departments as lower-level officers move up to match titles with their peers.

Even though the total number of leaders is often described as being an insignificant fraction of total federal employment, it creates a significant percentage of the layers between the top and bottom of federal departments and agencies. In 2002, for example, veterans hospital nurses reported upward through nine formal layers of command, including five at the Veterans Affairs Department's Vermont Avenue headquarters, while air traffic controllers reported upward through twelve, including six at the Federal Aviation Administration's headquarters on Independence Avenue in Washington (Light, 2018a).

Trump seemed to recognize the potential cost of the layers in February 2017 when *Fox & Friends* asked him to explain the slow pace of presidential appointments barely one month into the term: "Well, a lot of those jobs, I don't want to appoint, because they're unnecessary to have. You know we have so many people in government, even me, I look at some of the jobs and its people over people over people. I say what do all these people do? You don't need all those jobs. There are hundreds and hundreds of jobs that are unnecessary jobs" (Cillizza, 2017).

As for the president's complaint about people over people, Trump soon began adding his own people to the same hierarchy he criticized. Some were appointed as members of the Senior Executive Service, while others moved into lower-level positions as personal and confidential assistants to future Senate-confirmed appointees. Labeled by some observers as the "eyes and ears" of the White House, by others as "spies," and by at least one Defense Department official as "commissars," four hundred of these high-level officers were in place by late March 2017 according to ProPublica, including the president's picks for principal deputy assistant attorney general and principal deputy associate attorney general (Shaw and Kravitz, 2017).

The Hidden Pyramid

The United States has relied on a blended workforce of federal, contract, and grant-funded employees to advance its national agenda since the Revolutionary War and will continue to do so far into the future. However, this government-industry workforce involves a mix of incentives, oversight, and organizational authorities that can weaken the coordination needed for success.

Moreover, the failure to embrace the blended, or multisector, workforce as a whole reinforces the canard that the federal workforce is limited to employees who receive their paychecks directly from the Treasury. Table 1.3 shows two trends in this blended workforce. First, the total number of employees who received their pay directly or indirectly from the federal government hit more than seven million in 2017, down from the nine million in 2010 when the Obama administration's Iraq-war surge and economic stimulus package were still engaging large numbers of contract and grant employees. Second, the total number of federal, contract, and grant employees changed multiple times between 1984 and 2015: it decreased slightly from 1984 to 1994, dropped from 1995 to 1999, increased slightly from 1999 to 2002, surged to a record high between 2002 and 2010, then fell again between 2010 and 2015 where it held steady through 2017 (Light, 2018a). Although some experts might argue that contract and grant employees operate under different levels of inspection with different motivations, the two groups often provide goods and services as part of a multisector workforce that expands and contracts over time with changing national priorities.

The end of the Cold War and subsequent defense downsizing generated the first period of decline, while the drawdowns in Iraq and Afghanistan and the near-simultaneous spend-down of the Obama stimulus packaged spurred the second period of decline. What went up during war and economic stimulus fell when the wars and economic crises cooled.

There are many appropriate reasons for using contract and grant employees to faithfully execute the laws, but convenience is not one of them. (See Francis Fukuyama's chapter in this volume, "The Intrinsic Functions of Government," for a detailed discussion of the topic.) In theory, for example,

Table 1.3. The True Size of Government, 1984–2017

Employee sector	1984	1990	1993	1996	1999	2002	2005	2010	2015	2017
Federal[a]	2,083,000	2,174,000	2,139,000	1,891,000	1,778,000	1,756,000	1,830,000	2,128,000	2,042,000	2,062,000
Contract	3,666,000	3,427,000	3,245,000	3,042,000	2,398,000	2,791,000	3,882,000	4,845,000	3,702,000	4,128,000
Grant	1,234,000	1,352,000	1,344,000	1,351,000	1,415,000	1,236,000	1,578,000	2,344,000	1,583,000	1,189,000
Total	6,983,000	6,953,000	6,728,000	6,284,000	5,591,000	5,783,000	7,290,000	9,317,000	7,327,000	7,379,000
Ratio of contract + grant to federal employees	2.4	2.2	2.2	2.3	2.1	2.3	3.0	3.4	2.6	2.6

[a] Does not include active-duty military personnel or U.S. Postal Service employees.
Source: Light, 2018a.

federal employees must perform inherently governmental functions even if a commercial source is available at lower cost. Also, in theory, contract and grant employees can perform other functions deemed appropriate for outsourcing (Schooner, 2004). However, demographic realities, bureaucratic constraints, and political pressures play a prominent role in driving functions and headcount from one side of the government-industrial complex to the other as catch-22 pressure takes precedence over careful distribution of responsibilities.

Demography and history come together to reshape the federal hierarchy—employees grow older, missions expand and contract, personnel policies shift, new technologies emerge, and jobs evolve. The changes are easy to track by the number of technical, administrative, clerical, and blue-collar positions at any given point in history.

- In 1940, the federal hierarchy was shaped like a pyramid, with most employees at the bottom, smaller numbers of professional and technical employees at the middle, and even smaller numbers of career and presidential executives at the top.
- By 1960, the federal hierarchy was still shaped like a pyramid, but it was widening at the middle with more professional and technical employees while rising at the top with more career and presidential executives.
- By 1980, the federal hierarchy was shaped more like an isosceles trapezoid than a pyramid as departments and agencies began reducing the number of employees at the bottom while continuing to add professional and technical employees at the middle and more career and presidential executives at the top.
- By 2000, the federal hierarchy was shaped like a pentagon as the number of administrative, clerical, and blue-collar employees dropped below the growing number of professional, technical, and white-collar employees at the middle of government while the number of career and presidential executives continued to rise.
- By 2020, the federal hierarchy is almost certain to look like an ellipse, with far more federal employees at the middle levels and even more federal supervisors, managers, and executives at all levels. (Light, 2018a)

Public administration scholar Donald F. Kettl tracks this change by average federal employee grade, which rose from 6.7 in 1960 to 10.3 in 2014, and attributes the rise to a growing federal mission and the associated dependence on contract and grant employees: "The big story overall is that federal employment has hovered around two million workers, but spending, after inflation, has risen sharply. The same number of federal employees is leveraging an ever-growing amount of money. . . . This is a direct result of the federal government's increasing use of proxies, as more of its work was done outside the federal government—and by the accelerating underinvestment in the people needed to do the work" (Kettl, 2016, 51).

These changes reflect the rising number of contract employees who now fill many of the middle- and lower-level jobs once filled by federal employees. The federal hierarchy looks as if it is changing shape largely because contract and grant employees work in a hidden pyramid that allows Congress and presidents to address its demographic problems and its workload surges by hiring de facto federal employees. The couriers and stenographers may be gone, but the data suggest that the federal government still employs plenty of cafeteria workers, cartographers, groundskeepers, mechanics, security guards, and statisticians under contract. These employees may not carry federal government identification cards, but they help the federal government execute the law nonetheless. They are just hidden from view in contract firms, grant-funded agencies, and academic institutions.

The federal government may not know precisely how many employees work in this hidden pyramid, but millions of employees show up for work every day as part of a blended workforce nonetheless. The decision to separate these employees from the federal headcount perpetuates the conceit that government can do more with less ad infinitum, and it encourages departments and agencies to create their own systems for managing the workload. As the National Academy of Public Administration recently concluded, the absence of reform has produced chaos:

Among its many problems, the current civil service system is no longer a system. It is mired in often-arcane processes established after World War II, in the days before the Internet, interstate highways, or an interconnected global economy. Pursuit of those processes, many now largely obsolete, has become an end in itself, and compliance with them has tended to come at the expense of the missions they were supposed to support. As a result, the federal civil service system has become a non-system: agencies that have been able to break free from the constraints of the outmoded regulations and procedures have done so, with the indulgence of their congressional committees. (National Academy of Public Administration, 2017, 3)

Catch-22 Performance

The federal government produces more than enough data each year to prove its salutary effects on national health and welfare, but it is far from producing the broad measures that might show its achievements. Until then, catch-22 government continues to work its will on federal employee engagement, public distrust, and public divisions on the need for reform. (See Shelley Metzenbaum's chapter in this volume, "Good Government," for a review of recent progress in federal outcome measurement.)

The Engagement Gap

Employee engagement, and the productivity and morale that explain it, is essential for high performance in public service organizations. Engaged employees work harder and take greater pride in their work, and they often outperform their less engaged colleagues. The chance to make a difference may bring federal employees to work each day, but dedication rests in large measure on the reciprocal relationship between what individuals hope to accomplish and what their organizations allow. Employees must have confidence that their organization will provide the resources and opportunity to succeed (Bakker, 2015).

However, OPM's 2017 Federal Employee Viewpoint Survey (FEVS) revealed significant threats to this confidence. Although the report's subtitle celebrated departments and agencies for "empowering employees and inspiring change," the 485,000 federal employees who took the survey expressed doubts about both achievements (OPM, 2017).

Overall employee engagement did rise 4 percentage points to 67 percent between 2013 and 2017, and most of the eighty-four FEVS questions showed positive gains, but majorities of federal employees still gave their work units negative grades on recruitment, discipline, rewards, and innovation, and the effects of the Trump administration's budget cuts, hiring freeze, and targeted reorganizations were still unclear. Most of the trends moved in the right direction, but the absolutes had barely changed from 2015 when the House

Committee on Government Oversight and Reform summarized the FEVS in a hearing report titled, *The Worst Places to Work in the Federal Government* (2015).

Start with the FEVS questions about empowering employees. According to the survey, less than half of respondents were satisfied with the information they received from management (48 percent), had sufficient resources to do their jobs (47 percent), felt personally empowered with respect to work processes (45 percent), believed their organization recruited people with the right skills (43 percent), worked in units where employee performance was recognized in a meaningful way (34 percent), thought their work units took steps to deal with poor performers who could not or would not improve (29 percent), and said pay raises depended on how well employees do their jobs (22 percent).

Turn next to the FEVS questions about inspiring change. According to the survey, less than half of respondents were recognized for providing high-quality products and services (48 percent), felt acknowledged for doing a good job (48 percent), were satisfied with the policies and practices of their senior leaders (42 percent), worked for leaders who generated high levels of motivation and commitment (41 percent), felt rewarded for their creativity and innovation (38 percent), believed they had the opportunity to get a better job in their organization (36 percent), and thought promotions were based on merit (32 percent).

Moreover, further analysis of the 2017 data revealed a significant federal-private "engagement gap" that led the Partnership for Public Service (2017) to declare an urgent need for progress in the work environment. Although federal morale had increased from the recent lows that followed the 2011 congressional budget stalemate, federal employees still trailed their private-sector peers by more than 10 percent on average across a battery of other satisfaction questions: According to the partnership's side-by-side comparison, federal employees were slightly more satisfied with their pay (57 percent versus 55 percent) and much more likely to say they were willing to put in the extra work to get a job done (95 percent versus 83 percent). At the same time, they trailed their private-sector peers by at least 10 percent on twelve other items:

1. Supervisors in my work unit support employee development: −11 percent
2. I am satisfied with the training I receive for my present job: −12 percent
3. My workload is reasonable: −14 percent

4. I can disclose a suspected violation of any law, rule, or regulation without fear of reprisal: –14 percent
5. My supervisor provides me with constructive suggestions to improve my job performance: –14 percent
6. My training needs are assessed: –18 percent
7. I feel encouraged to come up with new and better ways of doing things: –18 percent
8. My talents are used well in the workplace: –20 percent
9. Awards in my work unit depend on how well employees perform their jobs: –23 percent
10. I have trust and confidence in my supervisor: –24 percent
11. I have sufficient resources (for example, people, materials, budget) to get the job done: –24 percent
12. I believe the results of this survey will be used to make my agency a better place to work: –31 percent

Irreconcilable Differences

Catch-22 government thrives in part on the public's shared distrust of government and demand for more of what the federal government delivers. Just as Americans distrust Congress but favor their own representatives, they distrust the federal government but favor most of its programs and even favor beleaguered federal agencies such as the Internal Revenue Service (IRS).

This less-and-more effect is clear in the Pew Research Center's long-running surveys of trust in government. Despite "rally-round-the-flag" surges during national crises such as 9/11 and longer rebounds during economic expansion, Pew's data show that trust has never fully recovered from the Vietnam War and Watergate. After hitting a post–World War II high at 77 percent in 1964, the percentage of Americans who said they trusted the federal government to do the right thing just about always or most of the time fell on a mostly straight line to 30 percent in 1980, recovered to 47 percent during the Persian Gulf crisis in 1991, dropped to 20 percent in 1994, steadily recovered to 49 percent just after 9/11, and eventually dropped to just 18 percent in December 2017 (Pew Research Center, 2017b).

Distrust is not the only measure of antigovernment sentiment. Pew also tracks long trends in public anger and frustration toward government and beliefs that government is almost always wasteful and inefficient, run by a few big interests looking out for themselves, in need of "very major" reform, and so poorly led that ordinary Americans could do a better job of solving the nation's problems than elected officials.

Americans have not allowed this distrust to weaken their support for big government, however. Even with trust near modern lows in 2015, Americans said the federal government should play a major role in addressing almost every problem on the agenda. They also gave the government high marks on responding to natural disasters (79 percent said government was doing a good job), setting workplace standards (76 percent), keeping the country safe from terror (72 percent), and ensuring safe food and medicine (72 percent). Although they also gave the federal government much lower marks on managing the immigration system (22 percent), helping people out of poverty (36 percent), ensuring basic income for older Americans (48 percent), and strengthening the economy (51 percent), they wanted the federal government to play a major role in those issues nonetheless.

Moreover, Americans also expressed favorable views toward most departments and agencies. The Postal Service had an 84 percent favorable rating in 2015, followed by the National Park Service (75 percent), the Centers for Disease Control and Prevention (71 percent), NASA (70 percent), the FBI (70 percent), the Department of Homeland Security (64 percent), the Department of Defense (63 percent), the CIA (57 percent), the Social Security Administration (55 percent), and the Department of Health and Human Services (54 percent) as the top ten. The Department of Justice, the Department of Education, the IRS, and the Department of Veterans Affairs were the only organizations ranked below the 50 percent mark, but even the IRS earned a 42 percent rating (Pew Research Center, 2017a).

Despite these positive marks for individual departments and agencies, Americans are sharply divided between competing visions of government reform. Asked in April 2018 to choose between a smaller government that provides fewer services and a bigger government that provides more services, Americans were evenly divided at 50 percent on the question. Asked next whether the federal government needs very major reform or is basically sound and needs only some reform, Americans favored major reform by a margin of almost two to one: 58 percent to 30 percent.

Once past these tight margins, Americans split into four distinct and sharply divided philosophies of reform: (1) the dismantlers, who want smaller government and very major reform, (2) the rebuilders, who want bigger gov-

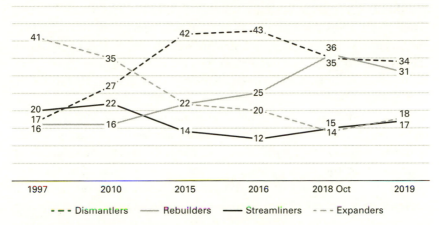

Figure 1.1. Dismantlers Versus Rebuilders, 1997–2019 (%)
Source: Light, 2018a.

ernment and very major reform, (3) the expanders, who want bigger government and only some reform, and (4) the streamliners, who want smaller government and only some reform (Light, 2018a).

The past twenty years have witnessed a dramatic reversal of fortunes among these four groups. The dismantlers surged from just 17 percent of Americans in 1997 to 43 percent in August 2016 before falling back to 34 percent in 2019, while the expanders steadily dropped from 41 percent in 1997 to just 18 percent in 2019, the rebuilders increased from 16 percent in 1997 to 36 percent just before the 2018 elections before dropping slightly to 31 percent in 2019, and the streamliners dropped from 20 percent in 1997 to 12 percent in 2016 before rebounding to 17 percent in 2019. (See Figure 1.1 for the trends in dismantling and rebuilding.)

This shift from traditional disputes over government's size reflects rising demand for major government reform—the percentage of Americans who said the federal government was basically sound and needed only some reform dropped from 58 percent in 1997 to just 31 percent in 2018, while the percentage who said the federal government needed very major reform jumped from 37 to 60 percent. In turn, this demand for reform reflected broad declines in trust in government and rising levels of anger and frustration. The decline in the number of dismantlers also appears to reflect growing dissatisfaction with Trump's performance in reducing the size of government and honoring his promise to "drain the swamp" (Light, 2018b).

This surge suggests continued support for hiring caps, cuts, and freezes, while the collapse of the reinventors suggests little support for "bringing back the bureaucrats," as public administration scholar John J. DiIulio Jr. recommends (DiIulio, 2014). Two out of three Americans now favor very major government reform and have left the reinventors and streamliners behind in the demand for action.

Party identification and political ideology divide each group from the others, but all share the general sense that their side has been losing more than winning on issues about which they care. Republicans changed places with Democrats on the winning-losing continuum by August 2017, but both groups were convinced that the next generation will be worse off than the present one. Both also remain equally skeptical about government performance and the need for reform (Pew Research Center, 2017c). The reinventors and streamliners must either embrace the need for major government reform or watch future elections from the sidelines.

A Cascade of Breakdowns

Name a domestic or international challenge since World War II, and odds are that the federal government helped address it, often achieving great success in reducing disease, promoting civil rights, strengthening the nation's infrastructure, ensuring access to higher education, helping veterans return from war, and increasing access to health care. There is still much to do in converting Hamilton's arduous and extensive enterprises into lasting achievements, but the nation can be proud of what the federal government has accomplished.

Yet, though the federal government achieved great things, catch-22 pressures appear to be creating a rising number of highly visible breakdowns. According to counts based on public opinion surveys of public news interest, the federal government generated 1.6 breakdowns per year that reached the public agenda in the fifteen years between 1986 and 2001, but 3.3 in the fifteen years from 2001 to 2017, including several of the most visible events recorded in the post–World War II era (Light, 2016). The federal government often recovered quickly as events unfolded, but it contributed nonetheless to national tragedies such as the September 11 attacks, the space shuttle *Columbia* explosion, the sluggish response to Hurricane Katrina, the 2008 financial collapse, the veterans waiting list scandal, the repeated security breaches, and other national embarrassments.

It is important to note that many of these breakdowns involved errors of omission, not commission. The federal government did not hijack the aircraft that killed so many Americans on September 11, 2001, but it also did not imagine the possibility in time to prevent the tragedy. It did not breach the levees when Hurricane Katrina came ashore in 2005, but it also did not have the leadership or plans to respond quickly. And it did not design the Byzantine instruments that triggered the banking collapse in 2008, but it also had little capacity to stop it.

It is also important to note that there was no single cause of the cascade. Staffing shortages and skill gaps in mission-critical occupations contributed to thirty-six of the fifty-three breakdowns, antiquated technology to thirty-one, broken chains of command to twenty-eight, funding shortages to twenty-four, duplication and overlap across agencies to nineteen, and contracting failures to seventeen (Light, 2016). Even as inflated expectations, ambiguous direction, conflicting statutes, and unattainable deadlines produced impossible policy, effective management was undermined by funding shortages, skill gaps, miscommunication, poor decisions, duplication and overlap, and misconduct. As the 9/11 Commission concluded, these problems framed the much broader "failure of imagination" that exposed the nation to the devastating attack.

The Tides of Tinkering

The trends just presented reflect unresolved tensions in past government reform. Congress and presidents enacted 195 major reforms since the end of World War II and the 2016 election, but they have never agreed on a single philosophy of improvement. As I argued in *The Tides of Reform* (Light, 1997, 2006), the problem with federal government reform has been not too little reform but rather too much.

My recent update to the post–World War II trend line of reforms shows continued competition among four philosophies of reform. As Table 1.4 shows, 43 percent of the post–World War II reforms embraced the supposed "scientific" principles of public administration articulated during the 1930s; 18 percent launched wars on waste through budget cutting, tighter monitoring, and bureaucratic restructuring; 24 percent encouraged more transparency and public access to information; and 15 percent promoted deregulation, employee empowerment, and broad liberation from the strictures of scientific management (Light, 2018a).

Table 1.4. Reform Philosophies by Decade, 1945–2017

Decade	Number of reforms	Scientific management (% of reforms)	War on waste (% of reforms)	Watchful eye (% of reforms)	Liberation (% of reforms)
1945–1954	22	82	9	9	0
1955–1964	17	82	0	12	6
1965–1974	35	43	3	29	26
1975–1984	30	30	37	27	7
1985–1994	40	17	28	33	23
1995–2004	34	41	21	21	18
2005–2017	17	35	24	29	12
Average	28	43	19	24	15

Note: $N = 195$ reforms.
Source: Light, 2018a.

The contest between the four tides increased after Watergate. Congress and presidents employed scientific management to reform Franklin D. Roosevelt's New Deal bureaucracy during the 1950s and build Lyndon Johnson's Great Society infrastructure in the 1960s, but they focused on watchful-eye reforms after Watergate and turned to wars on waste as the federal budget swelled in the 1980s. At the same time, the number of reform activities began to decline in the 1990s. Reform activity peaked from 1965 to 2004 with an average of thirty-five statutes per decade, then fell to seventeen between 1995 and 2017. (See Table 1.4 for the trend.)

The size and scope of government reform also drifted toward smaller-scale reforms over time. As Table 1.5 shows, the percentage of large reforms dropped steadily from a high of 50 percent in the first decade after World War II to a low of 29 percent from 1995 to 2017. The number of new initiatives varied over the 1945–2017 period but dropped to a low of just 18 percent of the total from 2005 to 2017. Although there are several post-9/11 reforms on the list of recent statutes, many of these are small or old reforms that express a general reluctance to confront the trends just listed with comprehensive action.

The decline in the amount of large-scale reform reflects broad changes at both ends of Pennsylvania Avenue.

At 1600 Pennsylvania Avenue, recent presidents initiated fewer reforms over time, and fewer of the reforms they produced were comprehensive. Presidents initiated 60 percent of all reforms before Watergate, compared with just

Table 1.5. Scale of Reform by Decade

Decade	New idea, not old (% of reforms)	Large idea, not small (% of reforms)	Small/old idea (% of reforms)
1945–1954	27	50	41
1955–1964	65	47	29
1965–1974	34	34	46
1975–1984	50	30	43
1985–1994	48	33	40
1995–2004	55	29	38
2005–2017	18	29	71
Average	44	35	43

Note: $N = 195$ reforms.
Source: Light, 2018a.

24 percent afterward. Presidential interest in large-scale reforms also fell from 55 percent of such statutes before Watergate to 40 percent afterward.

On Capitol Hill, Congress picked up some of the slack in the number of reforms as presidents stepped away, but it showed even less ambition. Although the congressional share of activity surged from 41 percent of all reforms before Watergate to 76 percent after, its interest in large-scale reforms fell from 47 percent to just 24 percent during the period (Light, 2018b).

However, even if Congress and the president decided to embrace large-scale reform, the question is where they would begin the drafting. This book offers a range of answers. This era of disruption may lack a name, as James L. Perry argues, but it is a period of disruption nonetheless. The technological revolution has created an algorithmic world in which governments at all levels must compete for high-demand skills, polarization has reinforced long-standing concerns about big government and hidden influence, new policy instruments have increased the need for agility in addressing domestic, economic, and international threats, and the government agenda is being tested by disputes about the intrinsic functions of government.

This book provides important context for resolving these pressures, but it also provides an outline of the institutional reforms that might move government toward a comprehensive response to these pressures through institutional repairs and a new public service equal to the complex challenges ahead. There is room for extensive reform of the federal bureaucracy, including long-overdue discussions of the federal agenda, organizations, the workforce, and the need for robust measures of performance that will create stronger accountability and more effective programs. There is also an urgent need for hard conversations about the changing nature of the public service, including the disruption in what constitutes a public-service career; how future public servants should be recruited, educated, trained, managed, and rewarded; and where the public service ends and the contract service begins.

Bibliography

Bakker, Arnold B. 2015. "A Job Demands-Resource Approach to Public Service Motivation." *Public Administration Review* 75 (5): 723–32.

Bolton, Alexander, John M. de Figueiredo, Charles M. Cameron, and David E. Lewis. 2015. "Grade Inflation in the U.S. Government." Unpublished draft, January 1, 2015.

Chamberlain, Andrew. 2017. "How Long Does It Take to Hire? Interview Duration in 25 Countries." Glassdoor, August 9, 2017. https://www.glassdoor.com/research/time-to -hire-in-25-countries/.

Cillizza, Chris. 2017. "Donald Trump's A+/C+ Presidency." *Washington Post*, February 28, 2017.

Committee on Homeland Security and Government Affairs, Federal Hiring Process Improvement Act of 2010, S. Rep. 111-184 (2010).

Davidson, Joe. 2010. "President Obama's Hiring Reforms Draw Applause at Personnel Agency." *Washington Post*, May 12, 2010.

———. 2016. "Federal Hiring, Fixed Before, Needs Fixing Again." *Washington Post*, April 13, 2016. https://www.washingtonpost.com/news/powerpost/wp/2016/04/13/federal-hiring -fixed-before-needs-fixing-again/?utm_term=.645d6b93509d.

DiIulio, John J., Jr. 2014. *Bring Back the Bureaucrats: Why More Federal Workers Will Lead to Better (and Smaller!) Government.* West Conshohocken, PA: Templeton.

GAO (U.S. Government Accountability Office). 2001. *High-Risk Series: An Update.* GAO-01-263. Washington, DC: U.S. Government Printing Office.

———. 2015a. *Federal Workforce: Additional Analysis and Sharing of Promising Practices Could Improve Employee Engagement and Performance.* GAO-15-585. Washington, DC: U.S. Government Printing Office.

———. 2015b. *Federal Workforce: Improved Supervision and Better Use of Probationary Periods Are Needed to Address Substandard Employee Performance.* GAO-15-191. Washington, DC: U.S. Government Printing Office.

———. 2015c. *Federal Workforce: OPM and Agencies Need to Strengthen Efforts to Identify and Close Mission-Critical Skills Gaps.* GAO-15-223. Washington, DC: U.S. Government Printing Office.

———. 2017. *High-Risk Series: An Update.* GAO-17-317. Washington, DC: U.S. Government Printing Office.

Jobs, Jobs, Jobs: Transforming Federal Hiring: Hearing Before the Subcommittee on Federal Workforce, Postal Service, and the District of Columbia of the Committee on Oversight and Government Reform. 111th Cong., 2d Sess. (May 19, 2010). Serial No. 111-91.

Kettl, Donald F. 2016. *Escaping Jurassic Government: How to Recover America's Lost Commitment to Competence.* Washington, DC: Brookings Institution.

Levine, Charles H., and Rosslyn S. Kleeman. 1986. *The Quiet Crisis of the Civil Service: The Federal Personnel System at the Crossroads.* Washington, DC: National Academy of Public Administration.

Light, Paul C. 1997. *The Tides of Reform: Making Government Work, 1945–1995.* New Haven, CT: Yale University Press.

———. 2006. "The Tides of Reform Revisited: Patterns in Making Government Work, 1945–2002." *Public Administration Review* 66 (1): 6–19.

———. 2016. *Vision + Action = Faithful Execution: Why Government Daydreams and How to Stop the Cascade of Breakdowns That Now Haunts It.* New York: Volcker Alliance.

———. 2018a. *The Government-Industrial Complex: The True Size of the Federal Government, 1984–2018.* New York: Oxford University Press.

———. 2018b. *Introducing the Next Government Reform Majority.* Washington, DC: Brookings Institution.

National Academy of Public Administration. 2017. *No Time to Wait: Building a Public Service for the 21st Century.* Washington, DC: National Academy of Public Administration.

National Commission on the Public Service. 1989. *Leadership for America: Rebuilding the Public Service.* Washington, DC: National Commission on the Public Service.

———. 2003. *Urgent Business for America: Revitalizing the Federal Government for the 21st Century.* Washington, DC: National Commission on the Public Service.

Neal, Jeffrey. 2014. "What Happened to All of the Young Federal Employees?" ChiefHRO .com, July 10, 2014. https://chiefhro.com/2014/07/10/what-happened-to-all-of-the-young -federal-employees/.

Oh, Seong Soo, and Gregory B. Lewis. 2013. "Performance Ratings and Career Advancement in the US Federal Civil Service." *Public Management Review* 15 (5): 740–61.

OPM (U.S. Office of Personnel Management). 2017. *Federal Employee Viewpoint Survey: Empowering Employees. Inspiring Change.* Washington, DC: U.S. Office of Personnel Management.

Partnership for Public Service. 2014. *Embracing Change: CHCOs Rising to the Challenge of an Altered Landscape.* Washington, DC: Partnership for Public Service and Grant Thornton.

———. 2017. *The Best Places to Work in the Federal Government: Overall Findings and Private Sector Comparison.* Washington, DC: Partnership for Public Service.

Pew Research Center. 2017a. *Beyond Distrust: How Americans View Their Government.* Washington, DC: Pew Research Center.

———. 2017b. *Government Gets Lower Ratings for Handling Health Care, Environment, Disaster Response.* Washington, DC: Pew Research Center.

———. 2017c. *Partisan Shifts in Views of the Nation, but Overall Opinions Remain Negative.* Washington, DC: Pew Research Center.

Romero, Henry. 2014. "Grade Inflation: Does It Matter?" Government Executive, September 5, 2014. https://www.govexec.com/excellence/promising-practices/2014/09/grade -inflation-does-it-matter/93218/.

Schooner, Steven L. 2004. "Competitive Sourcing Policy: More Sail than Rudder." *Public Contract Law Journal* 33 (2): 263–97.

Shaw, Al, and Derek Kravitz. 2017. "Here Are More than 400 Officials Trump Has Quietly Deployed Across the Government." ProPublica, last updated August 31, 2017. https:// projects.propublica.org/graphics/beachhead.

Uncle Sam Wants You! Recruitment in the Federal Government: Hearing of the Subcommittee on Oversight of Government Management, the Federal Workforce and the District of Columbia of the Committee on Homeland Security and Governmental Affairs. 111th Cong., 1st Sess. (May 7, 2009).

U.S. Bureau of Labor Statistics. 2018. *Job Openings and Labor Turnover Survey.* March 6, 2018. Rep. No. USDL-17-0590. https://www.bls.gov/news.release/archives/jolts_05092017.pdf.

The Worst Places to Work in the Federal Government: Hearing Before the Subcommittee on Government Operations of the Committee on Oversight and Management Reform. 114th Cong., 1st Sess. (April 16, 2015). Serial No. 114-35.

PART I

───────

Disruptive Influences

CHAPTER 2

Beyond the Financial Crisis

Regulators Confront New Challenges from Technological (R)evolution

Sheila Bair

Cryptocurrencies. Blockchain. Artificial intelligence. These new technologies promise tremendous economic and public policy benefits. They also create potential avenues to evade core tenets of financial regulation surrounding market integrity, consumer protections, and safeguards against illicit use of our payments system. Regulators will be struggling to address these challenges with an antiquated regulatory structure, still fragmented about whether an activity is a "security," "derivative," or "banking" product. The regime is poorly suited to rapid adaptation of regulatory approaches to entirely new asset classes such as cryptocurrencies and entirely new ways of providing financial services through artificial intelligence (AI). This technology can enhance regulation. But it can also disrupt it if regulators do not keep pace (World Economic Forum, 2015).

The financial industry is forging ahead. The hype surrounding these technological innovations in the media is surpassed only by the intensity of the discussions they are prompting in the management committees and boardrooms of the world's largest financial institutions. Will these innovations help or disrupt their business models? How do they position themselves strategically? With cautious eyes cast toward the thousands of financial technology, or "fintech," companies popping up across the commercial landscape, do they try to innovate as well, buy their potential disruptors, or partner with them? Build, buy, or buddy?

Regrettably, regulators in the United States, still struggling with unfinished reforms from the 2008 financial crisis (and now dealing with a tide-turning political wave to undo many of the reforms already put into place), have not focused on technology and its benefits and challenges with the same intensity. To be sure, there have been efforts to rethink regulatory approaches and adapt them to fintech firms, but they have been met with controversy and resistance from industry interests well entrenched in the status quo. To see how, one need only review the laundry list of issues identified by the Financial Stability Oversight Council, the interagency group created by the Dodd-Frank financial reform law to identify and mitigate systemic risks to the financial system. The council's 2017 annual report (U.S. Financial Stability Oversight Council, 2017), with the exception of cyber security, is still dominated by the types of postcrisis issues we were struggling with in 2010 when Dodd-Frank was enacted: systemic institutions, capital, liquidity, and counterparty risk. Notably, the council did admonish its member agencies to "monitor and analyze" (6) the effects of cryptocurrencies on system stability. A few regulators have tried to pioneer new structures suited to financial technology, two examples being the New York Department of Financial Supervision's groundbreaking work to construct a regulatory structure for cryptocurrencies and the Office of the Comptroller of the Currency's efforts to create a new national charter custom-built for financial technology firms. But those have been lonely efforts, met with skepticism by their fellow regulators.

Hopefully, regulators will bring more vigorous regulatory attention to financial technology in the future. The challenges are many, and meeting them in a coordinated fashion will be complicated by the Balkanized system of oversight we have in the United States, where long-standing interagency tensions and jurisdictional turf fights too often get in the way of timely regulatory responses to market evolutions—or, perhaps in this case, revolutions. The label "financial technology" should not be used as an excuse to compromise basic regulatory protections in the name of fostering innovation and competition. Any business performing the functional equivalent of the duties of a regulated entity or practice should be met with like-kind regulation, lest financial technology become a cover for simple regulatory arbitrage—putting regulated institutions at unfair competitive disadvantage and creating the risk of digital shadow structures forming beyond the reach of regulatory bodies. For instance, there is no reason why an entity providing services in cryptocurrency should be subject to less stringent anti-money-laundering and anti-terrorist-financing controls than an entity doing business with fiat currency. Similarly, a marketplace lender should be subject to the same consumer protections as a bank lender (though not to equivalent safety and soundness oversight, given the lack of deposits backed by the Federal Deposit Insurance Corporation and access to Federal Reserve lending). At the same time, regulation should not be used as a tool to block innovative technology. Many technological innovations have important consumer and, yes, regulatory benefits. Blockchain technology comes to mind, which could provide a more secure, fraud-resistant chain of title for a whole host of assets while eliminating errors and execution risks associated with lengthy settlement periods. Regulators should accommodate such positive innovations even if they promise to disrupt regulated monopolies, which currently intermediate settlement transactions. Similar, robo-advisors are already empowering retail investors to ferret out low-cost funds in the multitude of options frequently provided them in their 401(k)s and 403(b)s, threatening the revenue streams of high-cost, inefficient fund providers (Morrell, 2017). Regulators should not fear such innovations, but rather encourage and embrace them.

The rapidly growing array of transformative uses of technology in the financial sector is too vast for treatment in this chapter. As a consequence, I have chosen three areas that I think exemplify the promise and challenges of technology, particularly in forming regulatory policy. The first part of the chapter reviews cryptocurrencies and blockchain—both in nascent stages but promising to be radically disruptive. The second part discusses robo-advising, a technology-driven service already being provided by multiple firms but evolving and expanding in ways that provide both benefits and risks to investors and retirement savers. The third part analyzes marketplace lending, now maturing as an accepted and established platform for consumer and small-business lending but hardly representing the paradigm shift in democratizing credit extension its advocates originally envisioned. To be sure, marketplace lenders have provided benefits in terms of lowering origination costs and making responsibly priced credit more widely available, but they have also given rise to many of the same issues long associated with nonbank lending, including volatility of funding sources and skewed economic incentives for those who originate loans to sell to others as opposed to retaining the credit risk themselves. Moreover, we have learned that the use of algorithms to make credit decisions, while touted as being free of *human* bias, can nonetheless have disparate impact (see Chapter 3 for further discussion of algorithms and disruption). Thus, marketplace lending provides a good window to view how technology, once developed and applied, can evolve into something quite different from its original vision and present new variations of the problems it was supposed to solve.

Cryptocurrencies and Blockchain

The meteoric rise and wild swings in Bitcoin prices are symptomatic of the red-hot interest in cryptocurrency. However, as is usually the case with market manias, investor—and media—understanding of the risks and potential benefits of crypto money has been lacking, including massive confusion in differentiating between Bitcoin and the blockchain technology that underpins it. Their development and potential uses are different things and, as a consequence, will be discussed separately.

Bitcoin

Introduced in 2008 by its mysterious creator, Satoshi Nakamoto, Bitcoin is the oldest and most widely held cryptocurrency among an increasing number of crypto competitors. Originally envisioned as an "electronic cash system," Bitcoin was designed to permit peer-to-peer transactions anywhere in the world through a distributed ledger called blockchain, completely bypassing the banking system and the need to use government-backed, fiat currency. Using this decentralized network, anyone with internet access could join, making it easy to send Bitcoin between addresses. However, limitations were purposefully built into the system. The network could only process around five transactions per second, and the number of Bitcoin that could be "mined" was set at twenty-one million. These limitations have impeded Bitcoin's usefulness as a medium of exchange. However, they have increased its perceived value as a good place to store money, similar to gold. Its rapid rise in value in 2017 reinforced this perception. Bitcoin's decline in price more recently may yet again change perceptions of its value as a place to store money.

Bitcoin's limitations as a medium of exchange have spawned competitor crypto currencies such as Bitcoin Cash, Ripple, Ethereum, and Litecoin, which, in general, are governed by different mining algorithms and provide significantly larger transaction capacity. However, none have come close to overtaking Bitcoin in dollar volume. Of these competitors, Ethereum has been applied specifically to facilitate cross-border transactions, processing about $1 billion in transactions in 2016.

Regulatory Issues Presented by Bitcoin

Some argue that Bitcoin performs no socially useful function and thus should be banned. To be sure, it and its ilk present significant public policy issues. No doubt, too many unsophisticated investors have been drawn to its outsize run-up in value, likely investing more than they can afford to lose if the price plummets, as it did late in 2017 (Popper, 2017). In addition, the anonymity, and ability to bypass regulated banks and their customer screens, that Bitcoin and other cryptocurrencies provide to users makes it more susceptible to use for illicit purposes such as illegal drug trafficking. Finally, the fact that ownership of Bitcoin remains relatively concentrated gives rise to concerns of market manipulation.

While these issues are serious, they are hardly unique to Bitcoin. And the threshold question—Does Bitcoin have "value"?—is an issue generally left, for any asset, to markets, not the government. Value—like beauty—is in the eye of the beholder. Since the beginning of commerce, humans have assigned value to things of no readily apparent intrinsic worth. Particularly in the case of mediums of exchange, we assign value simply because those with whom we conduct transactions do so as well. Whether it is the cowry shells of ancient India or the thin green pieces of paper many of us still carry in our wallets today, worth depends more on psychology than physical attributes. This is also true of fiat currency, which is backed by governments and their taxing power, and central banks and their money-printing power. But when the public loses confidence in those institutions—whether in the Weimar Republic in post–World War I Germany or in Southeast Asia in the late 1990s—value evaporates. Regrettably, with reduced trust in government, the lack of central bank backing of Bitcoin and other cryptocurrencies may *add* value in the eyes of Bitcoin's more passionate investors, who boast that they have more faith in technology than their elected and appointed officials.

Though the number of businesses and individuals recognizing Bitcoin as a medium of exchange is limited, they are still of sufficient scale to belie attempts to label it as worthless as an exchange medium. And the *promise* of Bitcoin—of eventual widespread acceptance allowing direct, peer-to-peer transactions with anyone in the world—has a strong allure for many. More-over, this is hardly the first time markets have priced assets far above sane levels. The Netherlands did not ban tulips in the 1630s, nor did we ban tech stocks when they reached nosebleed levels in the early 2000s. Regrettably, asset bubbles are inherent in market-based economies, particularly when central banks, through low interest rates, make it so cheap to borrow for speculation.

Banning Bitcoin would surely set us on a slippery slope. What would be next? Penny stocks? How about synthetic collateralized debt obligations? I could certainly live without those, given the damage they created during the 2008 financial crisis. A better course would be to make sure government polic-ies do not feed the frenzy, as we did during the lead-up to the 2008 financial crisis through highly favorable regulatory capital treatment of mortgage se-curitizations and derivatives. Certainly, federally insured banking organ-izations should not be allowed to directly or indirectly support Bitcoin speculation. Stringent caps should be placed on the use of leverage to make cryptocurrency investments (if leverage should be allowed at all). Govern-ment should also take steps to help ensure that the Bitcoin price—wherever the market assigns it—is reflective of investors making informed decisions, free of fraud and manipulation, and that trading is not facilitating illicit uses such as money laundering or terrorist financing. Fortunately, regulators are already taking positive steps forward in these areas.

For instance, the New York Department of Financial Services has pro-vided a regulatory framework in which Bitcoin exchanges can operate, in-cluding as a regulated trust. This provides a vehicle for investors to trade on an exchange subject to bank-like supervision, including capital requirements, customer due diligence, and cybersecurity oversight. In addition, though the Chicago Board Options Exchange and Chicago Mercantile Exchange were criticized for "legitimizing" Bitcoin by launching Bitcoin futures trad-ing in 2017, they did create additional regulated venues to take a Bitcoin position through futures trading. And while most Bitcoin exchanges remain unregulated, the Commodity Futures Trading Commission has pressed both the Chicago Board Options Exchange and Chicago Mercantile Ex-change to institute information sharing with Bitcoin exchanges that will help them and the commission monitor for market manipulation and fraud in the underlying Bitcoin market.

The Securities and Exchange Commission (SEC) has also stepped up ef-forts to warn investors about risks associated with cryptocurrencies and quash attempts to evade securities requirements by offering what is essentially a security in the guise of an "initial coin offering" (Clayton, 2017).

Importantly, the SEC has warned investors about the difference between investing in Bitcoin—a cryptocurrency—and investing in companies that are trying to develop the blockchain technology that underpins Bitcoin trading. *Blockchain* refers to the distributed ledger used to create a highly secure, unalterable chain of ownership for Bitcoin (see the next section for a detailed discussion of its origins and regulatory implications). It is best to think of it as a database, not a medium of exchange. Many fintech firms are trying to apply blockchain technology to other assets, such as precious metals, securities, and mortgage titles, some with more credibility than others (Biella and Zinetti, 2016). This is highly sophisticated technology—promising but probably years off in terms of widespread application. But the important point is that investing in Bitcoin does not provide upside potential in blockchain adaptation to record ownership of other assets. They are two different things.

Finally, Congress is considering legislation to strengthen government oversight of the potential use of cryptocurrencies for illicit purposes, including money laundering and terrorist financing. Most Bitcoin exchanges are not subject to the regulation and reporting requirements that obligate banks to screen customers and detect and report suspected instances of illicit financing. They should be.

As helpful as these regulatory initiatives are, our siloed regulatory structure in the United States has impeded a holistic approach to cryptocurrency oversight and regulation. For instance, no federal regulator appears to have direct authority over manipulation and fraud in the underlying "cash" market. Confusion and ambiguity over a cryptocurrency—viewed as a commodity by the Commodity Futures Trading Commission—and an "initial coin offering"—viewed as a security by the SEC—will risk potentially inconsistent regulatory approaches for investors. No federal agency has clear authority over consumer use of Bitcoin. Though the Consumer Financial Protection Bureau (CFPB) will accept consumer complaints associated with Bitcoin use, its ability to regulate cryptocurrencies is unclear, and, to date, it has excluded them from its rules covering electronic fund transfers. Fortunately, the dollar volume invested in Bitcoin represents a tiny fraction of the financial system, making systemic impact extremely unlikely even if its value fell to zero. Expanded use of cryptocurrency, resulting in a shadowy payments system, could eventually pose systemic risks. However, at this point, that seems a remote possibility.

Bitcoin is not the first market mania, nor will it be the last. It may well eventually find its equilibrium price and stabilize. The best discipline for Bitcoin speculation is a precipitous fall in price—as we have seen many times. That is a healthy reminder to those who are investing in this highly volatile asset that prices can go down as fast as (or faster than) they go up.

Blockchain

Since 2008, when Bitcoin introduced the idea of a secure, decentralized distributed ledger to record transactions, a great deal of thought and analysis has been devoted to this technology's potential to be applied to other uses (Schneider et al., 2016). But what exactly is "blockchain" technology?

In its most basic form, blockchain is a database accessible to multiple parties instead of being held and controlled by a central repository. Each network participant has a file of transactions (blocks) on his or her computer. As any one participant initiates a transaction, a message is "distributed" to all others to inform them. Each then rushes to make sure that the participant has the capacity to transact, sending a message to all other network participants once he or she has done so, attaching the logic for verifying the transaction (proof of work). When a consensus is reached among network participants to verify, all ledgers are updated to reflect the completion of the transaction.

It should be emphasized that the ledgers underpinning Bitcoin and most other cryptocurrencies can be accessed by anyone through the internet. Thus, the encryption technology used for verification is highly complex and sophisticated, requiring significant computer power. Early verifiers are rewarded with additional Bitcoin. Contrast these public ledgers with what the industry calls "permissioned" networks that limit who can participate (and charge fees for that privilege). Most commercial uses currently in development for blockchain contemplate permissioned networks. The "gating" of network participants reduces the complexity required for network verification as participants have already gone through a series of screens before being permitted to join.

Distributed ledgers have a number of obvious advantages over centralized gatekeepers. The first is time. By cutting out intermediaries, transactions can be settled in close to real time. Errors are dramatically reduced, as the ledger can only be changed with the agreement of the counterparty and consensus support of the network. Similarly, fraudulent alteration of the ledger is virtually impossible, as ledger entries are only permitted with the consent of the other participants.

The highly centralized process currently used to clear and settle equity securities transactions provides a good example of the potential benefits of distributed ledger technology. While equities, for instance, *trade* in tiny fractions of seconds, the posttrade clearance and settlement process is cumbersome. A centralized counterparty such as the National Securities Clearing Corporation substitutes itself as the seller to the buyer and the buyer to the seller for securities trades once a trade occurs. Most securities are held by the Depository Trust Company, which facilitates book-entry transfers among its participants, with funds netted and settled at the end of the day. Thus, market participants each have to manage their own sets of books and records and reconcile them to other participants' ledgers, the National Securities Clearing Corporation, and the central ledger of the Depository Trust Company, a costly, inefficient, and error-prone process.

With so many parties involved across a single transaction, multiple versions of the trade are recorded, leading to inevitable inconsistencies among those many versions that usually require manual intervention to reconcile. This inefficient process requires two days to settle those trades, which ties up capital and liquidity among parties to the transaction, as well as exposing them to the risk that the transactions will fail. Adding to these inefficiencies is the fact that multiple records must be constantly updated as securities accounts are opened and closed, account numbers change, and custodians change, creating ever more opportunities for inconsistencies and errors that require manual intervention and communication among the various participants. Moreover, unlike a distributed ledger, centralized clearing and record keeping create single points of failure to operational errors or hacks, placing the security of the entire system at risk with a single breach.

It has been estimated that roughly 10 percent of equity trading volume involves some sort of entry error requiring manual intervention to correct. Typically, these involve incorrect settlement instructions or account details. By forcing agreement at *the time of entry*, a distributed ledger could eliminate the vast majority of these errors, saving financial firms billions over time in back-office functions. Shortening settlement times could also reduce the risk of failed transactions, freeing up capital that now must be posted with clearinghouses until trades are settled. Finally, the distributed ledger would eliminate concentrated risks at centralized clearing and settlement repositories because multiple network participants, instead of a single authority, serve as the gate-keepers for the data (Moody's Investors Service, 2017).

Securities settlement is far from the only area where fintech firms are working to apply blockchain technology. Potential areas of use currently being discussed include credit reporting (giving consumers access to and control over the distributed database where their credit records are stored); real estate titles (disintermediating title insurers by creating a distributed ledger for tracking title transfers); reputation management in the sharing economy (for instance, allowing Airbnb to address safety issues by creating a tamper-proof ledger for managing the credentials of guests and providers); energy grids (empowering individuals with excess capacity to be their own power providers); "know your customer" requirements for financial institutions (creating a highly secure, shared database of customer information and transaction data); and philanthropic uses such as creating and tracking digital identities for refugees.

A form of blockchain is also being developed for international currency transactions. Federal Reserve Board governor Lael Brainard (2016) has observed that adaptation of distributed ledger technology to cross-border payments could help decrease the time, costs, and counterparty risks associated with the current system while providing greater transparency.

Regulatory Issues Associated with Blockchain

Unlike Bitcoin and other cryptocurrencies that present a host of regulatory challenges, blockchain would seem to be mostly a win-win for regulators. For instance, dramatically reducing settlement times for securities transactions would also reduce regulated financial institutions' exposure to losses associated with trade errors or counterparty default, while providing capital relief to banks, which now must post capital against unexecuted transactions until completed. It would also alleviate the need for banks to extend short-term credit to customers needing cash pending execution of their securities transactions. While this might affect interest income for some of the large banks, it would also eliminate the huge amount of concentrated risks they take in supporting short-term funding markets, particularly in the trillion-dollar "repo markets."

Repos provide a significant source of daily funding for banks and other financial institutions. They are technically short-term purchases but function as collateralized loans. A borrower institution "sells" collateral—usually high-quality government securities—to a lender institution with an agreement to repurchase it at a higher price, usually in a matter of days. These markets proved to be highly fragile in the aftermath of the Lehman Brothers bankruptcy in 2008, necessitating massive government assistance in terms of capital investments, Federal Reserve lending, and Federal Deposit Insurance Corporation debt guarantees. Risks were exacerbated by the use of triparty repo, in which a small number of large clearing banks would intermediate the transactions on both sides, acting as custodian for the lenders' securities collateral and advancing cash to the borrowers, holding risk to both counterparties until the transaction settled. The need for triparty repo, and its attendant systemic risks, would essentially be eliminated through use of a distributed ledger providing for real-time settlement. It would also greatly improve counterparties' and regulators' ability to track the collateral supporting these trades.

Compliance and enforcement of anti-money-laundering and anti-terrorist-financing requirements could also be greatly enhanced through the use of distributed ledger technology. Banks spend billions of dollars on anti-money-laundering compliance, and billions more on regulatory fines for failure to adhere to the strict regulatory requirements in this area. *Money laundering* refers to the practice of bank customers camouflaging money generated from illicit purposes so that it appears to come from legal sources. Notwithstanding the cost and robust enforcement of anti-money-laundering rules, the World Bank estimates that 3–5 percent of the gross domestic product represents "laundered" money, with only a small percentage identified through anti-money-laundering compliance programs.

Pursuant to regulatory requirements, when a bank opens an account, it must conduct an exhaustive process to verify the customer's identity, determine the account's true beneficial owners, and check this information against government sanctions lists such as that issued by the U.S. Treasury Department's Office of Foreign Assets Control. Once the account is opened, it must be monitored for suspicious activity. Suspicious activity alerts usually generate a high volume of false positives and require further manual investigation. Suspicious activity must be reported to the government, as well as any large currency transactions. In addition, banks must keep detailed and accurate records of all transactions and customer due diligence to be made readily available to government authorities if needed to assist in investigations.

Blockchain could make this process less expensive and more effective in a number of ways. Distributed databases of customer information could be shared among institutions. This would eliminate duplication of effort and provide more complete access to information for banks in opening new accounts, as they could benefit from the due diligence already conducted by other banks. This would make it significantly more difficult for criminals or sanctioned individuals to evade detection by opening accounts at multiple institutions. For legitimate customers, this would ease documentation burdens in opening new accounts by allowing banks with which they have preexisting relationships to provide testament to their lawful associations. Legitimate bank customers would also benefit from the more secure and accurate records kept about them afforded by blockchain technology. Similarly, banks could use a distributed ledger to store records of all transactions tied to that client, making it cheaper and faster to assist regulators and law enforcement entities investigating suspected illegal behavior. By creating a unique identifier for each customer, banks would have a better understanding of a customer's complete transaction history, reducing the risk of false positives and freeing up bank compliance staff to identify and investigate true instances of illicit conduct.

Adaptation of distributed ledger technology to cross-border payments in particular could have important regulatory benefits, as the recordation of payment flows would be much more secure and transparent than in the current system, which relies on multiple levels of intermediation and is highly opaque. The highly secure, unalterable nature of the distributed ledger could greatly assist law enforcement in tracing sources of funding for illicit activity. For retail customers, the ability to transfer payments across borders directly could substantially reduce costs and speed up processing.

Reducing the risk of trade errors and counterparty failures in securities settlements and enhancing the efficiency and effectiveness of efforts to combat illicit financing—these are two examples of a growing number of areas being explored where blockchain technology could have important public benefits. Other areas include the use of blockchain to create distributed ledgers to hold secure and accurate credit information for consumers, the uses for which they could control. This would be a major improvement over the current triopoly of credit bureaus, which house and sell vast swaths of frequently erroneous consumer information for commercial purposes outside consumers' control or consent. Widespread adoption of a blockchain to record mortgage titles would vastly improve the ability to track ownership of securitized mortgages. The Mortgage Electronic Registration System used by the industry to track ownership of securitized mortgages proved itself to be error prone and frequently unusable during the 2008 financial crisis, impeding loan modifications for troubled borrowers that frequently depended on the consent of the owner to achieve. Similarly, the use of blockchain technology to track real estate ownership could save homebuyers thousands of dollars in title insurance fees that they currently pay for duplicative title searches each time property changes hands.

While blockchain offers potentially exciting public benefits, there are a number of potential obstacles. For instance, widespread adoption of permissioned blockchains for specific commercial purposes will depend on industry agreement about technical standards, including the inevitable need for multiple blockchains to interact with each other.

Entrenched industry incumbents exposed to disruption will likely use all their resources, and regulatory relationships, to delay blockchain adoption for as long as possible. Regulators must exercise extreme care to make sure the regulatory environment embraces positive blockchain innovations and is not used as a weapon to stop uses that could bring significant public policy benefits. This will be a major challenge, as essentially any inefficient, centralized system will be ripe for disruption.

At the same time, new issues will arise with blockchain adaptation. For instance, distributed ledgers will only be as good as the data entered into them. Controls and processes must be in place to ensure data entry is accurate. Protocols will need to be developed to define trusted sources. Similarly, privacy issues will arise regarding the sharing of customer information and the ability to permanently affect customer reputations through erroneous data entries. In this regard, one of blockchain's strongest attributes—the security and inalterability of the data once entered—might also be its greatest weakness. Hopefully this weakness can be overcome by thoughtfully designed technical standards.

Robo-Advisors

Robo-advisor is a loose phrase generally used to encompass an automated service that allocates investments through a computer algorithm. These algorithms will periodically rebalance an investor's portfolio to align it with the appropriate asset allocation given the investor's risk tolerance and retirement horizon. Some robo-advisors will also analyze fees charged by the different fund options provided in workers' 401(k)s or 403(b)s and make sure investments are allocated to the lowest-cost funds (Ayres and Curtis, 2015).

Robo-advisory firms must be registered as investment advisors with the SEC and must provide advice consistent with the best interests of their clients, as is the case with any investment advisor (SEC, 2017). To date, applying a fiduciary standard to robo-advisors has not been problematic, as the algorithms they use are based on standard, accepted investment guidance. However, as discussed later, as machine learning and AI are applied to financial advice—with more customized, idiosyncratic guidance given to investors from a "black box"—application of the fiduciary standard may not be so straightforward.

There seems to be a consensus, with a few caveats, that robo-advisors provide positive social benefits by widening access to basic, affordable financial advice for middle-income investors. Human financial advisors are expensive. Many have minimum asset requirements of $500,000 or more and typically charge an annual fee equal to 1 to 2 percent of assets. This is in addition to the fees charged by the funds they may recommend to their clients. In contrast, many robo-advisors have no minimum asset requirement, and the requirements of most that do are under $5,000. Fees generally range from 0.25 to 0.50 percent a year. Some charge monthly fees as low as $1 per month for very small accounts.

Though robo-advisors do not purport to put their clients in the best-performing fund (a difficult challenge for humans or computers, as past performance is no indicator of future results), they are designed to put their clients in the lowest-fee fund, typically passive index funds offered by Vanguard and others. Simply reducing fees can substantially improve the performance of an average investor's portfolio. For instance, compare a $10,000 investment over twenty-five years paying a 2 percent fee, for an actively managed fund, and 0.5 percent fee, typical of a passive index fund. The difference in that 1.5 percent over twenty-five years translates into $30,000.

Regrettably, a recent survey by Pew of 401(k) participants indicates that nearly one-third were not familiar with the fees charged on their investments, and two-thirds had not read investment fee disclosures over the past year (Pew Charitable Trusts, 2017). Four out of five wanted more information about investment fees. They need it! A 2015 *Yale Law Journal* study of 3,500 401(k) plans found that a significant portion established investment menus that led investors to high-fee portfolios. On average, investors were paying 0.78 percent more by being directed to actively managed funds (Ayres and Curtis, 2015).

Robo-advisors also take the emotion out of investing by regularly rebalancing their clients' investments to make sure their asset allocations are appropriate to their risk tolerances and retirement horizons. This entails selling a portion of those assets that have been performing well and buying underperforming assets—the classic buy low, sell high strategy. This is a time-tested strategy to maximize returns. Nonetheless, it is a strategy that is difficult to execute for many inexperienced (or even experienced) investors. Who wants to sell investments that are rising in value and buy ones that are falling? In addition to taking emotion out of investing decisions, robo-advisors solve the problem of the inattentive investor who simply does not have the time or inclination to periodically monitor and rebalance asset allocations on his or her own.

Though the benefits of robo-advisors are clear, particularly for younger workers with relatively small retirement nest eggs, they also have their disadvantages. They are good entry-level tools for the world of investing but are far from adequate in providing more advanced services such as estate planning, tax management, trust fund administration, and postretirement planning. They are also less well equipped to handle unexpected changes in an investor's financial situation—a large inheritance, perhaps. In light of this shortcoming, robo-advisor firms are increasingly offering human advice as part of their package of services.

As previously mentioned, robo-advisors are subject to the SEC's fiduciary standard. Since they rely on well-accepted investment principles in designing the algorithms that support their services, application of fiduciary principles has not impeded the growth of robo-advisories. In fact, the Department of Labor's proposed rule to expand the fiduciary standard to brokers who give retirement investment advice would have worked to robo-advisors' advantage as, unlike many of the (human) brokerage firms with which they compete, they were already compliant.[1]

However, robo-advisors are now turning to AI to provide more sophisticated counsel to their clients. As used in this chapter, AI refers to teaching a computer how to complete a given task by having it process a large set of data and "learning," through trial and error, how to connect the data with the desired outcome. (See Chapter 3 for more about AI.) This is in contrast to hard-coding a computer with all the various scenarios it may encounter when performing a given task. The coder preordains the result. With AI, the computer figures it out for itself. This kind of AI, machine learning, is already finding a host of applications with self-driving cars, prediction of disease, and even the movie recommendations you receive from Netflix (Rosov, 2017).

The challenge—as we have found with the AI long used to support high-frequency trading—is that computer "thought" can be a bit of a black box. Not even the engineers who design the programming can always understand the reasoning, and sometimes unpredictable outcomes, produced by AI. Thus, it seems unlikely that regulators will be able to evaluate and understand a robo-advisor's AI code to determine whether it was working in the customer's best interests.

A solution, however, might be found in the approach exchanges and the SEC have taken toward the unpredictable and opaque results of high-frequency trading. Regardless of how those computers make their trading decisions, they are subject to circuit breakers that halt trading when stock prices go into free fall. This approach does not directly attack the problem of errant AI, but it does limit the damage it could cause. Similarly, the SEC might want to consider putting some type of guardrails around AI investment advice, drawn from fiduciary principles applied to any investment advisor. This would give robo-advisors more flexibility to vary advice depending on data inputs relevant to the client, while preventing errant programming, for instance, from putting a twenty-five-year-old worker's 401(k) into money market funds, or a risk-averse retiree into Bitcoin futures.

A second regulatory issue presented by robo-advisors, but fortunately technically easier to solve, arises from robo-advisors' need to access their clients' account information to provide their services. Some robo-advisors provide account services and offer their own investment products, but most rely on access to clients' accounts and investment options that are provided at other firms. In the United States, to enable this access, clients usually have to give their security credentials to the robo-advisor. However, this creates risk that clients' security information could be compromised if the robo-advisors' own systems are breached. It also presents privacy issues, as the giving up of security credentials essentially allows the robo-advisor to see everything the client can see when he or she accesses the account. This may include a significant amount of data that are extraneous to the services the robo-advisor provides.

The challenge is made more complex by the economic self-interest of account providers to resist giving that access. Customer data are among financial institutions' most precious assets. Many are loath to share it. Robo-advisors in particular can help clients identify low-fee funds, potentially drawing them away from higher-cost funds provided by the account custodian. If you are Transamerica and administering accounts for 401(k)s that offer Vanguard funds as well, why would you want to help a robo-advisor tell a plan participant that Vanguard's funds are cheaper than yours?

The solution to this problem would seem to be for regulators in the United States to require financial institutions to provide access to third-party advisors through an application programming interface (API). This is already being done in Europe for bank customers wishing to use third-party service providers to manage their money. The use of APIs permits access without customers having to give up their security credentials and also confines access to data necessary to provide the services the customer has authorized. So, for instance, a robo-advisor authorized to rebalance a customer's 401(k) account could only view that account, not the customer's brokerage or 529 account. Many large U.S. banks have voluntarily decided to provide API access though it has not been required by U.S. regulators. The CFPB recently opined through a nonbinding statement of "principles" that consumers should have the right to grant "trusted" third parties access to their accounts and that agreements with their account providers should support safe, customer-authorized access that does not require consumers to give up their security credentials (CFPB, 2017).

Shortly after the CFPB's issuance of these principles, Fidelity—one of the largest record keepers for 401(k) accounts—announced that it would begin providing robo-advisors and other third-party providers with API access (Crossman, 2017). This is a trend that should be strongly encouraged, if not required, by U.S. regulators. However, here again, the lack of clear regulatory ownership may be an impediment to requiring API access. The CFPB is responsible for protecting consumers and has jurisdiction over banks, but it is not the primary regulator of mutual fund managers and investment advisors, a responsibility that rests with the SEC.

Marketplace Lending

Marketplace lending refers to lending provided by nonbank financial firms that use investment capital (instead of deposits) to lend through online platforms. Originally envisioned for "peer-to-peer" lending, linking individual lenders with individual borrowers, the platforms have evolved so that the vast majority of their investment capital now comes from institutional investors, including banks. Marketplace lending encompasses multiple business models. Some originate loans and hold them on their balance sheets. Some partner with a bank to originate loans, then buy those loans and sell them to investors as whole loans or as securitizations. Others use a hybrid model, retaining some portion of their loans in portfolio and selling the rest. All use automated, online loan applications and have no retail branches. Funding decisions are generally made within forty-eight to seventy-two hours.

When marketplace lending was first launched in the United States in 2006, the hope was that data-driven, automated underwriting would lower origination costs and expand credit eligibility beyond the traditional underwriting used by banks, while eliminating the risk of discriminatory bias in human judgment. Though some of these goals have been achieved, the algorithms used by marketplace firms have themselves presented regulatory issues.

The volume of loans issued by marketplace lenders has grown rapidly but still represents a tiny fraction of the consumer lending market. Research shows that online lenders have expanded access to credit for consumers and provided credit at lower rates, at least for prime borrowers. A substantial majority of consumer loans made by the major marketplace lenders are used to consolidate and refinance higher-cost credit card debt and home improvement loans. Similarly, SoFi—which specializes in student lending—refinances high-cost student loans once a student has graduated and secured employment. Thus, it does not support access to college, but it does help graduates who are safe credit risks lower their student loan repayments.

The evidence is more mixed regarding the cost of credit to near-prime and subprime borrowers, though a recent report analyzing data from Lending Club (Jagtiani and Lemieux, 2017)—the largest of platform lenders—suggests that Lending Club's data-driven underwriting is allowing many borrowers who would be classified as subprime using traditional criteria to qualify for prime rates. This research also indicates that consumers paid smaller spreads on loans from Lending Club than provided by traditional lending venues. Finally, it found that Lending Club's online lending had penetrated areas in need of additional credit supply, such as those that had lost bank branches.

While the weight of research suggests that marketplace lending has had positive benefits in expanding access to credit and lowering costs, there have been criticisms. Traditional banks argue that online lenders have an unfair competitive advantage because they are not subject to the same degree of regulatory oversight. Ironically, many marketplace lenders have expressed interest in obtaining federal banking charters because of their perceived advantages in securing low-cost, stable deposit funding and the ability to charge consistent rates nationwide through preemption of individual state usury laws. There would seem to be no good reason why fintech lenders should not be able to obtain bank charters if they are willing to comply with the same level of supervision and regulatory oversight applicable to banks. Indeed, bringing them under the regulatory umbrella could allay fears about an uneven playing field. At the same time, there appears to be no good reason why fintech firms should get special breaks as regulated, federally chartered depositories. For instance, they should be subject to the same capital, liquidity, and safety and soundness standards applicable to lending by traditional banks, as well as the same consumer obligations, including the Community Reinvestment Act.

Allowing marketplace lenders to become federally charted depositories—under the same rules that apply to traditional banks—could also have important benefits for system stability. As marketplace lending becomes a larger source of consumer credit—the U.S. Treasury Department report estimates the potential market at $1 trillion—it becomes a greater source of systemic risk if its funding is disrupted in an economic downturn (U.S. Department of the Treasury, 2016). Market funding is highly volatile, particularly during periods of economic tumult. As loan defaults increase, investors pull back on their willingness to finance credit. Deposit funding, on the other hand, is stable, as federally backed banks are viewed as safer than non-insured institutions. Bank deposits actually increased during the 2008 financial crisis. The more our economy relies on marketplace lenders for consumer credit access, the more important it becomes for that segment to have a resilient source of funding that can function through the cycle. Access to insured deposits would provide that resilience. At the same time, if marketplace lenders are to be brought under the safety net, they must accept the tradeoff: much tougher consumer and prudential standard oversight.

Another issue presented by marketplace lenders concerns the increasing use of more sophisticated AI to make credit decisions. Fintech lenders are subject to fair lending laws—as they should be—and, as established in recent court precedents, they must take care to use criteria that do not have a disparate impact on a protected class. The problem, however, as with the use of AI for investment advising, is that it is not always clear why outcomes based on machine learning of large swaths of data produce unintended results (Knight, 2017). Even the "smartest" computers do not distinguish between correlation and causation. For instance, a computer might find high levels of loan performance among borrowers whose social media friends also have good credit histories. However, such an algorithm might exclude otherwise credit-worthy loan applicants and reinforce systemic social bias by assuming that individuals who are creditworthy also have creditworthy friends.

When the use of AI in credit approvals results in disparate impact, it seems the onus should be on the fintech lender to identify the problem and correct it. It is their black box. They need to be held responsible for it. Sophisticated technology should not be used as an excuse for discriminatory lending practices. By imposing such accountability, fintech firms will presumably train their engineers on the front end about fair lending requirements and the need to avoid discriminatory outcomes in loan approval decisions. Fintech firms should also continually monitor patterns in lending decisions for disparate impact. Online lending platforms and the use of AI hold great promise for making responsible credit more widely available at lower cost. However, as the use of AI progresses, regulators need to be wary and ensure that robust fair-lending compliance programs are in place at these firms.

Conclusion

This chapter has sought to highlight only a few of the many regulatory issues associated with financial technology. The opportunities presented by fintech are exciting. For both businesses and consumers, it promises to make a wider array of services and data accessible in ways that are faster, more efficient, and less costly. There are also important public and regulatory benefits to much of this technology, whether it is reducing systemic risks inherent in our current, heavily intermediated financial markets; broadening access to cost-effective professional investment advice for middle-income savers; or making more credit-worthy borrowers eligible for reasonably priced loans.

At the same time, these benefits cannot be achieved without some disruption to established market participants, who will no doubt use all of their preexisting regulatory relationships to resist change (McCarthy, 2017). The difficult balance for regulators will be to make sure regulation is not used as a weapon against positive innovation, while at the same time making sure technology is not used as a weapon to undermine core regulatory protections that serve the public interest.

This is not a challenge unique to financial services. Uber may well be a positive catalyst for shaking up state and local licensing regimes that do more to erect barriers for entry to car-hiring services than to promote public convenience and safety. But this is not to say that all licensing and regulation of cars for hire is unnecessary. It is in the public interest to have some basic standards around safety, insurance coverage, and driver competence. If, over the long term, market disruptors such as Uber and Lyft can force a shakeup of inefficient, anticompetitive regulatory regimes, that will be a good thing. If, however, the disruption leads to wholesale deregulation, that will be a bad thing. If the disruption leads to smarter regulation for all car-hiring services that is focused on the public interest, not commercial self-interest, that will be a positive for all.

Similarly, fintech may serve as an important catalyst to rethinking and improving aspects of financial oversight for the public and those who provide financial services to them, both traditional and fintech (Jagtiani and Lemieux, 2017). For instance, better understanding of borrowers' capacity to repay loans based on broader data sets and AI technology could merit a rethinking of punitive capital requirements too often imposed on unsecured consumer loans when borrower FICO scores slip into "subprime" territory. Such capital requirements can discourage lending to low- and middle-income borrowers who may not have built strong credit histories based on traditional factors. Thus, technology may help regulators rethink and broaden their view of the characteristics of borrowers who are at risk of nonrepayment. However, the basic principle of requiring financial institutions to make credit decisions based on the borrower's ability to repay should remain sacrosanct: it is core to both consumer safety and soundness regulation. If we learned anything from the financial crisis, it is that the making of unaffordable loans can have horrific consequences for borrowers and their families, as well as the financial stability of banks and the financial system as a whole. But being open to evolving views of borrower credit capacity is not inherently inconsistent with a commitment to making sure loans are affordable. Done right, technology can help us broaden credit availability while reducing borrower defaults.

Poorly thought-out "self-regulating" approaches to financial oversight proved disastrous in the lead-up to the financial crisis. The lack of borrower protections in mortgage finance, a complete "hands-off" approach to derivatives markets, deference to big banks in setting their own capital requirements—these were all major contributors to the subprime debacle. The key challenge for regulators is to identify ways that fintech can lead to smarter regulation while preserving core regulatory protections. Technology may disrupt financial services, but we cannot permit it to disrupt financial services oversight.

Note

1. The Department of Labor's fiduciary rule was struck down in the courts before it was fully implemented, but the SEC has since proposed a similar rule.

Bibliography

Ayres, Ian, and Quinn Curtis. 2015. "Beyond Diversification: The Pervasive Problem of Excessive Fees and 'Dominated Funds' in 401(k) Plans." *Yale Law Journal* 124 (5): 1476–552.

Biella, Mateo, and Vittorio Zinetti. 2016. *Blockchain Technology and Applications from a Financial Perspective*. UniCredit Technical Report.

Brainard, Lael. 2016. "Distributed Ledger Technology: Implications for Payments, Clearing, and Settlement." Remarks before the Institute of International Finance Annual Meeting on Blockchain, Washington, D.C., Federal Reserve Board, October 7, 2016. https://www.federalreserve.gov/newsevents/speech/brainard20161007a.htm.

CFPB (U.S. Consumer Financial Protection Bureau). 2017. "Consumer Protection Principles: Consumer-Authorized Financial Data Sharing and Aggregation." October 18, 2017. https://www.consumerfinance.gov/about-us/newsroom/cfpb-outlines-principles-consumer-authorized-financial-data-sharing-and-aggregation.

Clayton, Jay. 2017. "Statement on Cryptocurrencies and Initial Coin Offerings." U.S. Securities and Exchange Commission, December 11, 2017. https://www.sec.gov/news/public-statement/statement-clayton-2017-12-11.

Crossman, Penny. 2017. "Fidelity Latest Financial Firm to Facilitate Data Sharing with Fintechs." *American Banker*, November 14, 2017. https://www.americanbanker.com/news/fidelity-latest-financial-firm-to-roll-out-customer-data-api.

Jagtiani, Julapa, and Catharine Lemieux. 2017. "Fintech Lending: Financial Inclusion, Risk Pricing, and Alternative Information." Federal Reserve Bank of Philadelphia Working Paper No. 17-17.

Knight, Will. 2017. "The Dark Secret at the Heart of AI." *MIT Technology Review*, April 11, 2017. https://www.technologyreview.com/s/604087/the-dark-secret-at-the-heart-of-ai.

McCarthy, ed. 2017. "Augmented Intelligence: Combining Human Intelligence and Technology." *CFA Institute Magazine* 28 (3). https://www.cfainstitute.org/research/cfa-magazine/2017/augmented-intelligence-combining-human-intelligence-and-technology.

Moody's Investors Service. 2017. "Credit Strategy—Blockchain Technology: Blockchain Has Potential to Transform Many Elements of Securities Trading." April 12, 2017. https://www.moodys.com/research/Moodys-For-financial-institutions-blockchain-has-great-potential-in-the--PR_364986.

Morrell, Alex. 2017. "How Even the Tiniest Change in Fees Can Devastate Your Retirement Savings, in 4 Charts." *Business Insider*, May 10, 2017. http://www.businessinsider.com/401k-fees-devastate-retirement-2017-5.

Pew Charitable Trusts. 2017. "Many Workers Have Limited Understanding of Retirement Plan Fees." Issue brief, November 15, 2017.

Popper, Nathaniel. 2017. "Bitcoin Hasn't Replaced Cash, but Investors Don't Care." *New York Times*, December 6, 2017.

Rosov, Sviatoslav. 2017. "Machine Learning, Artificial Intelligence, and Robo-Advisors: The Future of Finance?" Market Integrity Insights, CFA Institute, July 12, 2017.

Schneider, James, Alexander Blostein, Brian Lee, Steven Kent, Ingrid Groer, and Eric Beardsley. 2016. *Blockchain: Putting Theory into Practice*. Goldman Sachs Equity Research Report. https://msenterprise.global.ssl.fastly.net/wordpress/2017/07/Goldman-Sachs-Blockchain-putting-theory-to-practice.pdf.

SEC (U.S. Securities and Exchange Commission). 2017. "Inadvertent Custody: Advisory Contract Versus Custodial Contract Authority." Guidance Update No. 2017-01, February 2017. https://www.sec.gov/investment/im-guidance-2017-01.pdf.

U.S. Department of the Treasury. 2016. *Opportunities and Challenges in Online Marketplace Lending*. Washington, DC: U.S. Department of the Treasury. https://www.treasury.gov/connect/blog/Documents/Opportunities_and_Challenges_in_Online_Marketplace_Lending_white_paper.pdf.

U.S. Financial Stability Oversight Council. 2017. *2017 Annual Report*. Washington, DC: U.S. Department of the Treasury. https://www.treasury.gov/initiatives/fsoc/studies-reports/Documents/FSOC_2017_Annual_Report.pdf.

World Economic Forum. 2015. *The Future of Financial Services: How Disruptive Innovations Are Reshaping the Way Financial Services Are Structured, Provisioned, and Consumed*. June 2015. http://www3.weforum.org/docs/WEF_The_future__of_financial_services.pdf.

CHAPTER 3

Big Data, AI, and Algorithmic Platforms

Implications for Governing and Public Policy

Ramayya Krishnan

On April 10, 2018, Mark Zuckerberg, CEO of Facebook, testified to the House Committee on Energy and Commerce about the Cambridge Analytica scandal. The personal information of approximately eighty-seven million Americans who use Facebook had been breached. With over two billion monthly active users worldwide, Facebook is a global social platform widely used for communication and news consumption. The Me Too campaign[1] grew on Facebook, money has been raised on it after disasters such as Hurricane Harvey, and more than seventy million small businesses use it as their platform. Yet its ubiquity and use as a trusted tool for sharing personal information and consuming news were exploited to "hack" U.S. elections and democratic processes. House Energy and Commerce Committee chairman Greg Walden (R-OR) posed the following questions in his opening remarks: "How should we, as policymakers, evaluate and respond to these events? Does Congress need to clarify whether or not consumers own or have any real power over their online data? Have edge providers[2] grown to the point that they need federal supervision?" (Walden, 2018).

In this essay, I discuss these and related questions that are the nexus of information technology and public policy. These questions have arisen as a result of the convergence of big data, artificial intelligence (AI), and algorithmic platforms that power systems like Facebook that have achieved societal scale and are nearly ubiquitous. However, this technological convergence is by no means limited to social media. Driverless cars and popular applications such as IBM Watson and AlphaGo (Silver et al., 2017) have captured the imagination of the public and leaders alike. Watson defeated human *Jeopardy!* champions by using a question-answering system combined with cognitive computing over a large knowledge base. AlphaGo used a combination of pattern recognition and optimization algorithms along with a novel, simulated game-playing technique to defeat the best human players of what is widely regarded as the most difficult strategy board game ever devised. While these examples of cars and games may seem distant from organizational or societal decision-making, they are not.

These recent developments demonstrate that algorithms can perform tasks that require perception, cognition, and action at levels comparable to— or better than—those of performances by humans. The consequences for society are significant. Will algorithmic systems be deployed in an unbiased and fair manner that aligns with our societal values? How will these developments change the nature of work and the skills required to do work and provide economic opportunity for all?

I focus on both the challenges and the opportunities posed by this information-technology-led transformation of society. The questions listed here highlight the focal topics addressed in this essay. The topics have been chosen based on both the significant impact they are likely to have on society and the interest they have generated in public discourse.

- What are the consequences for communication and news consumption of algorithmic systems that shape the use of social media in privately owned platforms?
- How should algorithms and the data that they use be audited for explainability to ensure that they are free of bias?
- As algorithms develop the capability to perform certain tasks at human levels, the nature of work will change, as will the skills required to perform work. What is the future of work in an algorithmic world? How should government and public policy respond to help citizens prepare for a new economy and new modes of work?
- While being cognizant of the challenges arising in an algorithmic world, what opportunities can be harnessed to support the greater good?

- Given the important role that these technological changes have for governance, how should our law makers and public-sector leaders keep themselves informed about the technologies and their consequences?

Review: From Management Information Systems to the Algorithmic World

Early applications of computing in private and public organizations focused on management information systems (Laudon and Laudon, 2013). Numeric administrative data, often collected and entered manually, were processed in batches using centralized computing resources to produce reports on a weekly or monthly schedule. This was the world of "small data," with controlled mechanisms in place for data collection, processing, and distribution.

From these early days, computing evolved through generations of technology (for example, mainframes, minis, and the personal computer). Data management technologies and networking evolved in parallel. However, the advent of the World Wide Web in 1991 marked a turning point. In particular, it led to standardization. All types of content—numeric, data, graphic, audio, video, and text—could be formatted using the hypertext markup language (HTML), and all files had a unique address, the universal resource locator (URL). Thus, content could be universally shared, retrieved, and viewed using a device that had access to a web browser (Bhargava and Krishnan, 1998).

This standardization proved transformative. It resulted in a continually growing repository of data of various types residing in a networked collection of systems. The standardization also created an architecture for distributed computing. Data storage and computing centers required to host large volumes of data or to enable processing of the data could be interconnected with lightweight devices running web browsers at the edge of the network. Algorithmic processing could be located in the data centers (a.k.a. the cloud) or at the edge, depending on the needs of the application. This architecture led to the deployment of the "software as a service" model. Popular applications that are used widely today either by individuals (for example, Siri and Alexa) or by enterprises (for example, Salesforce Customer Relationship Management, enterprise resource planning systems such as SAP) are deployed using cloud computing.

From the perspective of societal systems, the web ushered in the world of big data with a focus on volume and variety. Its multimedia content and its scale resulted in massive movement of data on the internet, now estimated to be close to two zettabytes (one trillion gigabytes) per year. From a public policy standpoint, the big-data systems on the web focused attention on data privacy and confidentiality. In particular, given the extent of data collection about what content users consume via the web, public policy was concerned with data ownership, data security, and data-sharing practices. What was the notice given to users about whom data was collected? What were the limits placed on its use, and what permissions were given for linking or sharing the data with third parties or with other data sets? The Facebook data breach and the congressional hearing that I discussed earlier focused on these questions but in the context of social platforms that combine big data and algorithms. I will address these questions as they arise in the context of social media in the following section. The Federal Trade Commission is charged with monitoring and implementing data management, data privacy, and confidentiality policy in the United States.

The emergence of the smartphone a decade ago was the next turning point, and it presaged the deployment of sensors at a massive scale. Since sensors can stream data, this added the velocity dimension to big-data systems. The ubiquitous adoption of the smartphone created a large global platform for apps. On mobile devices, the app displaced the web browser as the user interface to enterprise applications in the cloud (for example, Siri or Salesforce). The app also enabled the creation of a peer-to-peer social media communication and collaboration platform. Sensors such as audio and video recorders, cameras, GPS, and accelerometers built into smartphones enabled data-rich communication via these app-based platforms. Facebook, Twitter, and Instagram are popular examples.

These app-based platforms have seen adoption rates rivaling those of the most successful inventions in human history. For example, there are more than two billion active users on Facebook. The sheer scale and the media-rich nature of the exchanges between users on the app-based platforms result in another large, societal big-data system (for example, phones and social platforms generate a zettabyte of traffic per year). As with the web, the app-based architectures provide mobile-device-based access to government services. However, from a public policy standpoint, the social dimensions of these platforms represent a fundamentally different challenge from that of the web.

Of particular relevance in this context is the role that social media platforms now play in our democracy. People disseminate news, share information, and debate social issues with one another using social media. Algorithms play a key role in mediating these conversations by curating and managing the exchange of news and information on these platforms. Therefore, new policies that consider the power of these algorithms are required for social media. This is in contrast to and represents a transition from the purely data-oriented policy relevant in the data privacy and data ownership discussion.

The need for this algorithmic policy lens extends beyond social media. It also applies to the general question of algorithmic accountability and bias, as well as the implications that the deployment of algorithmic decision systems holds for the future of work. In the rest of this essay, I will develop and discuss public policy issues that I outlined at the conclusion of the introduction, beginning with the case of social media.

Social Media, Algorithms, and Filter Bubbles

Social media is an edge service delivered over the internet. In August 2017, surveys conducted by the Pew Research Center (2018) revealed that more than 60 percent of American adults used social media sites as a source of news. The percentage was even higher for minorities. The social media platforms ranged from Facebook and YouTube to Twitter and Snapchat. This represented a significant shift from the world of broadcast television and radio to an era of narrowcast audio, video, and news.

The 1980s witnessed the shift from broadcast television to cable television and from AM/FM radio to satellite radio. This resulted in a vast increase in the number of channels offered to consumers. Consumers could select channels that most suited their preferences, opinions, and politics. There was no singular, authoritative Walter Cronkite news broadcast. This was the dawn of the era of narrowcasting. However, the emergence of the internet and mobile platforms over the last two decades and the emergence of algorithms have taken microtargeting to another level.

Social media platforms enable individual users to determine whom they want to connect with in the network. Many studies on the structure of social networks on platforms such as Facebook and Twitter document that some individuals are more highly connected, or have more followers, than others (Simsek and Jensen, 2008). Social media platforms and mobile technology have also lowered the barriers to entry for individuals to create and disseminate content. There are several advantages to these developments. Individuals can capture and share information both for entertainment purposes and to promote social welfare (for example, raise money for charity in the aftermath of Hurricane Harvey; share information that might result in attitude-changing discussions, as in the Me Too campaign; or hold elected officials or organizations accountable). However, this capability can also create problems. Jacobin mobs can emerge quickly as arbiters of opinion, influence, and, in the most pernicious extremes, repression. When individuals are highly connected, it is relatively straightforward to have influential nodes with high connectivity enable viral propagation of news (fact-checked or otherwise) over social networks such as Twitter and Facebook (Sekara, Stopczynski, and Lehmann, 2016).

Even more transformative has been the marriage of social algorithms and social networks. Information shared between individuals (that is, friends) in a social network is ranked using algorithms that take into account a variety of factors. These can include the user's prior clicks, the strength of his or her relationship with friends who are sharing the information, and other contextual factors, including location. Relevance scores computed by the algorithm determines which news feeds are displayed and their display order. This shapes the news and the information a citizen gets to consume. Clearly, personalization and recommendation algorithms have positive value to a user by reducing search costs and cognitive overload. However, emergent behavior results when individual choice exerted by users in what they choose to read and share interacts with algorithmic recommendations. This emergent behavior is not predictable from code reviews of the social algorithm in use on social media platforms, leading to concerns that social algorithms could create filter bubbles that are echo chambers. Essentially, users are exposed only to news and opinions entirely aligned with their politics or views.

Narrowcast, with its capacity to unicast news based on detailed data about individuals and their content preferences, can cause political polarization. Recent studies have begun to provide insight into the consequences of the interaction between social algorithms, individual choice pertaining to news consumption and sharing, and social networks. In 2015, a team of researchers from Facebook (Bakshy, Messing, and Adamic, 2015) studied the news consumption and sharing behavior of ten million users who self-reported their ideological affiliations (for example, liberal versus conservative). Roughly 20 percent of the friends of a conservative user were liberal, and this was approximately symmetrical for liberal users. The study found that the sharing of news content from traditional media was polarized. Conservatives shared conservative media stories with their friends, and liberals shared liberal ones with theirs. There was a larger willingness among conservatives to share liberal content than there was among liberals to share conservative content. Algorithmic recommendation and the social network did shape the availability and ranking of news on Facebook. However, the study found individual choice to be the key determinant of whether users wanted to limit exposure to or obtain access to content not aligned with their own opinions.

Recent work (Hughes and Lam, 2017) focused on the Facebook networks of and postings by congressional representatives and documented some interesting empirical facts. In comparison with lawmakers in the middle of the ideological spectrum, who have approximately nine thousand Facebook followers on average, lawmakers who are very liberal or very conservative have close to fourteen thousand followers. Further, as discussed in Messing, Van Kessel, and Hughes (2017), about 50 percent of the links to news outlets that were shared by members of the 115th Congress were predominantly news outlets linked to by members of just their own party.

While the discussion thus far has focused on polarization caused by the interaction between network structure and the role of algorithms in shaping the availability of legitimately generated news, there have also been concerns raised about the role of bots (that is, fake accounts controlled by computer programs) in social media. In a June 2014 Securities and Exchange Commission filing, Twitter acknowledged that close to 9 percent of its active users (or twenty-three million Twitter accounts) may be automated bots (U.S. Securities and Exchange Commission, 2014). The Defense Advanced Research Projects Agency created a competition in 2015 (Subrahmanian et al., 2016) to automatically detect social media bots, since this type of adversarial attack could further exacerbate polarization. Bots posing as users in a social network can algorithmically introduce content based on an analysis of "wedge issues" in an election, creating further divisions within society.

Our democratic processes rely on an informed populace. Thomas Jefferson's (1958) observation in his letter to Richard Price on January 8, 1789—"Wherever the people are well informed they can be trusted with their own government that whenever things get so far wrong as to attract their notice, they may be relied on to set them to rights"—holds true today. Ensuring that the algorithms that serve as gatekeepers permit the free and fair flow of information is therefore critically important. In the aftermath of the 2016 U.S. presidential election, there has been a good deal of attention paid to these issues. Most social media platforms rely on advertising-based business models. These platforms enable targeted advertising to their users (based on news consumption and sharing behavior, political affiliations, demographics, and location). This technology has been used by interest groups and politicians for the legitimate purpose of communicating with citizens. (Witness the barrage of ads before any election.) However, the same advertising platform can be used to target groups of users with "fake news" stories, and to promote events that can undermine our democratic processes.

On January 25, 2018, the Senate Intelligence Committee released information provided by Facebook following its investigation of alleged Russian interference in the U.S. presidential elections. Facebook reported that 129 Facebook events (a type of calendar ad that promotes a physical event) purchased by a Russian organization had been seen by three hundred thousand users on Facebook (Stretch, 2018). The events concerned highly contentious topics (for example, immigration, Islam in America) and used incomplete and incorrect information with the intention of pitting Americans against one another. Facebook has created a tool and action plan to take down fake accounts and to address the algorithmic manipulation of news and information on its platform. However, on account of the vast scale of Facebook, this is still a work in progress.

An important recent public policy development has been the introduction of the Honest Ads Act in the Senate and the House in 2017. Facebook and other social media platforms, in an attempt to self-police and in a bid to stave off regulation, are adopting some elements of the bill and have been supportive of this legislation.

Identity Verification and Know Your Customer

Following the 2016 presidential election, Facebook introduced steps to verify the identity and geographic location of buyers of political and issue-based advertising on Facebook. Since advertising can be purchased to microtarget users based on interests (for example, education, political support for President Donald Trump), Facebook introduced policies that would permit it to block ads, remove pages, or prevent content from being introduced into newsfeeds by prospective political and issue-based advertisers who did not reveal identity, funding, or location (Facebook Business, 2018).

Transparency

To increase transparency, particularly as it pertains to political advertising, social media platforms such as Facebook have created election commissions and a mechanism whereby ads will clearly specify who has paid for them. This is similar to the model used in television with political advertising. Facebook has also committed to hiring ten thousand employees to track down fake accounts. This is a difficult challenge and still very much a work in progress. To enable third parties to access information about such political ads, Facebook has created a searchable repository of all political ads that are run on Facebook, their price, and who is paying for them (Facebook, n.d.).

Clearly, the congressional hearings featuring Zuckerberg and the introduction of the Honest Ads Act have trained a spotlight on social media platforms. The steps being taken by companies such as Facebook are steps in the right direction. However, a major issue remains unresolved: the balance that is struck between an algorithmically driven content recommendation and a user engagement model that has revenue implications for the welfare objective of reducing echo chambers. A solution that provides incentives for innovation by the platform while promoting the public interest is challenging but will be required to protect civil discourse and our democratic processes.

Algorithmic Accountability and Bias

On December 11, 2017, New York City passed a law (New York City Council, 2018), the first of its kind in the nation, to establish a task force to develop a set of recommendations related to algorithmic accountability. Algorithms match kids to schools in New York City, allocate public housing, and are used by the police to predict where crimes may occur and to guide force deployment. The list of applications is long. The rationale underlying this widespread use of algorithms has been to improve efficiency and to make resource allocation more effective. Unfortunately, flaws or biases within the algorithms can precipitate injustice. Individuals can be denied bail or be disqualified from receiving a public benefit.

In her book *Weapons of Math Destruction*, Cathy O'Neil (2016) discusses some of the reasons that individuals trust mathematical models and algorithms, one of the main ones being that they believe these methods are free from human bias. However, recent research has documented multiple instances, in settings such as loan granting, criminal sentencing, and job advertising, in which algorithmic decisions are biased against minorities or women (Datta, Sen, and Zick, 2016). ProPublica (n.d.) monitors examples of "machine bias" in order to serve the public interest. Using algorithmically generated risk scores used in the criminal justice system as an example, they document instances in which the risk scores are biased, often affecting minorities disproportionately.

These documented examples have motivated questions about algorithmic accountability. When algorithms are "black boxes" and decisions made by them are opaque, it is difficult to build trust in algorithmic decision systems. Danks and London (2017) discuss different types of algorithmic bias. Two that are particularly relevant to this discussion are bias in training data sets and algorithmic processing bias. It is important to note that while bias usually has a pejorative connotation, the objective here is to understand it contextually. For example, a system that deploys a "neutral algorithm," which has been trained (that is, its parameters were estimated) with data from a human-controlled system, may learn the patterns of behavior implicit in the data. A common example in this setting is a field in the data set that is correlated with race (for example, number of times stopped by the police). If low thresholds on this field were used to decide who would get a loan, an algorithm trained using these data would likely grant fewer loans to minorities who, on average, might be more frequently stopped by police. This type of training data bias has been the subject of considerable attention in certain domains, such as financial services, where banks are required to provide data to federal government agencies in order to demonstrate the fairness of their loan-granting processes.[3]

The second kind of bias, algorithmic processing bias, relates to the characteristics of the algorithm itself and the steps it takes to arrive at a decision. In some cases, the model that is learned from the data can be analyzed and understood. Consider the case of a classification algorithm that takes multiple inputs and produces a binary decision (for example, to grant a loan or not to grant a loan). Drawing from an example described in Datta, Sen, and Zick (2016), let the loan-granting decision be based on two inputs: the debt-to-income ratio and race. How much did each of these inputs contribute to the decision? Establishing this will help us understand whether the system is fair or discriminating. When there are a small number of inputs, holding all but one of the inputs constant and perturbing it with values drawn randomly from a probability distribution could shed light on how that input influences the decision. Thus, in this simple example, holding the debt-to-income ratio constant and changing the race value randomly can determine how the classifier is using information about race. A more general and sophisticated version of the solution that permits multiple inputs to vary simultaneously is developed in Datta, Sen, and Zick (2016) and can be viewed as a response to an algorithmic transparency query: How much did each input contribute to the final decision?

While this is a powerful capability and works well for simpler classification models, more complex models do not lend themselves readily to explanation. This is the case with so-called deep-learning neural network models. While these models appear to learn and recognize patterns well, even the developer of the model has a difficult time explaining how the model arrived at its decision. In an *MIT Technology Review* article titled "The Dark Secret at the Heart of AI," Will Knight (2017) describes the example of a deep-learning neural network system called Deep Patient that was developed at the Mount Sinai Hospital using the vast amount of data available about seventy thousand patients in the electronic health record system. Deep Patient proved to be remarkably good at predicting disease and better than human physicians at predicting the onset of schizophrenia. However, the physicians who developed it did not understand how it worked. The interactions between the model elements made it too complex to explain. Recognizing the importance of this accountability problem, the Defense Advanced Research Projects Agency has launched the XAI, or explainable AI (Gunning, 2018), program, which is designed to create ways to explain the performance of algorithmic systems.

There is a need for policy innovation to work hand in hand with the development of better technical solutions to the problem of algorithmic accountability and bias. A recent report by the Federal Trade Commission (2016) provides a good overview of laws that an organization seeking to deploy algorithms in consumer-facing tasks should take into account. An example is the Fair Credit Reporting Act and associated eligibility determinations that are often used in loan-granting decisions. Traditional credit-scoring models use data about behaviors related to loan repayments or credit histories to determine a potential borrower's likelihood of meeting credit obligations and repaying loans. Predictive analytic models that have recently been introduced have begun to use new types of data to determine these same likelihoods. These data may include zip code, social media usage, shopping history, or late-payment history to determine the creditworthiness of a loan applicant. It is important for policymakers and developers alike to ensure that the inclusion of these data do not create biased data sets that disproportionately affect protected groups. It is also imperative that they assess the absence of bias in the algorithmic processing of these data. It is likely that the task force called for by the recently passed New York City law will recommend compliance testing, as has been the case with decisions pertaining to financial services and products. It is likely that a market will emerge to evaluate algorithmic decision systems (much like the auditing firms that audit financial statements to ensure that financial markets can trade with reliable and unbiased information). It is also conceivable that a nonprofit organization like Underwriter Laboratories may emerge to certify algorithmic accountability.

Algorithms and the Future of Work

On January 21, 2018, Amazon opened its first Amazon Go store (Amazon, n.d.). There are no cashiers or checkout lines in the store. Shoppers scan themselves into the store using the Amazon Go app. Computer vision, deep learning, and AI technologies are used to track what items a shopper adds to his or her shopping bag. Each item added to the shopping bag is then added to a virtual shopping cart. When the customer leaves the store, payment is made via the Amazon account. The application of AI technologies to transform our work, our lives, and our communities is no longer fiction. It is here.

In addition to the futuristic Go store, other examples include the first autonomous truck used by Anheuser-Busch to deliver beer, powered by Uber, which is conducting autonomous vehicle trials in Pittsburgh; robots winning the Amazon stocking and picking challenge, which seeks to automate the filling of e-commerce orders; and the emergence of robotic process automation, especially in domains such as financial services, with the objective of increasing efficiency and reducing costs. These technologies capture the imagination and inspire thinking about their potential value to society. At the same time, they also conjure fear about the job losses that might follow. How should society respond to this wave of technological advances?

In an editorial in the April 13, 2017, issue of *Nature* (Mitchell and Brynjolfsson, 2017), Tom Mitchell, a founder of the fields of machine learning and AI and a Carnegie Mellon faculty member, and Erik Brynjolfsson, a prominent economist at MIT, warned that policymakers are flying blind into what will almost certainly be massive economic, social, and personal upheaval as a result of the rise of AI in the workplace. In a National Academies report on the effects of technology on U.S. employment, they called for a data-intensive approach to evaluate policy options and create policy responses to help workers, organizations, and communities prepare themselves for current and future automation-driven disruptions. Three issues particularly relevant to this discussion are being investigated at the Block Center's Future of Work Initiative at Carnegie Mellon University.[4] The first issue pertains to the skill bias induced by algorithmic technologies. While algorithmic technologies like robotic process automation substitute some people out of a task, they also change the skill sets required for those that remain in the workplace. The cost savings and benefits to efficiency and effectiveness will result in the widespread deployment of these technologies within organizations. The societal question concerns how to identify the human skill sets needed in the algorithmic world and provide employees and workers with these skill sets in a cost-effective fashion in high school, college, and the workplace. This implies the need for widely available and inexpensive education (see https://learnlab.org/ for one example of education technology to support robust student learning at scale) to train the workforce in the skills that will be demanded in the labor market. In an insightful analysis of technological change and its implications for our society, economists Acemoglu and Johnson (2017) call for the use of internet-enabled education delivery models to reduce the cost of training and to prevent student debt from becoming a constraint on upward mobility. They also argue for a tax policy to favor investment in labor versus one that subsidizes investments in machines and algorithms. As they note, "We should not fear robots that can increase productivity and benefit us all—but we would be ill-advised to subsidize their deployment when this comes at the direct expense of workers" (Acemoglu and Johnson, 2017).

The second issue relevant to work relates to the spatial gap between where jobs are located and where people live—even in large, urban communities like Pittsburgh. Mobility, or the lack of mobility options, has been hypothesized as a reason for the inability of those "left behind" to find and retain jobs. Yet ride hailing is generating a new set of mobility options at a time when it is difficult to extend public transit. As Lee Branstetter, director of the Future of Work Initiative at the Block Center at Carnegie Mellon, has asked, could subsidized ride-hailing services make a difference in this long-running problem of spatial mismatch (Moore, 2017)?

The final issue relates to the emergence of the so-called gig economy and the growth of independent work enabled by digital platforms (Manyika et al., 2016). While platforms such as Upwork and TaskRabbit enable individuals to advertise their skills and services as independent workers, the lack of portable health insurance is a constraint that needs to be addressed. Combined with an enlightened education policy that makes full use of advances in learning science, alternative work models could grow to provide fulfilling opportunities to the 10–30 percent of American workers who engage in independent work.

Harnessing Algorithms for Societal Benefit

While discussing the policy challenges that algorithmic decision systems pose, it is important that we not lose sight of the considerable opportunity these systems offer to improve the efficiency and effectiveness of societal problem solving, including in government operations. Two examples demonstrate the impact of algorithms.

The New York Police Department's Domain Awareness System has been credited with reducing the incidence of crime and terror attacks in the city by 6 percent, enabling savings of over $50 million (Levine et al., 2017). The system is a citywide network of sensors, databases, and algorithms that informs decision-making by delivering analytics and tailored information to officers' smartphones and precinct desktops. This is a type of real-time decision-making and dispatching enabled greatly by the capacity to automatically collect and analyze unstructured data (for example, sounds of gunshots fired) via networked sensors.

In contrast to real-time decision-making in the Domain Awareness System, fraud detection leverages large volumes of structured and unstructured data to detect anomalies and patterns that enable state or federal government compliance agencies to screen claims before improper payment. The fraud prevention system deployed by the Centers for Medicare and Medicaid Services at the U.S. Department of Health and Human Services now processes more than 4.5 million claims and is credited with saving more than $4 billion (Centers for Medicare and Medicaid Services, 2018). A further testament to the importance of this capability is the creation and success of the Medicare Fraud Strike Force of the Office of Inspector General of the Department of Health and Human Services. The topic of fraud detection using pattern-mining techniques (for example, clever ways of detecting outliers that are robust to gaming) has received considerable attention from academic researchers. A discussion of these techniques in the context of fraud detection in social programs can be found in Pace and Pollak (2017).

A balanced approach to the deployment of algorithmic decision systems in an organizational setting should take into account these benefits while putting in place mechanisms to address the issues of algorithmic accountability and the implications of the changing nature of work I have already discussed in detail. But are there issues particularly relevant to the case of platforms that use these algorithmic systems to operate on a societal scale? One such issue I will conclude this essay with pertains to innovation and competition among platforms, and the role that data play in determining the trajectory of improvement of algorithmic decision systems.

In considering machine learning from a public policy standpoint, it is important to draw the distinction between the algorithms that power these systems and the data that they use to constantly improve their learning performance. In many of the machine learning systems with which consumers and citizens interact, the data are contributed by the consumers. Thus, the recommendation systems on Amazon improve as more data are collected from more users on the Amazon platform. This is true of Google (for example, Google Maps), Microsoft, Amazon, Apple, and Facebook, as well as future platforms, such as connected autonomous cars, that will gather vast amounts of data about people and their behaviors. Today, these data are contributed by users to the platform for "free" in exchange for use of their services. As a few dominant platforms have emerged, the returns to these platforms from having a critical and continually growing mass of consumer data confer an innovation advantage that will become insurmountable. We are already seeing the emergence of very large firms that are beginning to exhibit these returns to scale that accrue from the "data advantage." From a public policy standpoint, it would be beneficial to consider a model in which users have "property rights" over their personal data and "rent" use of their data to platforms for periods of time versus the current model, in which the platforms own the data. In their thought-provoking article in *Foreign Policy*, Acemoglu and Johnson (2017) draw a parallel between antitrust regulation and its application to break up monopolies in the late nineteenth and early twentieth centuries, on the one hand, and the need to rethink antitrust for the era of big data, on the other. They specifically argue for making data available to all competitors to prevent competition based on accumulating data and the associated processing capacity at scale. While this proposal requires more careful thought and discussion, it is quite clear that there is a need to better understand the drivers of competition and innovation in an algorithmic world to ensure that algorithms can be harnessed for the benefit of all global citizens.

Implications for Governance

When technological change has profound implications for the economy and society, it is important that policymakers and leaders understand its consequences. In this essay, I have discussed the changes being brought about by AI and social media, issues of algorithmic bias, the future of work, and the opportunities for effective and efficient public-sector service delivery enabled by developments in technology. However, as the Zuckerberg hearings demonstrated, our lawmakers are not sufficiently knowledgeable about these technological changes and how they help or hurt the public interest. From 1972 to 1995, Congress relied on the Office of Technology Assessment (OTA). The OTA focused on developing reports on technologies and their policy consequences. This was a valuable service to legislative staff. After the OTA was defunded in 1995, the only nonpartisan agency that could provide this service was the Government Accountability Office (GAO). The GAO, through its science and technology division, develops high-quality reports. Its recent report on AI covers material that complements this essay (GAO, 2018). The report provides detailed and expert input on technology developments, associated risks, and implications for regulation, accompanied by podcasts designed to be consumed by the interested citizen.

While GAO reports are of high quality, their production is not the focus or a priority at the agency as such assessments used to be at the OTA. Either some version of the OTA needs to be funded or the GAO will need additional resources from Congress to make its policy-relevant science and technology assessments a major part of its portfolio. It will be these assessments that our administrators, policymakers, and leaders will need to govern effectively in an algorithmic world.

Notes

1. The Me Too campaign spread to 4.7 million Facebook users in its first twenty-four hours (CBS News, 2017).

2. An edge provider is a privately owned, web-based service or online service that customers use to provide or obtain access to content. Facebook, Google, Twitter, and Instagram are all examples of edge providers. The Federal Trade Commission regulates edge providers in the United States.

3. For example, policies such as the Equal Credit Opportunity Act.

4. See Block Center for Technology and Society (n.d.) for information on this initiative.

Bibliography

Acemoglu, Daron, and Simon Johnson. 2017. "It Is Time to Found a New Republic." *Foreign Policy*, August 15, 2017. http://foreignpolicy.com/2017/08/15/its-time-to-found-a-new -republic/.

Amazon. n.d. Amazon Go website. Accessed April 25, 2019. https://www.amazon.com/b ?node=16008589011.

Bakshy, Eytan, Solomon Messing, and Lada Adamic. 2015. "Exposure to Ideologically Diverse News and Opinion on Facebook." *Science* 348 (6239): 1130–32.

Bhargava, Hemant, and Ramayya Krishnan. 1998. "The World Wide Web: Opportunities for Operations Research and Management Science." *INFORMS Journal on Computing* 10 (4): 359–383.

Block Center for Technology and Society. n.d. "The Future of Work Initiative." Accessed April 25, 2019. https://www.cmu.edu/block-center/future-of-work/index.html.

CBS News. 2017. "More than 12M Facebook Posts, Comments, Reactions in 24 Hours." October 17, 2017. https://www.cbsnews.com/news/metoo-more-than-12-million-facebook -posts-comments-reactions-24-hours/.

Centers for Medicare and Medicaid Services. 2018. "Medicaid Guidance Fraud Prevention." Last updated March 1, 2018. https://www.cms.gov/Medicare-Medicaid-Coordination /Fraud-Prevention/FraudAbuseforProfs/MedicaidGuidance.html.

Danks, David, and Alex London. 2017. "Algorithmic Bias in Autonomous Systems." In *Proceedings of the 26th International Joint Conference on Artificial Intelligence*, edited by Carles Sierra, 4691–97. Marina del Rey, CA: International Joint Conferences on Artificial Intelligence.

Datta, Anupam, Shayak Sen, and Yair Zick. 2016. "Algorithmic Transparency via Quantitative Input Influence: Theory and Experiments with Learning Systems." In *Proceedings of 37th IEEE Symposium on Security and Privacy*, 598–617. Los Alamitos, CA: IEEE Computer Society.

Facebook. n.d. "Facebook Ad Library." Accessed April 25, 2019. https://www.facebook.com /ads/archive/?active_status=all&ad_type=political_and_issue_ads&country=US.

Facebook Business. 2018. "The Authorization Process for US Advertisers to Run Political Ads on Facebook Is Now Open." April 23, 2018. https://www.facebook.com/business/news/the -authorization-process-for-us-advertisers-to-run-political-ads-on-facebook-is-now-open.

GAO (U.S. Government Accountability Office). 2018. *Artificial Intelligence: Emerging Opportunities, Challenges, and Implications*. GAO-18-142SP. Washington, DC: U.S. Government Accountability Office, March 28, 2018. https://www.gao.gov/products/GAO-18-142SP.

Gottfried, Jeffrey, and Elisa Shearer. 2017. "News Use Across Social Media Platforms." Pew Research Center, September 7, 2017. http://www.journalism.org/2017/09/07/news-use -across-social-media-platforms-2017/.

Gunning, David. 2018. "Explainable Artificial Intelligence (XAI)." Defense Advanced Research Projects Agency. Accessed April 25, 2019. https://www.darpa.mil/program /explainable-artificial-intelligence.

Hughes, Adam, and Onyi Lam. 2017. "Highly Ideological Members of Congress Have More Facebook Followers than Moderates Do." Pew Research Center report. https://www .pewresearch.org/fact-tank/2017/08/21/highly-ideological-members-of-congress-have -more-facebook-followers-than-moderates-do/.

Jefferson, Thomas. 1958. Letter to Richard Price, January 8, 1789. In *The Papers of Thomas Jefferson*, vol. 14, *8 October 1788–26 March 1789*, edited by Julian P. Boyd, 420–24. Princeton, NJ: Princeton University Press. https://founders.archives.gov/?q=Volume %3AJefferson-01-14&s=1511311112&r=224.

Knight, Will. 2017. "The Dark Secret at the Heart of AI." *MIT Technology Review*, April 11, 2017. https://www.technologyreview.com/s/604087/the-dark-secret-at-the-heart-of-ai/.

Laudon, Ken, and Jane Laudon. 2013. *Management Information Systems: Managing the Digital Firm, 13th Edition*. Upper Saddle River, NJ: Pearson Education.

Levine, Evan, Jessica Tisch, Anthony Tasso, and Michael Joy. 2017. "The New York City Police Department's Domain Awareness System." *Interfaces* 47 (1): 70–84.

Manyika, James, Susan Lund, Jacques Bughin, Kelsey Robinson, Jan Mischke, and Deepa Mahajan. 2016. "Independent Work: Choice, Necessity, and the Gig Economy." McKinsey Global Institute, October 2016. https://www.mckinsey.com/global-themes/employment -and-growth/independent-work-choice-necessity-and-the-gig-economy.

Messing, Solomon, Patrick van Kessel, and Adam Hughes. 2017. "Sharing the News in a Polarized Congress." Pew Research Center. https://www.people-press.org/2017/12/18/sharing -the-news-in-a-polarized-congress/.

Mitchell, Tom, and Erik Brynjolfsson. 2017. "Track How Technology Is Transforming Work." *Nature* 544 (7650): 290–92.

Moore, Daniel. 2017. "CMU to Study Potential Benefits of Ride-Hailing Apps in Poorer Neighborhoods." *Pittsburgh Post-Gazette*, October 11, 2017. https://www.post-gazette .com/business/career-workplace/2017/10/11/Carnegie-Mellon-Uber-Lyft-Ride-hail -apps-access-low-income-neighborhoods/stories/201710110028/.

New York City Council. 2018. "Automated Decision Systems Used by Agencies." Legislative Research Center. http://legistar.council.nyc.gov/LegislationDetail.aspx?ID=3137815&GUID =437A6A6D-62E1-47E2-9C42-461253F9C6D0.

O'Neil, Cathy. 2016. *Weapons of Math Destruction: How Big Data Increases Inequality and Threatens Democracy.* New York: Crown.

Pace, Nicholas M., and Julia Pollak. 2017. *Provider Fraud in California Workers' Compensation.* RR-1703-DIR. Santa Monica, CA: RAND. https://www.rand.org/pubs/research_reports /RR1703.html.

Pew Research Center. 2018. "Social Media Fact Sheet." February 5, 2018. http://www.pewinternet .org/fact-sheet/social-media/.

ProPublica. n.d. "Series: Machine Bias." Accessed April 25, 2019. https://www.propublica .org/series/machine-bias.

Sekara, Vedran, Arkadiusz Stopczynski, and Sune Lehmann. 2016. "Fundamental Structures of Dynamic Social Networks." *Proceedings of the National Academy of Sciences of the United States of America* 113 (36): 9977–82.

Silver, David, Julian Schrittwieser, Karen Simonyan, Ioannis Antonoglou, Aja Huang, Arthur Guez, Thomas Hubert, et al. 2017. "Mastering the Game of Go Without Human Knowledge." *Nature* 550:354–59.

Simsek, Ozgur, and David Jensen. 2008. "Navigating Networks by Using Homophily and Degree." *Proceedings of the National Academy of Sciences of the United States of America* 105 (35): 12758–62.

Stretch, Colin. 2018. Response to Committee Questions for the Record, Select Committee on Intelligence Hearing on Social Media Influence in the 2016 U.S. Elections. January 8, 2018. https://www.intelligence.senate.gov/sites/default/files/documents/Facebook%20 Response%20to%20Committee%20QFRs.pdf.

Subrahmanian, V. S., Amos Azaria, Skylar Durst, Vadim Kagan, Aram Galstyan, Kristina Lerman, Linhong Zhu, et al. 2016. "The DARPA Twitter Bot Challenge." Preprint, submitted January 20, 2016. Last revised April 21, 2016. https://arxiv.org/abs/1601.05140.

U.S. Federal Trade Commission. 2016. *Big Data: A Tool for Inclusion or Exclusion?* https:// www.ftc.gov/system/files/documents/reports/big-data-tool-inclusion-or-exclusion -understanding-issues/160106big-data-rpt.pdf.

U.S. Securities and Exchange Commission. 2014. "Form 10-Q—Twitter, Inc." https://www .sec.gov/Archives/edgar/data/1418091/000156459014003474/twtr-10q_20140630.htm.

Walden, Greg. 2018. "Facebook: Transparency and Use of Consumer Data." Opening Statement Before Energy and Commerce Committee Hearing, April 11, 2018. https://docs.house.gov /meetings/IF/IF00/20180411/108090/HHRG-115-IF00-MState-W000791-20180411.pdf.

CHAPTER 4

Political Disruption

Is America Headed Toward Uncontrollable Extremism or Partisan Goodwill?

Norman J. Ornstein

Kakistocracy is a term that was first used in the seventeenth century; derived from a Greek word, it means, literally, government by the worst and most unscrupulous people among us. More broadly, it can mean the most inept and cringeworthy kind of government. The term fell into disuse over the past century or more, and most highly informed people have never heard it before, but for kids familiar with the word *kaka*, it might resonate (Ornstein, 2017).

Today, *kakistocracy* may be the most apt term to describe public management and governance in the Donald J. Trump era. Consider an example. A *Washington Post* story in January 2018 started with the following:

In May 2016, Taylor Weyeneth was an undergraduate at St. John's University in New York, a legal studies student and fraternity member who organized a golf tournament and other events to raise money for veterans and their families.

Less than a year later, at 23, Weyeneth, was a political appointee and rising star at the Office of National Drug Control Policy, the White House office responsible for coordinating the federal government's multibillion dollar anti-drug initiatives and supporting President Trump's efforts to curb the opioid epidemic. Weyeneth would soon become [the office's] deputy chief of staff.

His brief biography offers few clues that he would so quickly assume a leading role in the drug policy office, a job recently occupied by a lawyer and a veteran government official. Weyeneth's only professional experience after college and before becoming an appointee was working on Trump's presidential campaign. (O'Harrow, 2018)

It is not unusual for an administration to fill some of its political appointments with campaign volunteers and workers. But it is far from typical to have a twenty-three-year-old with no substantive experience appointed to a critical high-level policy position.

The Trump administration in its first year was filled with many stories about unfilled positions and nominees unfit for their jobs. One of the most high profile and controversial was Sam Clovis, nominated to be chief scientist at the Department of Agriculture. Clovis, with no scientific background at all, withdrew after questions were raised about his ties to George Papadopoulos and Russian contacts. But before that, as CNN reported, "Clovis previously argued that protections for LGBT people would lead to protections for pedophilia, and as a radio host and political activist, he promoted the hoax that former President Barack Obama was not born in the US. Likewise, he called Obama a 'Maoist' and said Attorney General Eric Holder is a 'racist black'" (Perez et al., 2017).

The Worst Kind of Government

The Case of the State Department

Perhaps no department got more scrutiny than the State Department, where Rex Tillerson's tenure as secretary of state was characterized by summary dismissals of the most senior diplomats, including those with the most management experience; the failure even to nominate individuals to fill most of the critical policy positions, from undersecretaries and assistant secretaries to ambassadors; and Tillerson's attempt to remake the department by cutting the foreign service by a minimum of 8 percent even as the president's budget called for a 30 percent cut in diplomacy and development.

An October 2017 article in the *New York Times Magazine* was titled "Rex Tillerson and the Unraveling of the State Department." Author Jason Zengerle

(2017) wrote, "In a few short months, Tillerson had rid the State Department of much of its last several decades of diplomatic experience, though it was not really clear to what end." But, Zengerle noted, it was not entirely Tillerson's doing: "The new secretary of state, it soon became evident, had an easier time firing people than hiring them—a consequence of the election that delivered him to Foggy Bottom."

Because the vast bulk of Republican foreign policy experts and veterans had been part of the Never Trump movement, or had at least criticized Trump as a candidate, they were blocked from any consideration for posts. Tillerson's choice for deputy secretary, Elliott Abrams, was given a thumbs-up in an interview with Trump—but when Trump saw Senator Rand Paul criticize Abrams on television for his relatively mild criticism of the presidential candidate, he blocked the secretary's choice. A senior administration official told Zengerle, "The hiring pool is very different from your normal hiring pool. . . . The people the Senate would expect to confirm have all been taken off the table." Tillerson's tenure ended abruptly in the spring of 2018, as he was largely shut out of major foreign policy decision-making.

Management Woes

The dysfunction at top management levels goes well beyond State and is sharply greater than in previous administrations. The Partnership for Public Service, in collaboration with the *Washington Post*, tracks in real time the status of meaningful policy posts that require Senate confirmation. On January 17, 2018, three days from the one-year anniversary of the Trump inauguration, of the 633 critical positions, only 241—or 38 percent—had been filled. More positions (245) had no nominee than were occupied (Clark, 2018).

The unfilled posts were not second level or minor; they included the IRS commissioner; the ambassadors to critical countries like South Korea, Egypt, Australia, Venezuela, Jordan, and Qatar; the director of the Census; the heads of the Drug Enforcement Administration and the Bureau of Alcohol, Tobacco, Firearms and Explosives; the undersecretary of health at the Department of Veterans Affairs; and the inspector general at the Department of the Interior, where Secretary Ryan Zinke has been the focus of numerous investigations for his alleged misuse of government funds for his travel. Nearly two years in, in November 2018, less than 54 percent of the key positions had occupants, while more than 20 percent had no nominee (Power Post, 2018). A major embarrassment that fall was the fact that the United States had no ambassadors even nominated for Saudi Arabia or Turkey when we faced the dramatic controversy of the murder of *Washington Post* journalist Jamal Khashoggi by Saudi Arabian government operatives in the Saudi consulate in Istanbul.

In several instances in which nominations have not been made or have failed, the Trump administration has abused the Federal Vacancies Reform Act to install cronies in ways that at minimum skirt the law, including and especially by picking Office of Management and Budget director Mick Mulvaney to do double duty as acting head of the Consumer Financial Protection Bureau (Restuccia and Toosi, 2017), a move that has been challenged in the courts and was initially upheld but is headed to the Supreme Court at this writing. Even more controversial was Trump's pick to head the Justice Department after he forced out Attorney General Jeff Sessions. Matthew Whitaker had been serving as Sessions's chief of staff, a post that does not require Senate confirmation; constitutional lawyers as varied as John Yoo, Neal Katyal, and George Conway said the appointment violated the appointments clause of the Constitution, as well as statutes specifying the succession line at Justice.

More broadly, Trump, Mulvaney, and other cabinet officials have taken steps to dramatically cut back on civil servants in many departments. Trump's budget plan aimed at cutting the size of the workforce at the Environmental Protection Agency by 50 percent over five years. The IRS, which is tasked with implementing at breakneck pace the massive tax cuts and changes enacted in late 2017, is scheduled to have its already depleted staff hit by another deep budget cut in the range of $150 million. The IRS budget was $14 billion in 2010 and is set for $11 billion in 2018, an 18 percent cut while its responsibilities have grown. Enforcement personnel have been cut by 23 percent (U.S. Office of Management and Budget, 2017).

The impact of dysfunction has been broad and deep. As the *Washington Post* noted in January 2018,

> Errick King, a federal employee for 30 years, thinks he knows exactly what lawmakers will do next: more of the same.
>
> Congress has not balanced a budget in years, and King doesn't expect them to come February [when the new Congress was set to be

in place]. That has left the father of three feeling so hopeless that he has considered changing his family's lifestyle, including skipping the after-church meals out on Sunday afternoons and nixing the weekly bowling games they so enjoy.

The relentless instability, he said, is leading career employees to retire early and abandon agencies, leaving them increasingly thin on institutional knowledge.

"People are fed up," said King, an IT specialist with the Bureau of the Fiscal Service in Hyattsville, Md. "I think it hurts the government overall because you are losing that knowledge and skill. We are reliant on that to provide quality service." (Hernández, Hendrix, and Cox, 2018)

As the second year of the Trump presidency was about to begin, more effects of the Trump approach to governance appeared. The ambassador to Panama, John Feeley, a highly respected veteran diplomat and former Marine Corps helicopter pilot, resigned, saying he could no longer represent the United States with Trump as president. More broadly, a news story in January 2018 noted, "60 percent of the State Department's top-ranking career diplomats have left and new applications to join the foreign service have fallen by half, according to recent data from the American Foreign Service Association, the professional organization of the U.S. diplomatic corps" (Ordonez, 2018).

Meanwhile, ten out of twelve members of a federal board advising the National Park Service quit en masse, frustrated because Interior Secretary Ryan Zinke had refused to meet with them or to convene a single meeting of the group.

As for the broader federal workforce, an apparent plan to call for a pay freeze in 2019 following several years of pay freezes and 1 percent raises, and the budget plans to cut workforce sizes at most agencies, has left both managers and rank-and-file workers reeling. The second nominee for the Office of Personnel Management, Jeff Tien Han Pon (the first withdrew following widespread criticism from federal employee unions and others), pledged reform, but with few details. He was confirmed in March 2018—but barely seven months later, he was abruptly informed by the White House that he had "resigned" (directly firing him would have made a temporary appointment difficult under the Vacancies Act) and was replaced on an acting basis by Margaret Weichert, deputy director for management at the Office of Management and Budget. No reasons were given, but the rumors were that he had been too protective of the agency and not pliant enough to the wishes of the White House that the role and powers of the agency be sharply downgraded (Yoder and Rein, 2018).

Recent Historical Context for Government Reform

The challenge these failures of government performance pose to governance in the future, with our system of checks and balances hanging in the balance at some levels, and with enormous and complex problems for government and society to grapple with in coming decades, is immensely critical. But the issues here have tended to get lost in the broader conversation about the Trump presidency, Trump himself, and the tribal politics he encourages and is immersed in.

Of course, the reality is that issues of effective government management are almost always lost in the shuffle. Focusing on public management and a robust civil service has rarely been a priority in the political process. The deep American cultural distrust of government, the stereotype of bureaucrats as pampered, overpaid, unable to be fired, and insulated from the real America, makes any effort by politicians to improve the civil service or reward performance an uphill battle. Even if there were no headwinds, there are precious few incentives for politicians to devote time and resources to a subject that brings little acclaim and little direct benefit to constituents.

There have been exceptions, of course, more often than not driven by scandal or tragedy. The first major reform, in 1883, was a reaction to the corruption of the spoils system, but it was the tragic assassination of President James A. Garfield by a disappointed job seeker that made the difference, turning his successor, Rutherford B. Hayes, from a supporter of the spoils system into a reformer.

The next significant reform, the 1939 Hatch Act, had as its impetus a belief that government employees had been employed for political purposes by the Franklin D. Roosevelt administration in congressional elections in 1938; the Hatch Act prohibited such use while also providing protection for civil servants from pressure to act as political agents.

The last major reform came forty years ago with the 1978 Civil Service Reform Act, a signal accomplishment of the Jimmy Carter administration, driven to success in significant part by public frustration after Watergate, the Vietnam War, and a broader sense of government falling short of its promise. The bill was enacted with broad bipartisan support.

The Roots of Tribalism and Attacks on Governance

The year 1978, however also brought with it the seeds of a larger change in American politics, one that has set the stage for the crisis facing executive governance in Washington today—a crisis that was emerging long before Donald Trump, even if he has taken it to a new level. The dynamic has led to partisan tribalism, widespread disgust with politics and politicians, a broader sense that Washington and government are broken, and an ongoing attack on government, bureaucrats, government employees, and more. That year's congressional election brought to Washington an obscure history professor from a small college in Georgia, on his third try for the House, Newt Gingrich.

From the moment Gingrich arrived in Washington, he had a strategy and a panoply of related tactics to achieve his overriding goal: creating a Republican majority in Congress. Democrats had been in the majority for twenty-four consecutive years when Gingrich arrived on the Hill, and they showed no signs of losing it. A combination of factors had seemed to give a lock on that majority: incumbent lawmakers were skilled at separating themselves out from larger national trends or unhappiness with Washington; their name recognition and fund-raising prowess made a challenge uphill; and those advantages were much greater for members of the majority, who had the power.

For Gingrich, the goal meant nationalizing congressional elections, and creating so much anger at Congress, Washington, and government that voters would rise up en masse to throw out the "ins" and bring in the "outs"—which would mean electing more Republicans. From 1979 through 1994—over sixteen years—Gingrich managed to radicalize his own Republicans, gaining a top leadership position along the way despite the antipathy of the veteran Republican leader Robert Michel, and to tribalize American politics. He used allegations of ethics violations to enrage Democrats and create the sense of a corrupt institution, and he succeeded, among other things, in forcing the resignation of Speaker Jim Wright, who in his farewell speech warned about "mindless cannibalism" in Congress.

Populism and the Pay Raise

A populist surge in American politics in 1988–89 provided a major boost to his efforts. It was triggered by a broadly bipartisan pay raise for members of Congress, federal judges, and top executive officials recommended by a quadrennial commission and endorsed by outgoing president Ronald Reagan, incoming president George H. W. Bush, and all congressional leaders (including, ironically, Gingrich). The commission recommendation was to make up for a decade of no raises by accounting for inflation during that time—but its 25 percent raise caused a popular eruption. Most Americans struggled to get by, without any cost-of-living adjustment; the idea that politicians and bureaucrats making $87,500 a year were strapped for cash was too much.

In 1987, the Federal Communications Commission had repealed the Fairness Doctrine, which required radio and television stations to provide time for opposing points of view. The result was the creation of a new model, partisan talk radio, led by a former Sacramento, California, noontime radio host named Rush Limbaugh, who had moved to New York to try to create a national audience. The pay raise gave him the vehicle to do so, and he skyrocketed to fame on a virulently antigovernment platform.

The backlash to the pay raise also created populist candidates for president in 1992 on the right (Pat Buchanan), on the left (Ralph Nader), and in the center (H. Ross Perot), all attacking politics as usual, government, and its operations, but resulting in the election of Democrat Bill Clinton. With a Democratic president and Congress, Gingrich, now the Republican House leader, was able to unite his Republicans in implacable opposition, while Democrats divided over Clinton policies ranging from economic stimulus to health-care reform. Public dissatisfaction with government grew.

As the midterm elections loomed, Gingrich actively recruited candidates to run against House Democrats, giving them language and campaign themes to use, all focused on attacking government as evil and corrupt. It worked; a wave election in 1994 created a Republican majority in Congress and made Gingrich the first Republican Speaker of the House since 1954.

Gingrich made dramatic changes in the operation of the House. One move was to eliminate the Office of Technology Assessment, an arm of Congress that provided technical and scientific expertise to inform the legislative process. While he labeled it a cost-saving move, it was in reality the first major effort to discredit science and expertise in favor of ideology. Gingrich and his majority opposed Clinton and attacked government. Conflicts and confrontation with the president culminated in a government shutdown triggered by their demands for dramatic budget and policy cuts over the holidays at the end of 1995. The backlash to that shutdown created a brief period of bipartisan cooperation that ended once both Clinton and the Republican majority in Congress were returned in the 1996 elections.

Continued Partisanship and Tribalism

The twenty-plus years since then have been characterized by more bitter partisan and tribal competition that has caught governance in the crosshairs. Each party contributed to the impulse to discredit the other when out of the presidency, but it is clear that the more direct and sustained assaults have come from the Republican and conservative sides. Their more natural tendency to distrust, limit, and shrink government, joined with a ruthless pragmatism that saw efforts to delegitimize the Democratic president and Washington ramp up after Barack Obama's election, generally paid off in impressive midterm victories in 2010 and 2014. The intensity was greater for another reason; the GOP had moved from a conservative party, desiring a smaller but efficient and effective government, to a more radical one with the goal expressed pithily by antitax activist Grover Norquist: "I don't want to abolish government. I simply want to reduce it to the size where I can drag it into the bathroom and drown it in the bathtub" (Jeffery and Bauerlein, 2011).

As Thomas E. Mann and I detailed in our 2012 book *It's Even Worse Than It Looks*, updated in 2016 (Mann and Ornstein, 2012, 2016), Republican leaders developed an approach on Inauguration Eve 2009 in which they would get all their members in the House and Senate to vote in unison against every Obama and Democratic initiative, starting with the economic stimulus package and extending to everything else, including health reform, and move to block what they could and undermine whatever they could not. In his famous comment, Senate Republican Leader Mitch McConnell captured the approach:

"The single most important thing we want to achieve is for President Obama to be a one-term president" (Kessler, 2017).

House leaders, led by the self-proclaimed "Young Guns" Eric Cantor, Paul Ryan, and Kevin McCarthy, took the strategy one step further. They fanned out around the country in 2009 and 2010, recruiting Tea Party candidates to run for the House and, thus, inflaming the populist antigovernment anger that had created the Tea Party movement after the bailout that followed the financial collapse in the fall of 2008. They promised that if they recaptured a majority in the House they would use the debt ceiling as a weapon to force Obama to his knees, repeal Obamacare and Dodd-Frank, and dramatically cut government as we know it.

That strategy worked, insofar as it created a massive election victory for Republicans, the biggest gain in seats in more than sixty years. But the tactics, including using the full faith and credit of the United States as a hostage, did not work. Obamacare and Dodd-Frank remained in place, and while spending on discretionary domestic programs continued to shrink as a share of the economy, not a single agency was eliminated. But Republican control of the committees and the agenda in the House meant the ability to use hearings and the bully pulpit afforded by the majority to bash Obama and to discredit government and government employees.

Of course, the strategy did not result in Obama's defeat in 2012. But Republicans redoubled their efforts, continuing to discredit government and governance, including generating a government shutdown in 2013, and achieved more success in the next midterm, winning a majority in the Senate to go along with their control of the House. But again, the promises to repeal Obamacare and Dodd-Frank and blow up government went unfulfilled.

One effect, though, was to further public distrust of government. As the 2016 election loomed, the Pew Research Center found that only 18 percent of Americans said they could trust the government in Washington to do what is right "just about always" or "most of the time" (Pew Research Center, 2017).

Governance in the Trump Era

Conventional wisdom said that Republicans would still nominate a conventional establishment choice, as they had with George W. Bush in 2000, John McCain in 2008, and Mitt Romney in 2012. I was skeptical; in a column in the *Atlantic* in August 2015 titled "Maybe This Time Really Is Different"

(Ornstein, 2015), I suggested there would be an insurgent nominee like Trump and wrote, "Egged on by talk radio, cable news, right-wing blogs, and social media, the activist voters who make up the primary and caucus electorates have become angrier and angrier, not just at the Kenyan Socialist president but also at their own leaders. Promised that Obamacare would be repealed, the government would be radically reduced, immigration would be halted, and illegals punished, they see themselves as euchred and scorned by politicians of all stripes, especially on their own side of the aisle."

Trump, as we know, won the nomination and then, improbably, won the election. But he did not run on a radical antigovernment platform. His emphasis was more on nativist anti-immigration policies and protectionist trade approaches. He promised to protect the safety net, to keep Medicare, Medicaid, and Social Security from being cut. He did not endorse any of the radical cuts that had been proposed in a series of budgets by Paul Ryan, much less big tax cuts for the rich and corporations.

But once elected, with a transition run by vice president elect Mike Pence, a member of the radical Freedom Caucus when he had served in the House, Trump chose a cabinet filled with individuals who had little knowledge of public management and little respect for those working in government, and with deep desires to disrupt normal business and undo anything that had been done in the Obama years. From Budget Director Mick Mulvaney to Environmental Protection Agency administrator Scott Pruitt, Energy Secretary Rick Perry, Housing Secretary Ben Carson, and Interior Secretary Ryan Zinke, the disdain for government and the rejection of the rules and norms of behavior in politics, policy, and management have left low morale, shattered budgets, leadership vacuums, budget uncertainty, and the departure of the most-seasoned managers and policy experts. The reaction of the majority of Republicans in Congress has been, at best, indifference to the gaps in governance.

Trump's attraction for the many millions who voted for him was rooted both in tribal partisan identity and in the deep distaste for all things Washington that is partly in America's culture but has also been shaped by income inequality, social deterioration, and the sustained effort by Republicans in Washington to discredit all of government. The appeal to "drain the swamp," elect a rank outsider, and run government like a business resonated with a lot of voters. The lack of understanding about what government does and how it affects Americans in their daily lives contributed to the belief that Trump could blow up the town and it would not hurt people.

But to some who voted for Trump, the policy successes they see and his approach to getting there remain positives. On January 17, 2018, the *New York Times* gave over its editorial page to letters from continuing Trump supporters; this one, from Jason Peck of Holtsville, New York, expressed one view of that sort:

> I voted against Hillary Clinton more than I voted for Donald Trump. That said, President Trump has exceeded my wildest expectations. Yes, he is embarrassing. Yes, he picks unnecessary fights. But he also pushed tax reform through, has largely defeated ISIS in Iraq, has named a number of solid conservative judges, has prioritized American citizens over illegal immigrants, has gotten us out of several bad international agreements, has removed a number of wasteful regulations, is putting real pressure on North Korea and Iran, has reined in a number of out-of-control agencies, and so on and so on. I loved George W. Bush, but he failed on policy over and over again. If it takes putting up with Mr. Trump's brash ways to see things get done, that is a deal I'm willing to accept. To be honest, I'm not sure he would have accomplished what he has so far without being an unrelenting public bully. (Peck, 2018)

For others, the disruptions have created some second thoughts. The backlash against the efforts to repeal Obamacare, and the reaction to the disasters in many parts of the country that were created by devastating hurricanes, showed that some understanding of the importance of effective government is seeping through, albeit slowly. When budget cuts and leadership vacuums begin to impinge more directly on peoples' lives, maybe accompanied by scandal, there may be a reaction that will drive a new wave of reforms that might include the civil service and government employment but might also be more sweeping, to include the broader functioning of democracy, from redistricting reform, to voter registration and weekend voting, to campaign finance reform.

Looking Ahead

The political struggles over partisan control of Congress and the presidency that began with the stunning takeover of the House by Newt Gingrich's

Republicans in 1994 took on a new coloration—frequent changes in the majorities of at least one power center in Washington from one election to the next and majorities slender enough that the next election could easily bring another shift. The struggle for power was, of course, accompanied by sharper and sharper differences between the parties in their world view and view of the role of government.

For Gingrich, the tactic of defaming Washington and governance was equal parts strategic and ideological. The strategic part worked in 1994, with a giant backlash against Washington and government, and worked again in 2010 and 2014, with a populist backlash against all elites, especially those in Washington who had, in a bipartisan fashion, engineered the bailout of the financiers who caused millions to lose homes, jobs, and savings. And that backlash, which included condemnation of Republican elites, contributed to the nomination and election of outsider Donald Trump.

One consequence of all the battles, then, has been sustained efforts to delegitimize government, starve its resources, and trash its employees. Democrats, faced with deficits, have not been very successful at combatting the erosion of resources in most discretionary domestic programs or in areas like development and diplomacy, and they have often found themselves on the defensive when defending government and bureaucracy. The handful of Republicans who have championed the professional civil service, including longtime representatives Tom Davis and Frank Wolf, have retired and have not been replaced by comparable respected counterparts. And as this chapter details, the damage to governance and the professionalization of government management has only gotten worse.

Looking ahead, then, the larger questions are what damage will be done in the near future and whether it is reparable. On the inside, there are a few, occasional signs of a return to bipartisan agreement, cooperation, and compromise, including work on policies like immigration (Republican senators Jeff Flake and Lindsey Graham with Democrat Dick Durbin), health (Republican Lamar Alexander and Democrat Patty Murray), and the budget (Republicans Susan Collins and Lisa Murkowski with Democrats Joe Manchin, Mark Warner, and others). In addition, there have been bipartisan teams in the Senate working to protect the Mueller investigation, including Republican Richard Burr and Democrat Warner, Republican Graham and Democrat Cory Booker, and Republican Thom Tillis and Democrat Chris Coons.

On the outside, besides organizations like the Volcker Alliance and the Partnership for Public Service, groups like the Campaign Legal Center,

Citizens for Responsibility and Ethics in Washington, and the Project on Government Oversight have stepped up to protect democratic norms and government integrity. They have been joined by a host of conservative policy intellectuals like Bill Kristol, Jennifer Rubin, Max Boot, Tom Nichols, Evan McMullin, and David Frum who promote a more traditional conservative view of government—they may want less of it, but they also want it to function effectively and smoothly, run by professionals who respect science and facts.

While Congress has careered from one budgeting brink to another, operating on the fumes of continuing resolutions and deep uncertainties, it has also turned back some of the more radical and destructive defunding requests of Office of Management and Budget director Mulvaney and the Trump administration.

But the grim fact is that most Republicans in the House and Senate have supported the attacks on government and science and have, at best, turned a blind eye to the efforts to reduce the federal workforce by getting rid of its most senior experts, have failed to hold a single hearing on corruption and kleptocratic behavior in the White House and among cabinet appointees, and have largely joined in or condoned efforts to discredit the investigations into the role of Russia in the 2016 campaign and in American politics since. The eloquent outside voices of good government organizations and conservative opinion leaders have not been matched by many elected officials.

Elections matter, and the Democrats' impressive gains and new majority in the House following the 2018 midterms will provide a new impetus for oversight and investigations and new traction to fend off further damage. Committee chairs like Elijah Cummings at the House Committee on Oversight and Reform, Richard Neal at the House Ways and Means Committee, Jerry Nadler at the House Judiciary Committee, and others will turn their focus to the elements of poor governance and administration that I have labeled kakistocracy. Perhaps the next presidential election, in 2020, will provide a reversal of some of the disturbing and damaging trends. But the damage done to fundamental governance might take years, or decades, to undo.

Bibliography

Clark, Charles. 2018. "Trump Continues to Set Records for Agency Vacancies." *Government Executive*, January 16, 2018. https://www.govexec.com/oversight/2018/01/trump-continues -set-records-agency-vacancies/145218/?oref=river.

Hernández, Arelis R., Steve Hendrix, and John Woodrow Cox. 2018. "'A Huge Pain': Government Shutdown Briefly Idles Federal Workers Before Reprieve." *Washington Post*, January 22, 2018.

Jeffery, Clara, and Monika Bauerlein. 2011. "The Job Killers." *Mother Jones*, November/December 2011. https://www.motherjones.com/politics/2011/10/republicans-job-creation-kill/.

Kessler, Glenn. 2017. "When Did Mitch McConnell Say He Wanted to Make Obama a One-Term President?" *Washington Post*, January 11, 2017.

Mann, Thomas E., and Ornstein, Norman J. 2012. *It's Even Worse Than It Looks*. New York: Basic Books.

———. 2016. *It's Even Worse Than It Was*. New York: Basic Books.

O'Harrow, Robert, Jr. 2018. "24-Year-Old Helps Lead Trump Drug Policy Office." *Washington Post*, January 14, 2018, A1.

Ordonez, Franco. 2018. "Morale Disintegrates at State Department as Diplomats Wonder Who Will Quit Next to Escape Trump." McClatchyDC, January 13, 2018. https://www.mcclatchydc.com/news/politics-government/white-house/article194607714.html.

Ornstein, Norman. 2015. "Maybe This Time Really Is Different." *Atlantic*, August 21, 2015. https://www.theatlantic.com/politics/archive/2015/08/maybe-this-time-really-is-different/401900/.

———. 2017. "American Kakistocracy." *Atlantic*, October 9, 2017.

Peck, Jason. 2018. Letter printed in "'Vision, Chutzpah and Some Testosterone.'" *New York Times*, January 17, 2018. https://www.nytimes.com/2018/01/17/opinion/trump-voters-supporters.html.

Perez, Evan, Jeff Zeleny, Manu Raju, and Dan Merica. 2017. "Trump Nominee for Top Agriculture Post Withdraws Amid Russia Probe." CNN, November 2, 2017. https://www.cnn.com/2017/11/02/politics/sam-clovis-department-of-agriculture/index.html.

Pew Research Center. 2017. "Public Trust in Government: 1958–2017." December 4, 2017. http://www.people-press.org/2017/05/03/public-trust-in-government-1958-2017/.

Power Post. 2018. "Tracking How Many Key Positions Trump Has Filled So Far." *Washington Post*. Accessed November 2018. https://www.washingtonpost.com/graphics/politics/trump-administration-appointee-tracker/database/?utm_term=.790618346f65.

Restuccia, Andrew, and Nahal Toosi. 2017. "Trump Nominees Show Up for Work Without Waiting for Senate Approval." Politico, October 20, 2017. https://www.politico.com/story/2017/10/20/trump-nominees-working-senate-approval-243972.

U.S. Office of Management and Budget. 2017. *America First: A Budget Blueprint to Make America Great Again*. Washington, DC: U.S. Government Publishing Office. https://www.gpo.gov/fdsys/pkg/BUDGET-2018-BLUEPRINT/pdf/BUDGET-2018-BLUEPRINT.pdf.

Yoder, Eric, and Rein, Lisa. 2018. "Trump Abruptly Replaces Federal Personnel Director After Just 7 Months." *Washington Post*, October 5, 2018.

Zengerle, Jason. 2017. "Rex Tillerson and the Unraveling of the State Department." *New York Times Magazine*, October 17, 2017.

PART II

Emerging Government and Governance

CHAPTER 5

The Intrinsic Functions of Government

Francis Fukuyama

In this book, we have set a forward-looking agenda to think about the nature of government in the twenty-first century. What I hope to do is not to rehash arguments about the proper size and functions of government, which has been the central issue of American politics for the past several generations. Rather, I want to explore the question of what the intrinsic functions of government are, and which functions can safely be delegated to bodies outside the government. To anticipate my final conclusion, the intrinsic function of government that may not be delegated outside the public sector is the exercise of significant authority, not just as an agent of the sovereign people but as a proxy that can at times go beyond the law.

Increasing attention has been paid in recent years to the growth of outsourcing and the contracting out of government functions (Kettl, 2002, 2016; Freeman and Minow, 2009). Some observers have asserted that governance is something no longer necessarily performed by governments—indeed, that the very definition of governance is government-like services delivered by anything other than a government (Fukuyama, 2016). Others have raised grave concerns about the implications of this shift for the quality, accountability, and legitimacy of government functions (DiIulio, 2014; Verkuil, 2007, 2017). We need to understand both the reasons for this shift of functions out of government and the consequences of the shift, and to arrive at a normative framework for understanding when it is and is not legitimate to delegate government functions to private actors.

Historically, outsourced government is nothing new. In early modern Europe, conflicts like the Thirty Years' War were fought primarily by mercenaries. Much of South and East Asia were colonized not by states but rather by private companies operating under government charters, such as the British and Dutch East India Companies. Social services from poor relief to education were largely provided by the church in the Middle Ages; they came under state control only in the nineteenth and twentieth centuries. Contractors have been used in the United States since before the American Revolution, even for military functions; privateers (private ships used to raid hostile shipping) were employed up through the 1830s. Compared with Europeans, Americans were always much more ready to turn to the private sector to build what amounted to public infrastructure, such as early railroad, telegraph, and telephone networks.

These historical cases reflect many of the same imperatives that drive the use of private contractors today. The British and Dutch East India Companies were chartered because the governments of the time had neither the resources nor the state capacity to support colonization on their own. Private companies, by contrast, could be incentivized by the revenue stream that colonial exploitation offered. The limits of such public-private partnerships were also made evident: the British government took over direct control of the British East India Company's assets after the Indian Rebellion of 1857–58, when it became clear that the legitimacy of the British presence was being undermined by a private firm engaging in bloody military operations.

When we think about outsourcing in the present, we need to come up with a theoretical framework that can tell us which functions of government should be considered intrinsic to the state and which can be safely delegated to a private party. If the current mix of public and private provision of government services does not conform to the theoretical norm, we need to understand why, and whether it is feasible to bring about conformity. And if conformity is not possible, we perhaps need to rethink the norm itself. Only in this way can we get a sense of what twenty-first-century government will end up looking like.

Legal Considerations

A beginning point for this discussion concerns the legal framework for outsourcing, since both the Constitution and American law define what are considered "intrinsic" functions of government. Paul R. Verkuil's books provide a clear overview of this question, and I will be relying on them in this discussion (Verkuil 2007, 2017).

Article II of the Constitution provides that the president "take care" to see that the laws are faithfully executed and to demand the "opinion, in writing, of the principal officer in each of the executive departments." The president is also given the power, with senatorial concurrence in some circumstances, to appoint "Officers of the United States," those who exercise "significant authority" under the Constitution. Officers are distinguished from employees on this basis, and the former's powers cannot be delegated to private contractors, although case law has not established a clear boundary between the two. The extent of permissible delegation can be procedurally limited in important respects by congressional action.

The Subdelegation Act, passed by Congress in the wake of the Hoover Commission's findings, gives the president explicit authority to delegate powers within the executive branch without the express consent of Congress. Since this act enables subdelegation only to officers of the United States, it can trigger congressional concern when such powers are passed to private contractors.

The conservative turn that began in the Reagan administration gave rise to the view that privatization of many government functions was desirable, and this impulse was codified by Office of Management and Budget Circular A-76. It was amended in the early 2000s by the administration of George W. Bush to further encourage contracting out. The A-76 process requires all federal agencies to publicly distinguish between "inherently governmental" and "competitive" activities under their purview, and to open the latter for bidding by private parties. Inherently governmental activities are defined as ones that involve

1. binding the United States to take or not to take some action by contract, policy, regulation, authorization, order, or otherwise;
2. determining, protecting, and advancing economic, political, territorial, property, or other interests by military or diplomatic action, civil or criminal judicial proceedings, contract management, or otherwise;
3. significantly affecting the life, liberty, or property rights of private persons; or
4. exerting ultimate control over the acquisition, use, or disposition of U.S. property (real or personal, intangible), including establishing

policies or procedures for the collection, control, or disbursement of appropriated and other federal funds.

Private parties can challenge an agency's specification of competitive activities and sue it in the Court of Federal Claims if the internal review process does not support them.

The government has thus itself defined what it considers to be intrinsic functions, though this has come about not through any congressional action but rather through an administrative ruling. It is not clear that the distinctions made in Circular A-76 or the individual agency decisions mandated by it are linked to any body of theory, legal or otherwise, as to what constitutes an "intrinsic" government function. In any event, the A-76 process provides rather weak mechanisms for vetting or enforcing the guidelines that it sets.

While the existing constitutional and legal framework puts some boundaries around outsourcing, the actual degree to which government functions have been delegated over the years is driven by other considerations related to ideology, self-interest, efficiency, perceived deficiencies in the public sector, and, finally, simple hypocrisy, which I will consider in turn.

Drivers of Outsourcing

The first driver of outsourcing is ideology. The practice picked up dramatically in the Reagan administration and continued over the next generation as certain conservative ideas about the nature of government took hold in American political culture. Ronald Reagan came into office asserting that "government was the problem, not the solution," reflecting the belief that the private sector would always be more efficient than the public sector, and that government had grown too large. Reagan was part of a global move toward smaller government, supported not only by figures like his contemporary Margaret Thatcher but also by many market-oriented economists who argued that state sectors had become too large and were obstacles to economic growth.

This was not the exclusive province of conservatives, however; many groups on the left were also suspicious of government and were happy to see some of its functions delegated to the nonprofit sector. They were driven by suspicions that government regulators and agencies had been captured by powerful interest groups and were no longer representative of public interest. Many also believed that the nonprofit sector was inherently more public spirited than either private for-profit companies or the government, and more representative of the democratic public.

A second motive for increased outsourcing was a belief that private organizations were more efficient and effective than the government. There is certainly good reason for this. State-run organizations often do not face adequate incentives to perform efficiently for a variety of reasons: they may be monopoly providers of a particular service; they do not face the risk of bankruptcy for poor performance; they cannot control their own factors of production like private firms; and they are subject to complex mandates, which only intermittently include operational efficiency (Wilson, 1989). A private for-profit firm will not necessarily face similar constraints, though whether it actually could realize efficiencies is an empirical question that needs constant testing.

A third motive for privatization was simple self-interest. Many private firms either wanted to protect their existing relations with the government or hoped to win new contracts in areas not previously open to competition. Similarly, many people working for nongovernmental organizations saw their organizational survival as dependent on government contracts. This included not a few religious organizations that saw new roles for themselves as implementers of government-funded social services. These groups pushed for rules like Circular A-76 that gave them broader opportunities to bid on contracts.

A fourth motive had to do with deficiencies in the public sector. As the scope of government activities continued to grow over the decades, the capacity of the American state to take on new functions was often limited. Many of the constraints had to do with the excessive rigidity of personnel rules, which limited the government's ability to attract and retain highly skilled workers and to discipline those not meeting its standards.

Take the case of public-private partnerships. In contrast to other countries with developed democracies, such as Britain, Australia, and Canada, the United States undertakes relatively few public-private partnership projects. Part of the reason lies in the structure of the American municipal finance market, but there are also capacity constraints. The head of the Canadian public-private partnerships office (attached to the Finance Ministry) is a highly skilled individual recruited out of the financial sector who is paid a salary of nearly US$1 million a year. It would be very difficult to do this in the United States; although a number of agencies requiring special expertise have received "cut-outs"—that is, exemptions—from normal general schedule pay scales and hiring rules, there are limits to the political acceptability of this practice. Many of the hiring and accountability practices entailed by New Public Management that have become routine in Commonwealth countries like Australia, New Zealand, and Canada could not be put into effect in the United States.

These constraints mean that certain government functions necessarily get outsourced to private bodies. Karthik Ramanna gives the example of a number of what he labels "thin political markets," which involve activities so specialized that only a few dozen people with the requisite expertise exist in the entire country. The example he focuses on is the Financial Accounting Standards Board, a private nonprofit organization that sets corporate accounting standards with huge consequences for investors and corporate performance. The U.S. government has in effect outsourced the setting of accounting standards to this body because it does not have the requisite expertise. He argues that it has come to be dominated by the very large firms it regulates, and that the subject matter is so specialized that the government lacks the ability to even oversee its decisions (Ramanna 2015a, 2015b).

The rigidity of the civil service system encourages outsourcing in another way: because the rules for dismissing civil servants are so cumbersome, it is often easier to hire a contractor to undertake a job, which can be terminated when no longer necessary. Companies and nonprofits can obviously lobby to extend their contracts, but that system is still not as rigid as the employment conditions in most parts of the public sector. This rigidity is due to the risk aversion of the system's political principals, who do not want to be seen as permitting excessive discretion in routing hiring and firing decisions, and to public-sector unions that have sought to protect themselves from the same.

A final reason for the expansion of outsourcing in the United States is perhaps the most important: simple hypocrisy. Since the beginning of the republic, American politicians have been railing against bureaucrats and the excessive size of government. At a time when the U.S. government consisted of about three thousand individuals, Thomas Jefferson wrote, "We may well doubt whether our organization is too complicated, too expensive; whether offices and officers have not been multiplied unnecessarily and sometimes injuriously to the service they were meant to promote" (Jefferson, 1801). Countless other politicians, Republicans and Democrats, have since that time attacked the incompetence and size of the bureaucracy. At the same time, the demand for government services provided by bureaucrats has continued to expand. As John J. DiIulio Jr. has pointed out, federal employment has been essentially flat since the 1960s, while the amount of money passing through the U.S. government has increased fivefold (DiIulio, 2014). Offloading the work of civil servants onto contractors provides a convenient way for politicians to pretend that they are holding down the size of government while still delivering an ever-expanding array of services to constituents.

Constraints on Outsourcing

On the other side of the ledger, there are a number of reasons to be concerned about outsourcing and its consequences for the long-term effectiveness and legitimacy of the U.S. government. The first has to do with agency problems. Under principal-agent theory, corruption and other dysfunctions occur when agents have agendas other than carrying out the mandates of their principals. This can be the result of simple self-dealing, but it can also arise from the existence of multiple principals who impose different mandates on the agent. A contractor, whether for- or nonprofit, automatically has two principals, the government office contracting for its services and the owner or director of the organization for which he or she works. In the case of a private-sector contractor, the owner has a profit-maximizing objective; in the case of a nonprofit, the organization may be dedicated to goals that are different from those of the government principal. Privatization is often done for the sake of efficiency, but the savings for a contractor may redound to the private benefit of the company and come at the expense of public interest.

A second problem has to do with the very claims of superior efficiency that are often made on behalf of privatized services. Such results are much more likely to be realized for services provided by diverse and competitive markets, but many things that government does are the domain of monopoly or oligopoly providers. This is particularly the case for utilities like power, water, sewerage, and telecoms, where competition is often hard to come by. Some privatization experiments have been disastrous, like the privatization of Mexico's Telmex in the early 1990s, which turned a state monopoly into a private one. The privatization of British Rail in the United Kingdom was highly controversial and did not lead to clearly better services. Something similar can be said of a number of municipal water privatizations in Latin America. It is not clear that privatized prisons in states like California are operated much more efficiently than state-operated ones. Nor is it clear that the myriad of contractors working for the United States Agency for International Development are more effective than their federally employed counterparts. Many of the agency's workers take early retirement and continue doing essentially the same jobs as before, but at higher salaries as contractors; outsourcing serves to suck capacity out of government. When privatization has been successful, it has required the existence of states with sufficient capacity to regulate the private providers, something for which legislators do not always make provisions.

A third problem with contracting is related to transparency. The U.S. federal government is among the most transparent organizations in the world: there are a raft of statutes mandating transparency at an agency and individual level, including the Freedom of Information Act, the Government in the Sunshine Act, the Federal Advisory Committee Act, and a host of financial and political disclosure requirements imposed on anyone hoping to work for the federal government. None of these rules apply to contractors; indeed, the requirement that the government publish data on who its contractors and subcontractors are, and the terms of their employment, is not well established. The lack of transparency can then affect the legitimacy of government as a whole, as citizens are not sure who it is that is responsible for delivering services, or whom to hold accountable when things go wrong (James et al., 2016).

Transparency without accountability does not fix the oversight problem, which points to potential lack of accountability as the fourth problem with contracting. A case in point is the State Department's use of the mercenary firm Blackwater to provide diplomatic security in Iraq. If uniformed U.S. military personnel are accused of crimes against local civilians, there is a clear system of military justice that can hold these individuals to account. No such clarity exists when private contractors are allowed to make decisions regarding lethal force. The ultimate sanction that the government holds over most contractors is loss of the contract, which may not be a sufficiently severe penalty to deter behaviors that produce loss of life or other severe externalities.

A fifth problem with outsourcing has to do with its impact on state capacity. Pervasive outsourcing relieves the state of the need to maintain expertise and human capital on its own wage bill. This tends to shift the nature of government work away from substantive knowledge of the issue area for which the agency has responsibility to contract management. This problem is particularly acute for agencies like the Department of Energy or the United States Agency for International Development, where as much as 90 percent of the agency's work is done by contractors. It is an illusion to think that contractors can be managed effectively without extensive substantive knowledge of the issue area at stake, including on-the-ground experience dealing with the actual situations that contractors are likely to face. Without this direct experience, contract managers do not know what they do not know. This may account for the decline in some agencies' willingness to even manage contracts (Mahler, 2016). This is a problem that affects not just the executive branch but also other parts of the U.S. government like Congress.[1]

The Nature of Executive Authority

The list of arguments for and against the outsourcing of government functions to private parties may explain the historical reasons for this phenomenon, but it does not yet get to the theoretical question of what the intrinsic functions of government are. The following section outlines the beginnings of such a theory, which is rooted in the question of the nature of executive power in a liberal democracy.

In modern democratic theory, "the people" are sovereign. In a parliamentary system, the people vote for a legislature that represents their will by passing laws. That legislature then delegates to the executive the responsibility for implementing those laws. The executive itself contains multiple levels of delegation, from ministers to vice ministers all the way down to the frontline organizations that actually deliver services to and interact with citizens. This idealized understanding of democratic process is in line with current principal-agent theory, which is the primary framework within which economists understand the dysfunctions of hierarchical organizations.

The reality of the way that governments work is actually quite different from this idealized picture. All real-world organizations, whether governments, private businesses, or nonprofits, need to delegate substantial authority to lower levels of their administrative structures. The reasons for this are several. Substantive expertise in most organizations is held not at the highest administrative levels but rather lower down; authority over the right thing to do therefore often travels up the hierarchy rather than down as agents influence their principals (Simon, 1957; Friedrich, 1940). Lower levels of the organization are usually able to make decisions more quickly and accurately than higher levels, which often get distorted and untimely information as it travels through a complex administrative hierarchy. Finally, lower levels of an organization are usually in better touch with sources of local knowledge, providing the context necessary to make proper decisions (Hayek, 1945).

More importantly, the modern executive has never been seen simply as an implementer of decisions made by the legislature; rather, it is perceived as a source of authority in its own right. This is most true in presidential systems, where the president is directly elected, giving him or her a democratic mandate equal in legitimacy to that possessed by the legislature. But even in parliamentary systems, party discipline ensures that the prime minister is a powerful figure in his or her own right.

The central question for both administrative lawyers and organizational theorists is how to delegate discretion in a hierarchy and still maintain control over the behavior of the agents who constitute the organization. In theory, a hierarchy should delegate only the discretion needed to implement a particular mandate from the principal. In reality, principals often do not know exactly what they want: they may be excessively vague in their grants of authority, may mandate contradictory goals, or may simply seek to kick the policy problem down to the administrative agency and hope that the courts will clear up any problems later.

The problem of delegated discretion to administrative agencies was clearly understood in the United States in the wake of the huge expansion of government authority during the New Deal. The result was effectively a new constitutional settlement, the Administrative Procedure Act (APA) of 1946, that put boundaries around executive branch discretion (Skowronek and Orren, 2017). The APA recognized that the executive was not simply the implementer of legislative rules but often had the ability to write new rules on its own. Agency rule making was therefore made subject to notice and comment (transparency) and could be contested by the other branches of government (accountability). It is safe to say that much of the enormous body of case law and legal scholarship in this area since then has revolved around interpretations of the APA.

The APA offers procedural checks on the misuse of executive authority, reflecting an American political culture that has historically been highly suspicious of state power. There are, however, alternative points of view that have seen the benefits of executives being able to act outside the bounds of procedural rules or mandates imposed by legislatures. The first political theorist to describe the role of the modern executive was Niccolo Machiavelli. He argued that survival of the political community often necessitated quick, decisive, and memorable actions that could not be bound at all times by either morality or law. Laws were general and devoid of context; only an individual ruler could interpret that context and see what needed to be done. Harvey C. Mansfield Jr. has described the way that Machiavelli's prince was "tamed" by subsequent writers and incorporated into republican theory as the modern executive (Mansfield, 1989). The result, according to Mansfield, was a necessary equality of the executive and legislative branches: "The beauty of executive power, then, is to be both subordinate and not subordinate, both weak and strong. It can reach where the law cannot, and thus supply the defect of law, yet remain subordinate to law. This ambivalence in the modern executive permits its strength to be useful to republics, without endangering them" (xvi).

In a similar vein, the German legal theorist Carl Schmitt argued that the laws are general rules meant to apply to normal situations. The nature of human social life was, however, to be constantly subject to out-of-normal situations and emergencies, which required exceptions to general rules. He famously stated that the "sovereign is he who decides the exception"—that is, the leader who decides when circumstances merit going beyond the law (2005, 5). In classical Chinese thought, there was a long-standing argument between the Legalists and Confucians: the former argued that societies needed clear and strongly enforced rules to maintain social order, while the latter argued that no set of rules would ever be sufficient to cover all cases that might actually arise in practice (Fukuyama, 2014). Well-governed societies needed to rely on the judgment of a wise leader who could take contextual information into account to come to the right decision on behalf of the community. One of the ways in which Chinese political culture differs systematically from that of the West is, to put it in terms that an administrative lawyer would understand, that the Chinese put much more faith in executive discretion, while Westerners have tended to favor complex procedures for decision-making. This difference is not a stark binary choice but rather one of emphasis, since both cultures make use of both discretion and rules.

In the American tradition, the foremost exponent of executive authority was Alexander Hamilton, who in *Federalist Nos. 70–77* laid out the case for strong executive power. In *Federalist No. 70* he famously noted that "energy in the Executive is a leading character in the definition of good government." It is clear that Hamilton does not mean simply that the executive should be energetic in executing the law; he envisions many cases, mostly related to foreign policy, in which the law does not clearly enjoin action but action is needed. Energy implies initiative, the independent undertaking of actions that were not mandated by Congress.

In American history, executive discretion has been used at times not simply to interpret or extend an existing law but outside of or in contradiction to the law. We can of course think of many negative examples of this, such as Richard Nixon's efforts to use the CIA and FBI to protect his personal political interests. But this has also been done for more positive reasons: Abraham Lincoln famously suspended the right of habeas corpus during the Civil War to protect the Union against Confederate sabotage, while Franklin Roosevelt acted extralegally in extending lend-lease to Britain in the period before U.S. entry into World War II.

The last two are only some of the most famous cases. I suspect that virtually anyone who has occupied a senior executive position in the U.S. government will be aware of occasions in which an official skirted or actually violated the law in pursuit of a larger public goal. Let me just cite one case related to me by a friend and former colleague, who in the late 1970s was serving as head of the part of the U.S. Geological Survey responsible for regulating offshore oil leases. A major oil company held a farm-out lease in the Gulf of Louisiana that would expire on a certain date if exploration had not begun. The company was planning to do this by the deadline but was prevented from reaching the rig by an approaching hurricane. The president of the company asked for an extension of the lease, but the U.S. Geological Survey lawyers said definitively that the law would not permit this and that the lease would expire. My friend succeeded in delaying inspection of the tract for a couple of weeks and indirectly suggested to the company that it might begin exploration in the window between the end of the hurricane and the inspection. The company was thereby able to proceed with development of the tract.

My friend had, in effect, suggested that the company act illegally and then withheld this information, with collusion from his own agency. He believed, however, that in that period of oil shortage there was an overriding public interest in the rapid expansion of drilling in U.S. waters. I do not pass judgment on the rights or wrongs of his action but would only suggest that this type of discretionary judgment is frequently exercised by public officials to public benefit, and that American government would seize up from its own rigidities were this not the case.

One could argue that cases in which officials act extralegally in this fashion are rare, and one would certainly not encourage them to think that they should routinely do so. This can happen safely in a democracy under two conditions: first, there has to be a mechanism for holding officials accountable ex post such that abuses or cases of poor judgment are punished, and second, officials have to have a clear sense of public purpose that guides their decision-making. Nonetheless, in an effective government, you do not want officials who are so rigid and rule-bound as to never deviate from the letter of the law.

It is this type of discretionary authority that is least delegable to someone outside the government. Contractors are, in the first place, bound primarily by the terms of their contract. They are very unlikely to take the risks in the public interest—risks both to the public and to their own jobs—that such discretion entails. This is why Paul Verkuil has emphasized the importance of the oath of loyalty that all high U.S. officials must take, which forces those who take it to specify that their primary loyalty is to the Constitution of the United States.

My answer to the question of what constitutes an intrinsic government function would be this: a high government official exercises *authority* not simply to carry out mandates or instructions from the sovereign people but to exercise significant judgment on behalf of public interest, and to "go where the law does not." In doing so, that official has to be willing to risk his or her own personal reputation and standing for the sake of these larger public goals. This may not translate into clear rules about how an agency would distinguish between "intrinsic" and "competitive" functions, but it should at least help us to understand the essential meaning of government authority, and why it must be retained within the state itself.

The Nature of Twenty-First-Century Government

An answer to the theoretical question of what the intrinsic functions of government are may not, in the end, be a particularly good guide to how government will actually evolve in the twenty-first century. The government we get is not the government we deserve; the former is shaped by a host of political considerations that limit the realistic choices we face. If we could consistently elect wise leaders, appoint knowledgeable and responsible officials, pay them appropriately, and hold them properly accountable, then we could set clear boundaries around outsourcing (and also the proper size of government).

None of this is likely to happen, unfortunately; the reality we face is rather different. We can easily anticipate that the number of functions that citizens expect the government to perform will continue to increase, that the complexity of these functions will grow, that the American public will continue to be suspicious of bureaucrats and unwilling to grant them significant authority, except in extraordinary situations. We are in a sense trapped in a low-level equilibrium: citizens distrust government and are therefore unwilling to pay higher taxes or grant it greater authority, which then undercuts the ability of government to deliver the high-quality services they expect. This then confirms their original view that government cannot be trusted.

Thus, while it may be desirable in theory to follow John DiIulio's advice and hire a million new federal bureaucrats, this is very unlikely to happen. We are going to continue to rely on contractors because of dysfunctions in the existing, seemingly unfixable civil service system. Many of the defects of contractors have arisen as workarounds that were a response to the unreformability of the existing system. Rigidities in civil service hiring and termination rules create incentives to use contractors who are much easier to hire and fire. Use of contractors allows agencies to have access to talent that could not be induced to work directly for the federal government, either because of inadequate pay or burdensome compliance requirements. Even the lack of transparency for contractors can be an advantage, since current transparency rules like the Federal Advisory Committee Act have shut down internal agency deliberation as a result of the high costs of compliance.

The most obvious way to put boundaries around outsourcing is to reform the existing civil service system. We would need to do a number of things simultaneously: make hiring, promotion, and termination rules more flexible; remove pay caps for certain high-skill, competitive positions; modify individual disclosure rules to make them more comparable to those of the private sector; and finally, replace detailed ex ante rules and regulations with grants of greater authority in decision-making with an ex post system of accountability. The American public would need to pay increased respect to its public servants, and to trust government more.

Needless to say, the possibility of carrying out such a reform, comparable in scope to the 1883 Pendleton Act, is very low today. The American public is highly polarized, and a very substantial group sees the federal bureaucracy as a team player for the other side. The ideal, held in many other developed democracies, of the state as an impartial guardian of public interest standing above politics has always been foreign to American political culture, and it is even more so now. This means that the workarounds are likely to remain permanent fixtures of American government, and that, in the interests of simple functionality, we will need to preserve them—indeed, to expand on them as second-best solutions to our current dysfunctions. We will need to accept the fact that necessary types of expertise will necessarily exist outside the government and be tapped on an ad hoc basis; pay schedules will no longer be uniform but rather tailored to specific sectors, regions, and forms of expertise; there will have to be quasi-permanent exemptions from rules for particular parts of the government; and there is a general expectation that traditional government services will be delivered by states in partnership with nonstate actors. This means, in the end, that citizens will have to focus less on state performance than on final outcomes, which the government will help facilitate, but for which it will never in the end bear full responsibility.

Note

1. For example, congressional staffs often do not have the expertise necessary to write complex legislation; as a result, they outsource the drafting of legislation not to for-profit contractors but rather to the next best thing: the lobbyists with direct interests in the legislation at hand.

Bibliography

DiIulio, John J., Jr. 2014. *Bring Back the Bureaucrats: Why More Federal Workers Will Lead to Better (and Smaller!) Government.* West Conshohocken, PA: Templeton.

Freeman, Jody, and Martha Minow, eds. 2009. *Government by Contract: Outsourcing and American Democracy.* Cambridge, MA: Harvard University Press.

Friedrich, Carl J. 1940. "The Nature of Administrative Responsibility." *Public Policy* 1:3–24.

Fukuyama, Francis. 2014. *Political Order and Political Decay: From the Industrial Revolution to the Globalization of Democracy.* New York: Farrar, Straus and Giroux.

———. 2016. "Governance: What Do We Know and How Do We Know It?" *Annual Review of Political Science* 19:89–105.

Hayek, Friedrich A. 1945. "The Use of Knowledge in Society." *American Economic Review* 35 (4): 519–30.

James, Oliver, Sebastian Jilke, Carolyn Petersen, and Steven Van de Walle. 2016. "Citizens' Blame of Politicians for Public Service Failure: Experimental Evidence About Blame Reduction Through Delegation and Contracting." *Public Administration Review* 76 (1): 83–93.

Jefferson, Thomas. 1801. First Annual Message to Congress, December 8, 1801. Avalon Project of Yale Law School. http://avalon.law.yale.edu/19th_century/jeffmes1.asp.

Kettl, Donald F. 2002. *The Transformation of Governance: Public Administration for Twenty-First Century America*. Baltimore: Johns Hopkins University Press.

———. 2016. *Escaping Jurassic Government: How to Recover America's Lost Commitment to Its Competence*. Washington, DC: Brookings Institution.

Mahler, Julianne. 2016. "NASA Contracting and the Direction of Space Science." *Administration and Society* 48:711–73.

Mansfield, Harvey C., Jr. 1989. *Taming the Prince: The Ambivalence of Modern Executive Power*. New York: Free Press.

Ramanna, Karthik. 2015a. *Political Standards: Corporate Interest, Ideology, and Leadership in the Shaping of Accounting Rules*. Chicago: University of Chicago Press.

———. 2015b. "Thin Political Markets: The Soft Underbelly of Capitalism." *California Management Review* 57 (2): 5–19.

Schmitt, Carl. 2005. *Political Theology: Four Chapters on the Concept of Sovereignty*. Chicago: University of Chicago Press.

Simon, Herbert. 1957. *Administrative Behavior: A Study of Decision-Making Processes in Administrative Organization*. New York: Free Press.

Skowronek, Stephen, and Karen Orren. 2017. *The Policy State: An American Predicament*. Cambridge, MA: Harvard University Press.

Verkuil, Paul R. 2007. *Outsourcing Sovereignty: Why Privatization of Government Functions Threatens Democracy and What We Can Do About It*. New York: Cambridge University Press.

———. 2017. *Valuing Bureaucracy: The Case for Professional Government*. New York: Cambridge University Press.

Wilson, James Q. 1989. *Bureaucracy: What Government Agencies Do and Why They Do It*. New York: Basic Books.

CHAPTER 6

Reframing American Institutions

A Look Ahead to Midcentury

Donald F. Kettl

Over the last generation, there has been a growing, nagging worry: that American democracy has gradually become unmoored from its constitutional roots—and that Americans have lost confidence that their government can deliver. Of course, every generation believes itself in the midst of crisis, and it is always much easier to see the challenges of the present and to overlook those of the past. The hit Broadway musical *Hamilton* reminds us that every stage of American democracy has had to struggle with big, often fierce problems. And on one front, we have made great progress. Politicians no longer settle disputes with pistols at sunrise.

But, as Paul C. Light points out in his argument about catch-22 government, there is a very real sense that our current challenges are large and unprecedented. There is a rising distrust among Americans in their institutions, a declining willingness to match the appetite for government programs with the willingness to pay for them, an accelerating instinct to push big problems into the future, and rising political polarization that is, at once, both the cause and the effect of these big problems.

In 1988, Paul A. Volcker delivered the Francis Boyer Lecture and underlined the "quiet crisis" of public service, which served as the foundation for the Volcker Commission report (Volcker, 1988; National Commission on the Public Service, 1989). There are many explanations of its cause. Some analysts have pointed to broken institutions, especially Congress. Thomas E. Mann and Norman J. Ornstein argued that Congress has become "the broken branch"—and then argued, even more strongly, that the problem has become "even worse than it looks" (Mann and Ornstein, 2006, 2012). Others, like Francis Fukuyama (2014), have pointed to the decay in government's ability to represent citizens' views and administer government well. There is no escaping the conclusion that trust in government has declined to a perilous level (Kettl, 2017a).

But to these essential and discouraging conclusions, it is important to add another argument. To a large—but largely unrecognized—degree, these problems share a single root cause: throughout the twentieth century, American government has taken on a far broader array of functions, and it has chosen to govern them in ways that are out of sync with the structure, capacity, and public law of American institutions. We built our governmental institutions on a rule of law created to operate within the constitutional system. We have, however, evolved our policies through strategies and tactics with which the rule of law no longer fits; that cause our institutions to strain to govern and hold policies accountable; that cause us to struggle to deliver results; and that distort and break the line of sight from citizens to the elected leaders on many issues they care about. In particular, the closer we look at how American government has changed, where its money goes, and how government operates, the further elected officials appear to be from the key decisions that shape governance. This development poses a direct and stark challenge to American political institutions.

Given these challenges, it is little surprise that government struggles. If American democracy is to survive, let alone thrive, to midcentury and beyond, we need to refashion our governance institutions to match the policies that they are creating and pursuing.

The Strategies and Tactics of American Public Policy

A major challenge for our governance institutions is the increasingly complex layering of public policy strategies. Consider the following six points, building on the budget as the foundation for public policy decisions and the map of how those decisions flow.

Table 6.1. Federal Financial Footprint

Outlays in the budget	$3.85 trillion
Tax expenditures	$1.45 trillion
Loan disbursements	$0.62 trillion
Regulatory compliance costs	$1.89 trillion
Total	$7.81 trillion

Sources: Office of Management and Budget, 2017a, table 1.1; 2017b; Rogers and Toder, 2011; Crews, 2016.

The Budget Is Only Half the Federal Government's Financial Footprint

Most debate about the federal government's scope and size centers on the budget. Budgets, of course, are always good road maps of the government's activities. For the federal government, however, the $4 trillion budget captures only about half of the government's overall size. However, the federal government's financial footprint is about double that, roughly $8 trillion. The exact numbers are difficult to determine, and the fuzziness of the accounting itself creates even bigger challenges for assessing the true size and scope of government. That is because it produces good numbers for its outlays but does not carefully collect information about the size and cost of its other tools. For example, it calculates tax expenditures in different ways and does not add up the total amount of revenue lost. Loan disbursements are hard to track. And estimates of the costs for complying with federal regulations vary widely. Table 6.1 represents a reasonable, if rough, estimate of the total size of the federal government's financial footprint—and it is about twice the level of its direct expenditures.

Not only is the footprint far larger than is commonly appreciated, but there is no assessment, produced either within government or outside it, of the government's total financial activity, no debate about how large it *ought* to be, and no analysis of which tools are more likely to produce the best results. Moreover, there is a wide gulf between the actual federal financial footprint and the way the federal government governs it. Broken as it is, the federal budget process provides rough leverage over half of the federal government's financial activity. For the other half, embracing tax, loan, and regulatory policy, there is no real governance at all. One half of the footprint operates in sharp relief, cast against the background of ferocious battles. The other half operates in a shadow world of the dimmest transparency, oversight, and accountability. There are constant debates about the role of the

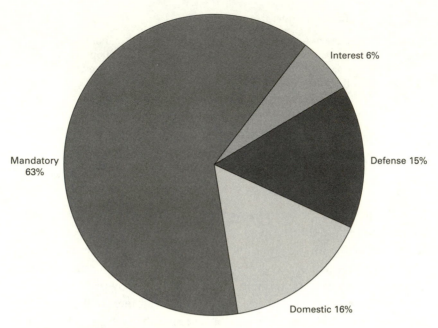

Figure 6.1. Composition of Federal Spending
Note: Data are for fiscal year 2016.
Source: Office of Management and Budget, 2017a.

"deep state," but this is the deepest state of all (Rucker and Costa, 2017). As a result, the structures and institutions of American government are increasingly distanced from the strategic decisions shaping its financial footprint.

Budget Battles Focus on a Small Part of the Federal Budget

In recent decades, the battles over the budget itself have grown increasingly fierce. From apocalyptic shutdowns of the government to recurring battles over spending ceilings, sequestration (automatic cuts if the government breaches those ceilings), continuing resolutions, and "dead on arrival" budgets, lines for skirmishes are drawn and then drawn again. But most of this fighting centers on a very small part of the budget. Mandatory programs— entitlements like Social Security, Medicare, and Medicaid—account for al-

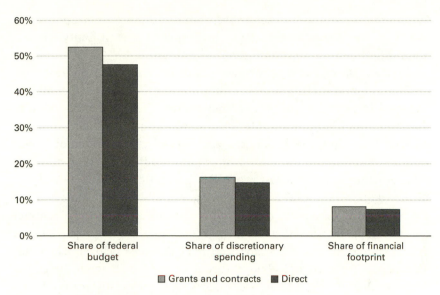

Figure 6.2. Federal Spending by Strategy: Direct, Grants, Contracts
Source: Derived from Figure 6.1.

most two-thirds of the budget. Interest on the debt is about 6 percent. That leaves only about 30 percent of the budget that gets regular review, split about equally between defense and domestic programs (Figure 6.1). And since the budget is only about half of the federal financial footprint, that means the intense scrutiny and high drama in the budget focus on only one of every six dollars in the footprint.

The Federal Government Directly Delivers Little of What It Spends

Much of the discretionary money that the federal government spends goes through mechanisms it does not directly control. A large piece of federal discretionary spending goes through grants to state and local governments, to programs other than entitlements (14 percent), and through contracts (39 percent). The federal government's bureaucrats directly account for just half of all discretionary spending, 15 percent of spending in the budget, and just 7 percent of the federal financial footprint (Figure 6.2). As Francis

Fukuyama points out in his chapter, there is a limit—practical and political—to how far we can go in delegating government's responsibility without threatening the integrity of our constitutional system.

Consider the case of Medicare, Medicaid, and the Children's Health Insurance Program (CHIP). Together, they account for 25 percent of all federal spending. But the number of employees who manage the programs, in the Centers for Medicare and Medicaid Services, an agency of the Department of Health and Human Services, account for just 0.2 percent of all federal employees. The Centers for Medicare and Medicaid Services manages these programs through a vast network of grants (to state governments for Medicaid and CHIP) and through contracts (for Medicare). State governments, in turn, manage Medicaid and CHIP through their own contract systems. About 90 percent of the budgets for NASA and the Department of Energy go to contracts, and analysts estimate that the intelligence community spends 70 percent of its budget through contracts (Lofgren, 2014). The deeper we drill into the federal government's activities, the further top elected officials appear from the key decisions and operations.

Federalism Is Part of Every Nook and Cranny of Domestic Policy

Most of the media—and most of the national debates—center on the federal government's role in public policy. And, indeed, the federal government surely is responsible for the broad strategies that shape the national debates. But state and local governments play an enormous role in these strategies, far larger than is often recognized. Indeed, there is no part of domestic policy in which state and local governments are not central. In 2017, President Donald J. Trump announced a tougher immigration policy, but hundreds of local communities declared themselves "sanctuary cities" and refused to cooperate. Environmental policy reforms have often bubbled up from the states, especially California. Infrastructure policy depends on the decisions, investment, and management of state and local government officials. Economic development is local, as is the implementation of social service policy.

And, perhaps most fundamentally, Medicaid—the federal government's program to provide health care for the poor and disabled—draws its real meaning from decisions made by the states. Federal grants flow to the states, state governments add their own funds, states decide which elements of the core national program to emphasize and add on their own pieces, and

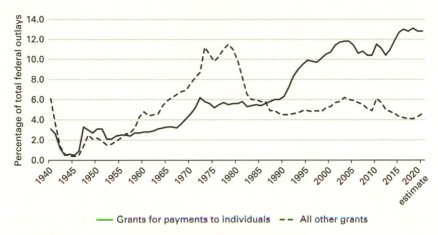

Figure 6.3. Federal Grants to State and Local Governments
Source: Office of Management and Budget, 2017a, table 6.1.

the states are then largely responsible for administering the program, through a vast and complex network of for-profit insurance intermediaries, who manage the payment system, and private and nonprofit medical providers, who actually deliver the care. The federal government in 2016 paid for 63 percent of Medicaid costs. The state share nationally is 37 percent, but it ranges from 49 percent in Virginia, Wyoming, and Nebraska, to 21 percent in Arkansas, Kentucky, and New Mexico (Henry J. Kaiser Family Foundation, 2017).

In fact, federal grants to state and local governments rose from 1 percent of all federal spending in 1945 to a projected 17 percent in 2020. The composition of grants, however, changed dramatically, with grants for payments to individuals (mostly for Medicaid, but also for CHIP, welfare, and other transfer programs) steadily rising. In 1985, more-traditional grants for infrastructure and social services equaled grants for transfer programs. Since then, grants for transfer programs have soared as health-care spending has risen, and more-traditional federal grants have declined (Figure 6.3). This is a sign of the deep interconnection of federal, state, and local finances; of the critical role that state and local governments play in administering federal programs—and, as Martha Derthick so clearly pointed out in a series of essays (2004), of the enormous challenge of keeping the "compound republic" that the nation's founders so proudly established. Republican reformers view these trends with alarm. Their solution is to reduce the federal role by

Table 6.2. Government Spending and Employment, 2014

	Full-time employees (millions)		Spending (trillions)	
Federal	2.08	12.9%	$3.51	53.9%
State	3.47	21.5%	$1.43	21.9%
Local	10.58	65.6%	$1.57	24.1%
Total	16.13	100.0%	$6.5	100.0%

Note: Percentages do not add to 100% due to rounding.
Sources: USGovernmentSpending.com; Office of Personnel Management, various reports; Census Bureau, various reports.

shifting responsibility to the states. That would dramatically transform the politics of the programs—and redefine the roles of both federal and state institutions in shaping policy decisions. It would surely boost the importance of federalism—and create new debates about just how much variation in national programs the country is prepared to accept.

The rising importance of federalism spills over into the patterns of spending and employment across the levels of government. The federal government accounts for a bit more than half of all government outlays in the United States but for just one of every eight government employees (Table 6.2). Local governments, on the other hand, spend just one of every four dollars but account for two-thirds of all government employees. State governments serve as the shock absorber in the system, sitting in between. Like the devices in our cars, they transmit the power of policy to the ground while absorbing the variations that flow back from the road. That, in fact, is the critical but often-overlooked role of the states in policy implementation: translating broad goals into specific results.

As the bruising battles over health reform in 2017 showed, intergovernmental tensions are hard-wired into the American system. That is precisely the way the founders intended it. Rather than drawing clear lines over the division of power, they created an arena in which combatants could struggle over where those lines ought to be—and within which the boundaries could shift. As policymakers worked through the challenges of the Great Depression (through the New Deal), postwar recovery (through the interstate highway system and urban renewal), the rising social pressures of the 1960s (through the Great Society), and the growing intermingling of functions (especially through shared responsibility for environmental policy, social services, and health policy), federalism has provided a fabric in which federal, state, and local functions have become far more interwoven and where the boundaries among responsibilities have become much more blurred.

Global Policy Is Shared to the Point of Blurring Sovereignty

The same phenomena that have increasingly shaped American federalism have spilled over into global governance. There are few, if any, areas in which nation-states are any longer truly sovereign. That is the case for the vastly complex world of military superpowers. It is even more the case for arenas ranging from climate change to financial regulation, where problems cross national boundaries and where national governments must deal with a complex web of nongovernmental players if they are to exert any real influence.

Sovereignty once meant supreme power, in a usage that dates from at least the fourteenth century. By the twenty-first century, critics wondered whether the term had become "loaded," "a favorite expression of authoritarian leaders," "imperialist," or a "dog whistle." The debate proved especially heated following a 2017 speech by President Trump to the United Nations in which he used variations of *sovereign* twenty-one times in framing a new strategy for American foreign policy (Lowry, 2017; Perlman, 2017). But with the rising interconnection of the global community, the very notion of sovereignty has evolved from one of absolutes—kings proclaimed themselves sovereign as a way of asserting their ultimate power—to one of degree, since increasingly complex policy puzzles have pushed nations into sharing responsibility for solving or, at least, trying to regulate them.

Sovereignty is no longer the province of a single official or a single country. It no longer shapes the development of any policy that matters. It is less the stipulation of power than the creation of arenas of action—and political conflict. And it is a marker of the changing role of American institutions in an increasingly globalized world. It is harder to control the nation's physical borders. Moreover, the borders themselves have far less meaning in an era when the globe's stock markets never close, when travel has created a global melting pot, and when many products do not have a clear national identity. At the core, it makes it increasingly hard for governments to govern.

These Patterns Have Erased the Line of Sight Between Citizens and Their Government

The first five points lead to a penultimate sixth: American policy and institutions are stuck in a deepening spiral of strategies that disconnect Americans from the government that serves them. This fundamental challenge to governance builds on a series of issues.

Americans do not like big government—or at least most of them will not admit publicly to supporting a large and powerful government apparatus. There is nothing new here. The United States retains deep roots in its revolutionary origin, which heavily flavors its governance in ways that continue to make politics in the United States very different from politics in other spinoffs from the British Crown like Australia, Canada, and New Zealand. But Americans surely do like—and demand—what government does for them. The unholy trinity of "waste, fraud, and abuse" invariably are labels applied to programs that someone else gets. On the other hand, even small-government conservatives like—and demand—that government step in to solve problems from which they are suffering. And, of course, there is no sense of self-aware irony in this paradox.

And how does American government respond to this paradox? Since World War II, there has been a common strategy, among both Republicans and Democrats: pursue the five previous points by expanding federally funded programs but relying heavily on nonfederal proxies to deliver these programs (Kettl, 2016a). This has allowed advocates to expand government programs without expanding government—or at least the federal government bureaucracy. Relying on nongovernmental proxies to do government's work provided a fig leaf for the expansion of government in the latter half of the twentieth century. Government's programs could grow without growing government, at least according to the metrics that catch the most attention.

If this fig leaf has provided a bit of rhetorical cover, it has disguised a far more fundamental problem. It convinced many policymakers and citizens alike that they could follow a strategy that allowed them to have their cake and eat it too: more government without a bigger government.

Both parties have been complicit in this fiction. Democrats allowed themselves to increase government programs without thinking through how to manage them. That problem was at the core of the collapse of Obamacare's website on the day it launched. Having won the fierce battle to pass the program, the administration did not pay enough attention to how to make it work. Republicans, on the other hand, convinced themselves that they could allow the new programs to pass and then strangle them by fighting their administration. That problem plagued George W. Bush in his struggle to deal with Hurricane Katrina. The two parties struggled to govern an increasingly complex system by finding compromise on ambitious goals—but with Democrats not paying enough attention to management and Republicans deciding they could reverse policies by starving management.

This dance had three important effects. First, it undermined the performance of government programs, because how well government worked became increasingly disconnected from what government tried to do (see Paul C. Light's Chapter 1 for more details).

Second, it undermined the confidence of citizens in their government's work, because the gap between policymakers' results and their capacity to deliver increased. The more indirect the tool used to deliver federal programs, the more likely it is to be plagued by problems of performance (Kettl, 2016b).

Third, it undermined democracy, because it reduced the line of sight between citizens and their government. Many citizens increasingly fail to see government programs hiding in plain sight because government's role is largely invisible to them. There is no better example than the story of the demonstrator carrying a sign saying, "Keep government's hands off my Medicare!" Cynics snidely pointed out that the woman obviously did not know that Medicare is one of the federal government's biggest programs. But, in a broad sense, the woman had an important point. There was no way that she could *see* the government in Medicare. Most Medicare and Medicaid recipients never see a government employee, because nongovernmental proxies deliver the services (Kettl, 2009).

This last point might well be the most important of all. Political debates have become increasingly disconnected from the process of governing. Governing has increasingly become disconnected from the process of delivering results. Government's institutions have increasingly become disconnected from the programs they are charged with overseeing. And citizens, not surprisingly, have felt increasingly disconnected from them all—except from the programs they want and expect. Here, they too often distrust government's connection with the things they care most about.

Now, to be sure, this does not apply to all of government. Local governments, in particular, continue to manage key frontline programs. Most of their employees are teachers and sanitation workers, firefighters and police officers. These government workers are responsible for fundamentally important programs that citizens want and appreciate. Moreover, trust in government tends to increase the closer services are to citizens. In 2016, trust in local government was 71 percent, and in state government trust was slightly lower at 62 percent. At the federal level, in contrast, trust was just 20 percent (McCarthy, 2016; Pew Research Center, 2017).

These differences focus the main point: especially at the federal level, the growing disconnection of governmental institutions from the actual processes of governing is having a deep and profound impact on government's ability to govern.

Reframing America's Institutions

These are large and daunting challenges. The nation's founders did not foresee the costs of pushing their inventions to the edge, and we are far past the point of solving the problem by tinkering with institutions or asking elected officials to reform their behavior. We are not likely to solve these challenges by falling into more money or easier problems, and the consequences for failing to address them well could be deep and profound. If the history of the decline of the American experience has to be written in the coming century, its roots will likely be found in the big issues here. What remedies might aid America's institutions in coping with these fundamental twenty-first-century governance challenges?

The task of reconciling America's institutions with the jobs we expect them to perform is richly illustrated by a plaintive email I received not long ago from a very senior federal official. She wrote about the obstacles she faced in accomplishing the work of her agency. She also complained about the enormous challenge of complying with the law. But she talked about these as two *separate* propositions. For her—and for many other government officials—there is a growing gap between the rule of law and the steps required to administer public programs. We want accountability, and for that we look to the rule of law, a view that John A. Rohr (1986) held as upholding the Constitution. We want effectiveness, and for that we look to our administrative institutions. But one of the central challenges of governance in the mid-twenty-first century is that our institutions have become unmoored from the rule of law and our policies have become disconnected from the basic governing institutions.[1]

Paul R. Verkuil's insightful and fascinating book *Valuing Bureaucracy: The Case for Professional Government* (2017) provides a foundation for exploring why this gap exists. He is among the very few scholars and public intellectuals to press the importance of the rule of law—and to identify where it falls short in governance. In fact, he argues, the rule of law "is too limited a frame from which to view the practice of government" (10). The implications are enormous—and growing.

The rule of law requires a government to be both accountable and transparent. The laws in place must be fair, and the public must have access to *workable mechanisms to resolve disputes*. The World Justice Project (n.d.) has laid out fundamental principles that it believes form the rule of law, and one of the most important is that "laws are clear, publicized, stable, and just; are applied evenly; and protect fundamental rights." The underlying problem is that both the management of government programs and the process of holding government accountable are rooted in the rule of law. We empower government officials to do their jobs but then constrain the power those officials exercise through the laws we pass and the rules we create. But this process is linear, with new laws carefully building on old ones and new regulations flowing from new laws. In fact, an important foundation of the rule of law is its utter predictability.

However, as Verkuil points out, the tools of administering the law are increasingly nonlinear. They build on the patterns of proxy-based administration described in this chapter. And by placing more responsibility in the hands of nonfederal actors, this approach to governance creates strategies and tactics far more complex to administer than in more traditional programs managed through the government's hierarchy. It outsources sovereignty, as Verkuil has powerfully argued, by placing far more governmental responsibility in the hands of nongovernmental actors.

Perhaps even more important, it creates fundamental challenges for the rule of law, because we do not have a good legal system for governing or managing a system that relies so heavily on proxies. Now, to be sure, there is a rich rule of law for government contracts and a strong base in administrative law for the government's management of its acquisition process. There are two problems here, however. One problem is that government contracts, important as they are, constitute a small fraction of the federal financial footprint—about 15 percent of the federal budget in 2016 and just 7 percent of the federal government's entire financial footprint. The areas in which there is established law govern only a small part of the federal government's proxy-based activities.

Moreover, contract law stipulates rules for bargaining among relatively equal parties. In many contracts, the government is a somewhat junior partner because it, too often, lacks sufficient expertise to know what it is buying or what it ought to pay—even though the prime purpose of these contracts is to advance the government's goals as the lawmaking process defines them. That is the critical puzzle of outsourcing government's sovereignty. As the government's capacity to act as a smart buyer has eroded, so too has its capacity to exercise its sovereignty.

The rich administrative law provisions that cover the basics of contracting do little to set the boundaries for which services should be contracted out and which are "inherently governmental" and therefore ought to be performed by government. They do little to answer the basic question of who is sovereign when government contracts with nongovernmental partners. For noncontract activities, such as loan programs and regulations, the rule of law is often far thinner, especially in establishing the foundation for the government's governance of these areas. Moreover, as Mahler points out (2016), contracting has evolved from one tool among many—how can we best carry out government's mission?—to an end in itself—since we do not trust government to do the people's work, how can we shift more of that work to private contractors?

Thus, we face a series of interlocking challenges. Our society places great weight on the rule of law, but the gap between the principles of the rule of law and the actual strategies for governing is growing. We do not have a good managerial model for ensuring the effectiveness and efficiency of government programs we implement through an increasingly complex set of proxy tools. The existing rule of law does not adequately cover many of those tools. And government's ability to exercise power on behalf of its citizens, in ways that serve the public interest instead of the narrow interests of its proxies, has weakened.

We often tend to brush aside concerns about governing capacity because we tend to fall back on an underlying assumption that the rule of law, quietly working below the surface, will, in the end, protect us. As we saw in the previous chapter, we rely on Friedrich's notion (1940) that the personal responsibility of administrations is the best route to accountability. But the tools of governance have evolved so dramatically since then that many of those exercising power on behalf of government are not part of government itself, and their sense of responsibility might connect only partly to the public interest. In contrast, Finer (1941) argued the need for far greater accountability of administrations to elected policymakers, but that is becoming far more difficult, as those who exercise power on behalf of government often have a tangential relationship, at best, to those policymakers. As a result, the strategies of governance, accountability, and the rule of law are becoming unmoored from each other, and from the theories that have guided the practice of government for a century.

As with the government official who saw getting her job done and complying with the law as separate propositions, we have slid into truly dangerous territory. The core of the problem is the growing gap between the rule of law, as it now exists, and the proxy-based tools of government action, for which there often is not a strong rule of law. The implications of this gap—the struggle to build government's capacity to produce results and to be held accountable for how it does so—are enormous and growing. They promise to be central to reframing American institutions for the mid-twenty-first century.

What options are there for solving this problem?

1. *More government bureaucrats.* John J. DiIulio Jr. (2014) has powerfully made the case for hiring a million more federal bureaucrats. We could allow governance to shift increasingly to governmental hands, he argues. Or we could strengthen government's capacity to govern by increasing the number of people who can act with government's authority. There is great power and logic in DiIulio's argument. But there seems little chance that enough political support would emerge, in an era of cutting government, to grow it—even if that growth would make government more focused and, in all likelihood, less intrusive.

2. *More transparency into who does what.* If deproxifying the federal government is unlikely, then we might strengthen governance at least by clarifying who contributes what to public policy. In particular, we might increase our ability to identify and measure the role of proxies in the administrative system. In his chapter for this book, DiIulio calls for a "Volcker Rule" for public administration. This strategy would at least make clear the true size of the workforce, both within and without government, to expand on Paul Light's pathbreaking work; to identify the consequences for government's outcomes that flow from proxy administration; and to follow a practice invented in New Zealand—relying on nonfederal actors when their work is more efficient and responsive, and relying on federal

managers when it is not. If we are to rely heavily on proxy administration, we can at least know how large our reliance on these tools is—and we can examine whether citizens and taxpayers are actually getting a good deal.

3. *More focus on the rule of law.* We are unlikely to slide away from the heavy reliance on government contractors and other forms of proxy government. But if we are to rely on these tools, we need to build a more robust rule of law to guide them. That, indeed, is a guiding principle of Fukuyama's argument in this book.

4. *More attention to data.* The more we drift from hierarchy to networks, from government-managed programs to proxies, the more we need to replace the central nervous system of authority with a strategy mapped to government's new operating realities. In her chapter for this book, Shelley Metzenbaum points to the power that evidence-based policy reforms can bring to government. Such reliance on evidence is important not only to improve policy decisions. It also provides a strategy for creating a tool that effectively follows the contours of government's proxy-based system, by providing feedback on just who is doing what—and how well.

5. *More citizenship by citizens.* The more important that nonfederal partners have become in governance, the less connected citizens have felt to government. This is an ironic consequence of the rise of proxy government. Interweaving government more into society has made society feel less tied to government (Perry, 2007). Reframing American institutions requires rediscovering and reinforcing the role of citizens. And that, in turn, builds on the previous four points.

These options, of course, will surely fall short of fully resolving a problem that has been several generations in the making. But they point at the kinds of transformation that the evolving system of governance will require. They point to the fact that strategies of governance have evolved faster than our ability to govern them. And, perhaps most important, they define just how large and fundamental this transformation is. America's system of governance has become unmoored from its traditional roots—and the system of accountability that has long shaped and dominated it. That system is a poor match for the challenges of mid-twenty-first-century governance.

Restoring the health of American democracy requires reframing American institutions to reinvent the connection between government and its capacity to govern. A more robust answer requires developing a government with stronger capacity—in particular, with human capital matched to the challenges of governance, equipped with the agility to move at the speed of technology. The nature of government's work is changing as fast as the nature of governance itself, and building government's capacity to govern, in a world of growing complexity, requires far more emphasis on the fundamentals: building the capacity of government's managers (National Academy of Public Administration, 2018). This is all a very tall order, but there is little doubt that the success of government in the twenty-first century—indeed, the ability of government to deliver services to citizens and to be held accountable to policymakers—requires at its core a rededication to building its most fundamental capacity to govern, in the role of government's administrator leaders and their ability to lead. This is the foundation on which the Volcker Commission was originally built (National Commission on the Public Service, 1989). This foundation becomes ever more important with each passing year.

Note

1. Portions of this section of the chapter originally appeared in the *Regulatory Review* (Kettl, 2017b).

Bibliography

Crews, Clyde Wayne. 2016. "Ten Thousand Commandments 2016." Competitive Enterprise Institute, May 3, 2016. https://cei.org/10KC2016.

Derthick, Martha. 2004. *Keeping the Compound Republic: Essays on American Federalism.* Washington, DC: Brookings Institution.

DiIulio, John J., Jr. 2014. *Bring Back the Bureaucrats: Why More Federal Workers Will Lead to Better (and Smaller!) Government.* West Conshohocken, PA: Templeton.

Finer, Herman. 1941. "Administrative Responsibility in Democratic Government." *Public Administration Review* 1 (4): 335–50.

Friedrich, Carl J. 1940. "Public Policy and the Nature of Administrative Responsibility." *Public Policy: A Yearbook of the Graduate School of Public Administration* 1 (1): 1–34.

Fukuyama, Francis. 2014. *Political Order and Political Decay: From the Industrial Revolution to the Globalization of Democracy.* New York: Farrar, Straus and Giroux.

Henry J. Kaiser Family Foundation. 2017. "Federal and State Share of Medicaid Spending: FY 2017." http://www.kff.org/medicaid/state-indicator/federalstate-share-of-spending/?currentTimeframe=0&sortModel=%7B%22colId%22:%22State%22,%22sort%22:%22desc%22%7D.

Kettl, Donald F. 2009. *The Next Government of the United States: Why Our Institutions Fail Us and How to Fix Them*. New York: W. W. Norton.

———. 2016a. *Escaping Jurassic Government: How to Recover America's Lost Commitment to Competence*. Washington, DC: Brookings Institution.

———. 2016b. *Managing Risk, Improving Results: Lessons for Improving Government Management from GAO's High-Risk List*. Washington, DC: IBM Center for the Business of Government. http://www.businessofgovernment.org/report/managing-risk-improving -results-lessons-improving-government-management-gao%E2%80%99s-high-risk-list.

———. 2017a. *Can Governments Earn Our Trust?* New York: Polity.

———. 2017b. "The Growing Gap in the Rule of Law." *Regulatory Review*, December 6, 2017. https://www.theregreview.org/2017/12/06/kettl-growing-gap-rule-law/.

Lofgren, Mike. 2014. "Essay: Anatomy of the Deep State." Moyers and Company, February 21, 2014. http://billmoyers.com/2014/02/21/anatomy-of-the-deep-state/.

Lowry, Rich. 2017. "Sovereignty Is Not a Dirty Word." *Politico Magazine*, September 20, 2017. http://www.politico.com/magazine/story/2017/09/20/rich-lowry-sovereignty-trump-un -215629.

Mahler, Julianne. 2016. "NASA Contracting and the Direction of Space Science." *Administration and Society* 48 (6): 711–35.

Mann, Thomas E., and Norman J. Ornstein. 2006. *The Broken Branch: How Congress Is Failing America and How to Get It Back on Track*. New York: Oxford University Press.

———. 2012. *It's Even Worse Than It Looks: How the American Constitutional System Collided with the New Politics of Extremism*. New York: Basic Books.

McCarthy, Justin. 2016. "Americans Still More Trusting in Local over State Government." Gallup, September 19, 2016. http://news.gallup.com/poll/195656/americans-trusting-local -state-government.aspx.

National Academy of Public Administration. 2018. *No Time to Wait, Part 2: Building a Public Service for the 21st Century*. Washington, DC: National Academy of Public Administration. https://www.napawash.org/studies/academy-studies/no-time-to-wait-part-2-building-a -public-service-for-the-21st-century.

National Commission on the Public Service. 1989. *Leadership for America: Rebuilding the Public Service: The Report of the National Commission on the Public Service*. Washington, DC: National Commission on the Public Service.

Office of Management and Budget. 2017a. *Budget of the United States Government, Fiscal Year 2017: Historical Tables*. https://www.whitehouse.gov/omb/budget/Historicals.

———. 2017b. "Credit and Insurance." Chapter 20 in *Analytical Perspectives: Budget of the U.S. Government, Fiscal Year 2017*. https://obamawhitehouse.archives.gov/sites/default /files/omb/budget/fy2017/assets/ap_20_credit.pdf.

Perlman, Merrill. 2017. "A War of Words over Sovereignty." *Columbia Journalism Review*, September 25, 2017. https://www.cjr.org/language_corner/sovereign-trump-united-nations .php.

Perry, James L. 2007. "Democracy and the New Public Service." *American Review of Public Administration* 37 (1): 3–16.

Pew Research Center. 2017. "Public Trust in Government: 1958–2017." Pew Research Center: U.S. Politics and Policy, December 14, 2017. http://www.people-press.org/2017/05/03 /public-trust-in-government-1958-2017/.

Rogers, Allison, and Eric Toder. 2011. "Trends in Tax Expenditures, 1985–2016." Tax Policy Center, Urban Institute, and Brookings Institution, September 16, 2011. https://www.urban.org/sites/default/files/publication/27561/412404-Trends-in-Tax-Expenditures---.PDF.

Rohr, John A. 1986. *To Run a Constitution: The Legitimacy of the Administrative State*. Lawrence: University Press of Kansas.

Rucker, Philip, and Robert Costa. 2017. "Bannon Vows a Daily Fight for 'Deconstruction of the Administrative State.'" *Washington Post*, February 23, 2017.

U.S. Census Bureau. Various reports. "Government Employment and Payroll." https://www.census.gov/programs-surveys/apes.html.

U.S. Office of Personnel Management. Various reports. "Federal Employment Reports." https://www.opm.gov/policy-data-oversight/data-analysis-documentation/federal-employment-reports/#url=Overview.

Verkuil, Paul R. 2017. *Valuing Bureaucracy: The Case for Professional Government*. New York: Cambridge University Press.

Volcker, Paul A. 1988. *Public Service: The Quiet Crisis*. Francis Boyer Lectures on Public Policy. Washington, DC: American Enterprise Institute for Public Policy Research. https://www.aei.org/publication/public-service-the-quiet-crisis/.

World Justice Project. n.d. "Advancing the Rule of Law Worldwide." Accessed April 26, 2019. https://worldjusticeproject.org/.

CHAPTER 7

Is Federal Public Service Reform Still Possible?

Toward a "Volcker Rule" for Federal Contractors

John J. DiIulio Jr.

In 1989, the National Commission on the Public Service, led by former Federal Reserve Board chairman Paul A. Volcker and popularly known as the Volcker Commission, issued its report, *Leadership for America: Rebuilding the Public Service* (National Commission on the Public Service, 1989). The National Commission on the State and Local Public Service, led by former Mississippi governor William F. Winter and widely referred to as the Winter Commission, picked up where the Volcker Commission left off. Its 1993 report, *Hard Truths/Tough Choices: An Agenda for State and Local Reform* (National Commission on the State and Local Public Service, 1993), found that the public service problems identified by the Volcker Commission ran no less deep in state and local governments. In 1994, the two leaders coauthored an introductory essay for a Brookings Institution volume on government reform: "As the chairpersons of two recent national commissions assessing America's public service, we are keenly aware of the need to make government at all levels more responsive, more accountable, and cost-effective. The question, however, is what, if anything, can be done to achieve this elusive goal?" (Volcker and Winter, 1994, xi).

Their answer to that question was guardedly optimistic: "While our experiences in chairing national commissions on the public service have made us more conscious of the need for meaningful reform, they have done even more to make us mindful of the political, fiscal, and social obstacles to reform" (xii). Under the subheading "Educating the Public," they concluded,

"Of one thing we are positive: effective public service is essential to our democracy. Yet the American people are not getting the quality of service to which they are entitled and upon which confidence in government rests" (xvii).

Today, nearly a quarter century after those words were written, even guarded optimism regarding "meaningful reform" makes one sound like a Pollyanna, and "educating the public" regarding the public service seems like a quaint aspiration.

Still, many eminent public administration scholars and practitioners see a way forward to improving government performance, rebuilding the public service, and restoring public trust and confidence in government. Three outstanding examples are featured in this very volume: Paul C. Light documents the trends that undermine government performance but identifies remedies that could slow and maybe even reverse those trends; Donald F. Kettl highlights the gap between government policies and the institutions that are supposed to translate them into effective action but identifies ways that the mismatch between policies and institutions might be bridged; and Paul R. Verkuil offers an unsparing assessment of how excessive outsourcing has harmed the public service, followed by a brief on how contractors, if properly recruited and managed, could promote "professional government."

Besides, Chairman Volcker's own public service ethos would have us neither whistle past nor whine about the many profound, seemingly implacable present-day obstacles to public service reform. Rather, a Volcker-inspired analysis would reflect the high-minded but clear-eyed brand of leadership that the chairman demonstrated at both ends of Pennsylvania Avenue, and on the world stage, during his 1979–87 tenure at the Fed's helm and many times thereafter, including during the global financial crisis of the 2000s. As Kettl has observed, Chairman Volcker never blinked or winked at hard empirical truths, deftly navigated around rough political realities, and did so whether people applauded him or instead chose to "praise him with faint damns" (Andrew H. Bartels quoted in Kettl, 1986, 188).[1]

Fences and Cow Bells

In the pragmatically idealistic spirit that makes Chairman Volcker's own public service legacy a timeless lesson in intellectual and civic leadership, we must be forthright but not despairing in recognizing the many obstacles to public service reform. In what follows in this essay, I shall briefly address three such challenges:

- Profound public disaffection toward the federal government
- Runaway growth in federal bureaucracy by proxy
- Misplaced faith in "big data" and other technological fixes

Also in this volume, Francis Fukuyama, a world-renowned thinker, perceptively explores various criteria for deciding what is and is not an inherently governmental function. Fukuyama, in Chapter 5, posits that the "most obvious way to put boundaries around outsourcing is to reform the existing civil service system."

It might, however, be no less right to posit the reverse: the most obvious way to reform the existing civil service system is to put boundaries around outsourcing—building new fences around federal contractors and putting cow bells around the necks of the congressional committee members that clang when their "oversight" of federal agencies amounts to ensuring that federal contracts go where they wish, with zero real regard for the existing civil service and little, if any, actual concern for government performance and results.

Thus, in the penultimate section of this chapter, I outline a preliminary case for a Volcker Rule for federal contractors, loosely defined as legislative, administrative, and public education measures that are intended to advance federal public service reform either by reining in federal contractors or by outing members of Congress whose support for outsourcing reflects self-dealing, or both.

Massive Public Mistrust

Since the late 1950s there has been a more or less steady decline in the proportion of Americans who say they trust the government in Washington. This massive public mistrust of the federal government has only increased since the days of the Volcker and Winter Commissions (Wilson et al. 2017, 87–90).[2]

Following the September 11, 2001, terrorist attacks on the United States, there was an extraordinary spike in public trust in government. In November 2001, about half of all Americans of both political parties said they trusted Washington officials to do what is right most of the time. But just a half year later, by the summer of 2002, only 40 percent expressed such trust in the federal government. In the fall of 2006, the percentage that trusted the federal government to do what is right most of the time had fallen below 30 percent. In the fall of 2011, the trust-in-government figure dropped to an all-time low of 15 percent. In April 2017, the percentage had risen from that all-time low, but only to a still-dismal 20 percent. From January 2010 through April 2017, the percentage of Americans who said they trusted the federal government to do what is right "always" or "most of the time" never exceeded 24 percent.

Massive public mistrust, however, is only the tip of the antigovernment opinion iceberg. In January 2013, for the first time, a majority of Americans believed that the federal government threatened their personal rights and freedoms (Pew Research Center, 2013a). In October 2016, as they had over most of the preceding nine years, more Americans named "government" as "the most important problem facing the country" than named the economy, health care, guns, or other issues or problems (Brenan, 2017).

There are, however, a few silver linings in the thick clouds of antigovernment public sentiment. One is that, when pressed to be more specific about the antigovernment sentiment, many respondents cite a particular elected leader they dislike rather than denouncing government itself; and another is that few respondents bash particular government agencies or trash the civil service (Newport, 2017). For example, in a September 2015 survey, a majority expressed a "favorable" opinion regarding thirteen of the seventeen particular federal agencies about which they were polled (Pew Research Center, 2015; see Table 7.1).

How much wider and deeper might favorable public sentiment toward particular federal agencies (and perhaps even toward "the federal government," "government bureaucracy," or "government" as a whole) become if the public knew more about (to borrow the subtitle of James Q. Wilson's 1989 magnum opus on the subject) "what government agencies do and why they do it"?

For instance, what if more people knew that from big-budget government programs like Medicaid to small-budget government programs like free school meals, 90-plus percent of government program dollars go to program beneficiaries, not to federal or state government bureaucracies (Greenstein and CBPP Staff, 2012, 2)? Might greater public awareness regarding such facts about government make a positive difference, and could "public education" campaigns move the needle a tad on such knowledge?

I think so. The plural of *anecdote* is not *data*, but I have educated (shocked, but educated) several different live audiences over the last few

Table 7.1. How the Public Views Particular Federal Agencies

Agency	Unfavorable (%)	Favorable (%)
U.S. Postal Service	14	84
National Park Service	11	75
Centers for Disease Control	19	71
NASA	17	70
FBI	19	68
Homeland Security	30	64
Defense Department	29	63
CIA	27	57
Social Security Administration	37	55
Health and Human Services	31	54
National Security Agency	31	52
Environmental Protection Agency	38	52
Food and Drug Administration	39	51
Justice Department	47	46
Education Department	50	44
IRS	52	42
Veterans Affairs Department	52	39

Note: Survey conducted September 22–27, 2015.
Source: Pew Research Center, 2015.

years by reciting "federal government fun facts" such as these: In 2014, the federal government spent (or, more precisely, borrowed and spent) about $250 billion a year in wages and benefits for *all* two million full-time federal bureaucrats, which was less than the $350 billion or so it spent on for-profit defense contractors, and less than the $600 billion it spent on Medicare beneficiaries (DiIulio, 2017). And both defense contracting and Medicare have had well-documented administrative problems going back a quarter century—almost all of the problems over all of those years implicating *not* their full-time federal workers but rather their paid private contractors (DiIulio, 2014, 68–69).[3]

Still, where present-day mass public mistrust of the federal government is concerned, behind every seeming silver lining there lurks a thicker, darker cloud. For the problem is not only that most contemporary Americans do not trust the federal government but also that most do not know even the most rudimentary historical and institutional facts about the federal government or, for that matter, the representative democracy established by the Constitution. In fact, by some measures, mass public support for representative democracy itself is in decline. For instance, as detailed in a 2016 report by the Century Foundation, only one-third of Americans can name all three branches of the federal government; one-third cannot name even one branch; and there has been a decline in the proportion who say that free elections are important in a democratic society and who support protecting civil rights and liberties for all (Kahlenberg and Janey, 2016).

Runaway Proxy Bureaucracy

Certain steps that might serve to stem, if not reverse, massive public mistrust—steps like actually improving citizens' experiences with federal agencies—are difficult, if not impossible, to take precisely and perversely because so much of federal public administration is not, in fact, in the hands of federal civil servants. As Kettl has keenly observed, "It's an intricate puzzle: building retail-level trust is the most effective strategy for earning trust; earning retail-level trust depends on improving citizens' experiences with government; but the more that for-profit and nongovernmental contractors, instead of government's own workers, are the ones who connect with citizens in delivering public services, the harder it is for government to earn trust, because it's harder for citizens to see their government at work" (Kettl, 2017, 99).

Of course, the federal government has always used contractors, but the era of runaway proxy bureaucracy began in the mid-1960s. It was then that the federal government began to expand in ways that were unprecedented. Today, Washington, DC, is headquarters for what Kettl has aptly characterized as "leveraged government" (Kettl, 2016, 172–73, 186–88) or what I have labeled "Leviathan by Proxy" (DiIulio, 2014, 13–28). The leveraging is evident in the two federal government deficits, one financial (routine debt financing) and the other administrative (routine proxy administration). With the national debt circling $20 trillion, the federal government's financial deficit is easily dramatized, widely known, and much debated. But the federal government's administrative deficit is difficult to dramatize, little known, and debated by experts but not by average citizens.

To elaborate just a bit,[4] from 1965 to 2015, annual federal government spending (adjusted for inflation) increased about fivefold. Seven new federal cabinet agencies were established, from Housing and Urban Development in 1965 to Homeland Security in 2002. Dozens of subcabinet agencies were also established, such as the Environmental Protection Agency in

1970 and the Federal Emergency Management Agency in 1979. Numerous new federal laws, regulations, and programs were enacted on issues that were virtually absent from the pre-1960 federal policy agenda—crime, drug abuse, campaign finance, sexual status, gun control, school quality, occupational safety, the environment, health insurance, and others. As federal spending increased fivefold, the number of pages in the *Federal Register* increased about sixfold.

For all the post-1965 growth in Washington's spending, agencies, policies, and programs, the federal government has had roughly the same number of full-time workers, not counting uniformed military personnel and postal workers, for the past six decades. For instance, when John F. Kennedy was elected in 1960, we had about 1.8 million full-time federal bureaucrats— the same number as when George W. Bush was elected president in 2000. When Ronald Reagan was reelected in 1984, there were about 2.2 million full-time federal bureaucrats—more than when Barack Obama left office in 2017.

In short, for the last half century, the full-time federal workforce has been shrinking relative to the size of the national population, the level of federal spending, the number of laws on the federal books, and the number of paid federal administrative proxies of all types.

Forsaking direct public administration, for five decades now the federal government has increasingly used state and local government workers, for-profit contractors, and nonprofit organization employees as de facto federal bureaucrats and, in effect, turned ever more full-time federal workers into contract administrators and grant supervisors.

State and Local Government Workers

Since the mid-1960s, while the federal workforce hovered around two million full-time bureaucrats, the total number of state and local government employees tripled to more than eighteen million workers. This subnational government workforce expansion was fueled by federal laws and dollars. Adjusted for inflation, between the early 1960s and the early 2010s, federal grants-in-aid for the states increased more than tenfold. For instance, at the Environmental Protection Agency, with its fewer than twenty thousand employees spread across ten administrative regions, more than 90 percent of agency programs are administered *A* to *Z* by state government agencies that employ thousands of environmental protection workers. Measurements and estimates vary, but, conservatively estimated, there are about three million de facto federal subnational government workers.

For-Profit Contractors

As Paul C. Light has taught us, for-profit businesses are used by every federal department, bureau, and agency. The data issues here are many and thorny, but Light's state-of-the-art research indicates that the number of federal contract employees increased from about 5 million in 1990 to about 7.5 million in 2013. For instance, in 1961 President Dwight D. Eisenhower warned about the military-industrial complex, but today it exists as the massive Department of Defense (DOD)–private contractor complex. Over the last decade or so, DOD has had the full-time equivalent of 700,000 to 800,000 federal civilian workers, plus the full-time equivalent of 620,000 to 770,000 for-profit contract employees—nearly 1 full-time contract employee for every DOD civilian bureaucrat.

Nonprofit Employees

Finally, in the nonprofit, tax-exempt, or independent sector, employment more than doubled between 1977 and 2012 to more than eleven million people. Just the subset of nonprofit organizations that files with the IRS has more than $2 trillion a year in revenues. Roughly a third of those nonprofit revenues flows from government grants plus fees for services and goods from government sources. Each year, tens of billions of federal "pass-through" dollars flow from Washington through state capitals and into the coffers of local government and nonprofit organizations—nonprofit hospitals, universities, religious charities, and others.

Again, the data are incomplete, but if the third of nonprofit revenues that comes from government translate into just a fifth of all nonprofit workers being funded by public dollars, then about 2 million nonprofit workers join the 7.5 million for-profit workers and the 3 million subnational government workers as de facto federal workers. That sums to 12 million de facto federal workers flanked by 2 million full-time federal bureaucrats, or a "real federal workforce" of some 14 million people.

Table 7.2. Americans' Attitudes Toward Spending

Would you increase, decrease, or keep spending the same for . . .	*Increase (%)*	*Same (%)*	*Decrease (%)*
Agriculture	34	42	20
Aid to needy in United States	27	44	24
Aid to world's needy	21	28	48
Antiterrorism defenses	32	45	19
Combatting crime	41	41	14
Education	60	29	10
Energy	36	38	21
Environmental protection	33	43	22
Food and drug inspection	33	50	14
Health care	38	34	22
Medicare	36	46	15
Military defense	32	41	24
Natural disaster relief	34	50	12
Roads and infrastructure	38	43	17
Scientific research	37	40	20
Social Security	41	46	10
State Department	14	46	34
Unemployment aid	24	41	32
Veterans' benefits	53	38	6

Source: Pew Research Center, 2013b.

There are at least three separate but related reasons for the federal government's two deficits: public opinion, lobbying by proxies, and congressional politics.

For all the mass public mistrust, for all the bad-mouthing of Washington, most Americans want the very government benefits and programs that the post-1965 federal government has enacted. The only thing a near majority wants to cut is foreign aid (Table 7.2).

While the mass public expects big-government benefits without paying big-government taxes, the three federal proxies exert nonstop pressure in favor of federal policies that pay them to administer federal business, with as few strings attached as possible, and with lots of paperwork but little real accountability for performance and results: state and local governments and their governors associations, mayors associations, state legislatures, corrections commissioners, and more; big- and small-business lobbies; and nonprofit organization or "independent-sector" lobbies. For reasons summarized perfectly by Martha Derthick, Congress needs little coaxing to give these proxy lobbies what they want: "Congress has habitually chosen the medium of grants not so much because it loves the states more but because it loves the federal bureaucracy less. Congress loves action—it thrives on policy proclamation and goal-setting—but it hates bureaucracy and taxes, which are the instruments of action. Overwhelmingly, it has resolved this dilemma by turning over the bulk of administration to state governments or any organizational instrumentality it can lay its hands on whose employees are not counted on the federal payroll" (Derthick, 2001, 63).

No Tech Fixes

Despite runaway proxy bureaucracy and all of its attendant problems, the federal public service is hardly beyond hope for reforms predicated on big data or, to use the more apt term, data and analytics innovation (DAI) (U.S. Government Accountability Office, 2016).

Examples of DAI helping the federal government to work better and cost less are starting to mount, not least in relation to such persistent proxy-administration problems as contractor fraud and improper payments. For instance, as early as 2006, DOD used the day's DAI technologies to identify shenanigans by a vendor that over the preceding decade had used clever billing tactics to get away with $20 million in improper payments (U.S. Government Accountability Office, 2017b).

Still, we must be cautious about placing too much faith in technological fixes as a path to federal public service reform. Let me craft a brief case for such caution by discussing four superb and suitably tech-friendly recent books: Stephen Goldsmith and Neil Kleiman, *A New City O/S: The Power of Open, Collaborative, and Distributed Governance*;[5] Kettl, *Little Bites of Big Data for Public Policy* and *Escaping Jurassic Government: How to Recover America's Lost Commitment to Competence*; and Verkuil, *Valuing Bureaucracy: The Case for Professional Government*.

Goldsmith and Kleiman make a compelling case for a tech-savvy approach to public administration that results in what they term "distributed governance," a "socio-technical ecosystem that . . . mines and integrates data from a wide range of sources then analyzes and presents the information in a way that is suited to support outcomes, share information, and serve administrative systems that support those who do the public's work" (Goldsmith and Kleiman, 2017, 6).

The Goldsmith-Kleiman case for this new "operating system" approach to public administration is addressed to local governments, but it can be generalized to state governments and the federal government as well. "Government systems," they suggest, "developed when bureaucrats owned and controlled data," but in the direct public administration "processes and programs that were the pride of the progressive era now often choke innovation and efficiency" (12). Those processes and programs, they contend, can and should be replaced by systems of "open, collaborative" governance utilizing "new digital tools" that enhance our "capacity to truly manage those who spend the public's resources or utilize public authority" (13).

Amen; but, as Goldsmith and Kleiman duly acknowledge throughout their treatise, there is no skirting or squinting past the human capital and workforce development issues that must be addressed in order for anything resembling a revitalized public service to become more than a pipedream. Indeed, Kettl makes clear that while utilizing new technologies in new ways can be an administrative tonic, it is very far from a cure: "There's often a strong belief that more and better information is the answer to many of the tough issues that government faces. . . . That ought to make the twenty-first century a golden era for government. . . . Big data provides vast new opportunities. . . . Yet trust in government remains low and polarization has increased. . . . Better information can often produce more effective government. The road to doing that, however, isn't an easy one. It begins by remembering that . . . the process is ultimately a political one, not an analytical one" (2018, 77).

Goldsmith and Kleiman argue persuasively that the best government tech uses and systems are yet to come, and Kettl would surely agree. (See Chapters 2 and 3 in this volume for additional discussion of some emerging technologies that offer opportunities and challenges.) Verkuil is likewise persuaded that new technologies and more-open systems can help to improve public administration in myriad ways, but he underlines the fact that many a government agency has already undermined that happy prospect by outsourcing so much relating to "technology" (Verkuil, 2017, 135–38).

Moreover, the relationship between better information management technologies and data analysis capacities, on the one side, and overcoming the administrative difficulties and performance maladies associated with public administration by proxy, on the other side, remains at best ambiguous and at worst nonexistent or negative.

For example, Kettl (2016) has analyzed the federal programs on the U.S. Government Accountability Office's list of programs (U.S. Government Accountability Office, 2015) that have suffered the worst cost overruns, management meltdowns, or other acute or chronic failures. Some have been on the list for decades. Kettl found that twenty-eight of the thirty-two programs on the Government Accountability Office's high-risk list were among the very federal programs with the highest proxy-administration quotients—all the ones in bold in Table 7.3.

Reexamining Kettl's list in light of calls for "distributed governance" approaches and the like, it becomes readily apparent that some of the biggest and most persistent problems have occurred within agencies and programs (most notably, perhaps, DOD) that have, in fact, made notable progress in integrating DAI into their respective management systems.

Of course, the counterfactual might be that the programs would be even more troubled were it not for their respective tech fixes; but there is as yet no compelling empirical evidence to suggest that DAI makes more than marginal performance management differences where federal public administration equals federal proxy bureaucracy.

With or without more "open systems" and bigger, better DAI, many federal agencies simply do not have all the full-time, well-trained workers (tech or other) they need to do a good job. To cite just two examples among dozens, consider the respective workforce plights of the Social Security Administration (SSA) and the Federal Aviation Administration (FAA).

The SSA is losing a third of its veteran workforce at a moment when its beneficiary population is booming, its disability claims are exploding, and it is on a trajectory to disbursing $1.8 trillion a year (DiIulio, 2014, 60–62). Long wait times at SSA offices, long hold times on calls to the SSA, and long delays in processing claims by retirees, disabled citizens, and others have become the unfortunate norm. Yet, rather than shore up the SSA's full-time federal workforce, in January 2018, Senate Republicans actually proposed cutting $492 million from the SSA budget (Economic Policy Institute, 2018).

Goldsmith and Kleiman cite the FAA as an example of a federal agency that practices what "new O/S" preaches, including "gathering data and making predictions" with the airline "industry in a collaborative fashion" and effecting concomitant changes in the agency's organizational culture (Goldsmith and Kleiman, 2017, 93).

All good as far as it goes, but a January 2016 Office of Inspector General report on the FAA (U.S. Department of Transportation, Office of Inspector

Table 7.3. High-Risk Federal Programs/Hyperproxy Federal Programs, 2015

Limiting the federal government's fiscal exposure by better managing climate change risks

Management of federal oil and gas resources

Modernizing the U.S. financial regulatory system and the federal role in housing finance

Restructuring the U.S. Postal Service to achieve sustainable financial viability

Funding the nation's surface transportation system

Strategic human capital management

Managing federal real property

Improving the management of information technology acquisitions and operations (new)

DOD approach to business transformation

DOD business systems modernization

DOD support infrastructure management

DOD financial management

DOD supply chain management

DOD weapons systems acquisition

Mitigating gaps in weather satellite data

Strengthening Department of Homeland Security management functions

Establishing effective mechanisms for sharing and managing terrorism-related information to protect the homeland

Ensuring the security of federal information systems and cyber critical infrastructure and protecting the privacy of personally identifiable information

Ensuring the effective protection of technologies critical to U.S. national security interests

Improving federal oversight of food safety

Protecting public health through enhanced oversight of medical products

Transforming the Environmental Protection Agency's processes for assessing and controlling toxic chemicals

DOD contract management

Department of Energy's contract management for the National Nuclear Security Administration and Office of Environmental Management

NASA acquisition management

Enforcement of tax laws

Managing risks and improving Veterans' Affairs health care (new)

Improving and modernizing federal disability programs

Pension benefit guaranty corporation insurance programs

Medicare program

Medicaid program

National Flood Insurance Program

Note: Bold indicates a high proxy-administration quotient.
Sources: U.S. Government Accountability Office, 2015; Kettl, 2016.

General, 2016) tells another story. The report documented that about a third of the 13,800 air traffic controllers will turn over by 2021, and that the FAA has an air traffic control system that is so badly antiquated technologically that nobody truly knows how to begin to modernize and patch it.

The Contractor Swamp

So long as we have too few well-trained full-time federal bureaucrats administering too many programs, handling too many dollars, and managing far, far too many administrative proxies (subnational government agencies, for-profit firms, and nonprofit organizations)—or, put another way, unless and until we expand the federal civilian workforce—no far-reaching federal public service reform plan can have a true prayer.

To reference one crude but suggestive measure, today we have about one federal bureaucrat for every 150 citizens. Elsewhere, I have prescribed hiring an additional one million full-time federal bureaucrats by 2035, which would bring the federal civilian workforce to three million with an estimated ratio of one bureaucrat for every 125 citizens—still below the 1965 ratio of one bureaucrat for every 100 citizens, but far better than if the ratio were to drop by then (as it would if it continued to hover around two million) to one bureaucrat for every 180 citizens (DiIulio, 2014, 98–103).

It is, of course, no surprise to anyone that a proposal to hire a million more federal bureaucrats has been embraced by neither party while being eschewed by many liberals and conservatives alike. As Fukuyama and other contributors to this volume aver, we cannot "bring back the bureaucrats" now or anytime soon. Agreed; but perhaps we can at least do more to regulate and rein in the legions of federal contractors that feast on our deficit-financed, proxy-administered national government.

All told, from 2011 through 2015, the federal government spent, on average, nearly $500 billion a year on contractors (Figure 7.1). How did we end up with a federal government that spent trillions of dollars on federal contractors in just the last decade, and that spends more on federal contractors each year than it does on its own entire full-time, flat-lined federal civilian workforce?

The crux of any answer, in one word, is Congress. As Wilson emphasized, the present-day federal bureaucracy is in every key particular more the creature of Congress in committee than it is of the chief executive, the cabinet

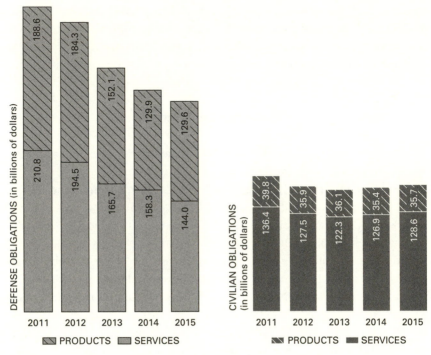

Figure 7.1. Nearly $2.5 Trillion in Federal Spending on Contractors, 2011–2015
Note: Total 2011–15 federal spending on contractors rounds to $2.48 trillion.
Source: U.S. Government Accountability Office, 2017a, 5.

secretaries, or the White House staff. Congress and its committees and sub-committees, supported by more than twenty thousand congressional staff members, controls the federal bureaucracy's "major day-to-day decisions" and determines the "conditions under which an agency operates" (Wilson, 1989, 236).

With respect to administrative "oversight," those committees' overlapping and competing jurisdictions reflect a system of self-dealing in which each member, no matter which party is in control of which chamber, can flack for favored contractors and fill campaign coffers. Between 1990 and 2011, federal contractors were thirty-one of the forty-one largest disclosed corporate contributors to federal campaigns and elections (Weiner, Norden, and Ferguson, 2015, 2). Thus it is that, "even after controlling for past contracts and other factors, companies that contributed more money to federal candidates subsequently received more contracts" (Witko, 2011, 761). And federal contractors supply "services" and "products" subject only to outsourcing laws like the Competition in Contracting Act of 1984—laws that were outmoded and weak when they were passed—plus a bewildering array of major to minute acquisition regulations and procurement rules that are quite often toothless in practice.

Volcker Rules

Containing, if not draining, the federal contractor swamp would be good in its own right and satisfy what is, at least in my view, the necessary but insufficient condition for far-reaching federal public service reform. But how?

I wish I knew, but in reflecting on that challenge, I have found both inspiration and a few clues in the story surrounding the Volcker Rule. In brief, in 2010, two years after the financial crisis of 2008, Congress passed the Wall Street Reform and Consumer Protection Act, better known as the Dodd-Frank Act, a 1,500-page law that forced major changes in how the nation's financial institutions did business. In a highly detailed and generally dour account of that law and its consequences, Robert G. Kaiser (2013, 238, 256, 310–12, 340–41, 347–49) casts one of the law's provisions, the Volcker Rule, in a more positive light—and rightly so.

During his service as chairperson of President Barack Obama's President's Economic Recovery Advisory Board, Chairman Volcker tutored Congress and the nation on how the financial system had been bollixed by a rapid expansion in the use of money-making instruments that were Greek to average citizens (most notably, perhaps, the rapid expansion in the use of so-called derivatives, which are essentially contracts that derive their value from the performance of an "underlying" asset, index, or interest rate). Basically, the Volcker Rule was intended to keep financial institutions from gambling wantonly, either with their own money or with other people's money.

More specifically, the Volcker Rule limited banks' proprietary trading (no investing in hedge funds, no plumping for private equity firms, and no other patently high-risk shenanigans). It took all sorts of extraordinary legislative gymnastics to keep the Volcker Rule in the 2010 bill. Even before the Volcker Rule took effect in mid-2015, it was the object of lawsuits by banks, critiques by Wall Street loyalists and conservative think tank analysts, and constant congressional calls for repeal. Through it all, Chairman Volcker stood tall. As of this writing, the Volcker Rule looks like all that might stand between average Americans and a Trump-backed, radical deregulation of the financial system.

By analogy, a "Volcker Rule for federal contractors" might be conceived as any legislative, administrative, or public education measure that advances one or more of the following objectives:

- Requires federal contractors and their most highly paid executives to disclose *all* donations and contributions, including funds given to unions, trade associations, and other organizations that can receive unlimited donations from individuals and corporations and spend money on elections without disclosing their donors
- Places a lifetime employment ban on *all* former federal employees, including former employees, political or career, of the White House or Congress, earning more than $100,000 a year (in 2018 dollars) in total from any for-profit organization that receives more than half of its annual revenues via federal contracts
- Curtails outsourcing in cases in which there is no empirical evidence regarding the costs and benefits of outsourcing versus insourcing
- Protects the public from both innocent and insidious shrouding of the true size of the federal contactor workforce
- Restricts federal contractors to work that does not involve inherently governmental functions
- Regulates federal contractors so that they conduct business in ways that render truly transparent and public where, for what, and to whom any tax dollars they receive go
- Subjects all large federal contractors to stringent federal performance and results reporting requirements and protocols
- Tweaks the Government Performance and Results Modernization Act of 2010 to incorporate attention to federal contractors into the annual budgeting process and strategic planning processes
- Establishes a network of nonprofit organizations like the Volcker Alliance and the Brookings Institution Center for Effective Public Management, plus congressionally chartered bodies like the National Academy of Public Administration, to address and publicize the role of federal contractors through research, analysis, and advocacy

Whether one likes or loathes them, none of these proposals is a snap, and the measures prescribed in the first two bullet points—requiring full financial disclosure of donations by federal contractors and placing a lifetime ban on federal employees earning more than $100,000 a year from federal contract-dependent firms—are probably impossible nuts to crack; but permit me to elaborate a bit on the need for each of those two just the same.

Starting in 2011, President Obama initiated efforts to require all federal contractors to disclose *all* of their campaign contributions, including so-called backdoor or "dark money" contributions to groups that are not required to disclose their donors (Weiner, Norden, and Ferguson, 2015; also see Weiner, 2016). In response, Congress attached a rider to the 2012 appropriations act prohibiting any federal agency from requiring any contractor to disclose all its donations (Weiner, Norden, and Ferguson, 2015, 5).

The straight-faced public rationale for that contractor-coveted prohibition, as for several subsequent ones enacted through 2016, was that forcing past or prospective federal contractors to disclose all donations would itself politicize procurement and curb free speech. Never mind that federal contractors had lobbied for that very 2012 prohibition. Never mind that they had lobbied over the preceding several decades to subvert Federal Acquisition Regulation provisions so as to virtually forbid procurement officials from taking data on cost overruns, compliance failures, and overall past vendor performance into account (Kelman, 1994). And never mind that they often took federal agencies to federal court or before "boards of contract appeal" to contest and overturn adverse performance evaluations (Manuel, 2015, 6–9).

When President Obama did not deliver on a new law to force federal contractors to disclose all donations, some among those who supported the measure called on him to act via executive order. As one group of advocates asserted, an executive order "requiring disclosure of dark money spending by contractors would help citizens hold their elected representatives accountable, strengthen confidence in government, and safeguard taxpayer dollars" (Weiner, Norden, and Ferguson, 2015, 6). But President Obama left office without signing any such executive order; and, of course, even had he done so, it might have been undone by his successor, who, during just his first year in office, reversed dozens of his predecessor's executive orders (Bump, 2017).

The existing post–federal employment "revolving door" rules for federal personnel are numerous, complicated, and vary greatly in specificity and stringency from one category of federal employment to the next, from the lifetime ban on former federal bureaucrats "switching sides" to represent a private party with which they dealt "personally and substantially" while in federal service, to the two-year "cooling off" period during which former U.S. senators may not lobby Congress after leaving the Senate (Maskell, 2014).

But this fog cannot hide the fact that the "revolving door" rules are plainly written to avoid the appearance rather than the reality of former federal officials using their public offices for private gains. Nothing could be more evident from the story of the legislation that included debates over the actual Volcker Rule, an epic legislative struggle that featured and enriched many among the nearly two hundred ex-senators and former House members who are part of the multi-billion-dollar lobbying industry (Kaiser, 2013, 131–32; also see Kaiser, 2009).

Nothing short of absolute, unambiguous, and universal lifetime restrictions or bans on post–federal employment influence-peddling will do much to reform how Congress relates to federal contractors or make congressional administrative oversight something more than a reliable rubber stamp for outsourcing unto runaway proxy bureaucracy.

Looking past America's own shores and experiences, one finds hopeful examples of democratic nations that seem to be doing a more robust job of managing contractors in the public interest. One especially hopeful example is Australia's Public Service Act of 1999. Over the last two decades, Australia's laws and regulations have increasingly required contractors to comply with "public service values" in such domains as responsiveness to government officials, fair and impartial treatment of all members of the public, public accountability and performance protocols, and merit appointment, including equal employment and workplace diversity (Mulgan, 2005).[6]

Another especially hopeful example from abroad is New Zealand's experience. Over the last decade or so, the New Zealand Ministry of Business, Innovation and Employment has articulated and begun to institutionalize "competitive sourcing," which explicitly directs government agencies to examine whether contracting out is more efficient and effective, and to do so in relation to "rules of sourcing" that preserve all due contractor flexibility while ensuring all necessary contractor accountability (New Zealand Government Procurement, n.d.).[7]

Taken together, the Australian and New Zealand cases should serve to remind us that while government can relate to its administrative proxies as partners, it must never relate to them as equal partners, let alone as junior partners: contractors can and should be required to comply with "public service values" and held to the same democratic accountability standards that full-time government workers must respect in all phases of their work.

Conclusion: "Don't Quit!"

In the early 1990s, Chairman Volcker and I were together on the faculty of a certain well-heeled public policy school located in central New Jersey. With a few notable exceptions, most other members of its faculty had absolutely no intellectual or civic interest in public administration, either as a field of study or as a profession. I became deeply frustrated with the situation, but the chairman counseled, "Don't quit—try something else!" Shortly thereafter, in 1993, the Brookings Institution's Center for Public Management was born. With unwavering support from the chairman and unfailing leadership from its founding codirector, Donald F. Kettl, the center immediately came to play a consequential role in analyzing and mediating the era's major federal public service reform initiatives (DiIulio, Kettl, and Garvey, 1993) and produced more than a dozen well-publicized reports and volumes in just its first few years.

"Don't quit!" is the ultimate Volcker Rule. May we persist with the chairman in believing that public administration matters, that a public-spirited federal bureaucracy can and should be the hands and feet of our great nation's representative democracy, and that federal bureaucrats can and should be selected better, trained better, respected better, and given all the support and tools they need to perform better in the public interest.

Notes

1. Also see Kettl (1986, 177, 184–88, 190–92).

2. This paragraph and the next one are derived in part from the relevant section of Wilson et al. (2017, 87–90).

3. Also see U.S. Government Accountability Office (2013b, 1) and U.S. Government Accountability Office (2013a, 9).

4. The material in the remainder of this section, including all facts and figures, is derived from DiIulio (2014, chapters 1–3).

5. *O/S* is short for "operating system."

6. I am grateful to James L. Perry for bringing this article and the Australian case to my attention.

7. I am grateful to Donald F. Kettl for bringing this website and the New Zealand case to my attention.

Bibliography

Brenan, Megan. 2017. "Dissatisfaction with Government, Direction of US Persists." Gallup News, October 19, 2017. https://news.gallup.com/poll/220703/dissatisfaction-government-%20direction-persist.aspx.

Bump, Philip. 2017. "What Trump Has Undone." *Washington Post*, December 15, 2017. https://www.washingtonpost.com/news/politics/wp/2017/08/24/what-trump-has-undone/?utm_term=.11f1b9c04e2b.

Derthick, Martha. 2001. *Keeping the Compound Republic: Essays on American Federalism.* Washington, DC: Brookings Institution.

DiIulio, John J., Jr. 2014. *Bring Back the Bureaucrats: Why More Federal Workers Will Lead to Better (and Smaller!) Government.* West Conshohocken, PA: Templeton.

———. 2017. "10 Questions and Answers About America's 'Big Government.'" Brookings Institution, February 13, 2017. https://www.brookings.edu/blog/fixgov/2017/ 02/13/ten-questions-and-answers-about-americas-big-government/.

DiIulio, John J., Jr., Donald F. Kettl, and Gerald J. Garvey. 1993. *Improving Government Performance: An Owner's Manual.* Washington, DC: Brookings Institution.

Economic Policy Institute. 2018. "The New Battle for Social Security." *EPI Policy Center Newsletter,* January 9, 2018.

Goldsmith, Stephen, and Neil Kleiman. 2017. *A New City O/S: The Power of Open, Collaborative, and Distributed Governance.* Washington, DC: Brookings Institution.

Greenstein, Robert, and CBPP Staff. 2012. "For Major Low-Income Programs, More Than 90 Percent Goes to Beneficiaries." Center on Budget and Policy Priorities, January 23, 2012. https://www.cbpp.org/research/romneys-charge-that-most-federal-low-income-spending-goes-for-overhead-and-bureaucrats-is.

Kahlenberg, Richard D., and Clifford Janey. 2016. "Putting Democracy Back into Public Education." Century Foundation, November 10, 2016. https://tcf.org/content/report/putting-democracy-back-public-education/.

Kaiser, Robert G. 2009. "Outlook: Stuck in the Revolving Door." *Washington Post*, February 2, 2009. http://www.washingtonpost.com/wp-dyn/content/discussion/2009/01/30/DI2009 013002445.html.

———. 2013. *Act of Congress: How America's Essential Institution Works, and How It Doesn't.* New York: Vintage Books.

Kelman, Steven. 1994. "Deregulating Federal Procurement: Nothing to Fear but Discretion Itself?" In *Deregulating the Public Service: Can Government Be Improved?*, edited by John J. DiIulio Jr., 102–28. Washington, DC: Brookings Institution.

Kettl, Donald F. 1986. *Leadership at the Fed*. New Haven, CT: Yale University Press.

———. 2016. *Escaping Jurassic Government: How to Recover America's Lost Commitment to Competence*. Washington, DC: Brookings Institution.

———. 2017. *Can Governments Earn Our Trust?* Malden, MA: Polity.

———. 2018. *Little Bites of Big Data for Public Policy*. Thousand Oaks, CA: CQ.

Manuel, Kate M. 2015. *Evaluating the "Past Performance" of Federal Contractors: Legal Requirements and Issues*. Congressional Research Service Report R41562. February 5, 2015. https://fas.org/sgp/crs/misc/R41562.pdf.

Maskell, Jack. 2014. *Post-employment, "Revolving Door," Laws for Federal Personnel*. Congressional Research Service Report R42728. January 7, 2014. https://fas.org/sgp/crs/misc/R42728.pdf.

Mulgan, Richard. 2005. "Outsourcing and Public Service Values: The Australian Experience." *International Review of Administrative Sciences* 71 (1): 55–70.

National Commission on the Public Service. 1989. *Leadership for America: Rebuilding the Public Service*. Washington, DC: National Commission on the Public Service.

National Commission on the State and Local Public Service. 1993. *Hard Truths/Tough Choices: An Agenda for State and Local Reform*. Albany, NY: Nelson A. Rockefeller Institute of Government.

Newport, Frank. 2017. "Deconstructing Americans' View of Government as Top Problem." Gallup News, October 27, 2017. http://news.gallup.com/opinion/polling- matters/221072/deconstructing-americans-view-government-nation-top-problem.aspx.

New Zealand Government Procurement. n.d. "Government Rules of Sourcing." Accessed April 29, 2019. https://www.procurement.govt.nz/procurement/principles-and-rules/govern ment-rules-of-sourcing/.

Pew Research Center. 2013a. "Majority Says the Federal Government Threatens Their Personal Rights." January 31, 2013. http://www.people-press.org/2013/01/31/majority-says -the-federal-government-threatens-their-personal-rights/.

———. 2013b. "A Sequester Deadline Looms, Little Support for Cutting Most Programs." February 22, 2013. http://www.people-press.org/2013/02/22/as-sequester-deadline-looms -little-support-for-cutting-most-programs/.

———. 2015. "Beyond Distrust: How Americans View Their Government." November 23, 2015. http://www.people-press.org/2015/11/23/beyond-distrust-how-americans-view-their -government/.

U.S. Department of Transportation, Office of Inspector General. 2016. *FAA Continues to Face Challenges in Ensuring Enough Fully Trained Controllers at Critical Facilities*. AV-2016-014. Washington, DC: U.S. Department of Transportation, January 11, 2016.

U.S. Government Accountability Office. 2013a. *Health Care Fraud and Abuse Control Program: Indicators Provide Information on Program Accomplishments, but Assessing Program Effectiveness Is Difficult*. GAO-13-7469. Washington, DC: U.S. Government Accountability Office, September 30, 2013. https://www.gao.gov/assets/660/658344.pdf.

———. 2013b. *Medicare Program Integrity: Increasing Consistency of Contractor Requirements May Improve Administrative Efficiency*. GAO-13-522. Washington, DC: U.S. Government Accountability Office, July 23, 2013. https://www.gao.gov/assets/660/656132 .pdf.

————. 2015. *High-Risk Series: An Update.* GAO-15-290. Washington, DC: U.S. Government Accountability Office, February 11, 2015. https://www.gao.gov/assets/670/668415.pdf.

————. 2016. *Data and Analytics Innovation: Emerging Opportunities and Challenges.* GAO-16-659SP. Washington, DC: U.S. Government Accountability Office, September 20, 2016. https://www.gao.gov/assets/680/679903.pdf.

————. 2017a. *Contracting Data Analysis: Assessment of Government-Wide Trends.* GAO-17-244SP. Washington, DC: U.S. Government Accountability Office, March 9, 2017. https://www.gao.gov/products/GAO-17-244sp.

————. 2017b. *Data Analytics to Address Fraud and Improper Payments.* GAO-17-339SP. Washington, DC: U.S. Government Accountability Office, March 31, 2017. https://www.gao.gov/assets/690/683859.pdf.

Verkuil, Paul R. 2017. *Valuing Bureaucracy: The Case for Professional Government.* New York: Cambridge University Press.

Volcker, Paul A., and William F. Winter. 1994. "Introduction: Democracy and Public Service." In *Deregulating the Public Service: Can Government Be Improved?,* edited by John J. DiIulio Jr., xi–xvii. Washington, DC: Brookings Institution.

Weiner, Daniel I. 2016. "Obama's Last Chance to Take on Dark Money." Brennan Center for Justice at New York University School of Law, November 23, 2016. https://www.brennancenter.org/blog/obamas-last-chance-take-dark-money.

Weiner, Daniel I., Lawrence Norden, and Brent Ferguson. 2015. "Requiring Government Contractors to Disclose Political Spending." Brennan Center for Justice at New York University School of Law. March 27, 2015. https://www.brennancenter.org/publication/requiring-government-contractors-disclose-political-spending.

Wilson, James Q. 1989. *Bureaucracy: What Government Agencies Do and Why They Do It.* New York: Basic Books.

Wilson, James Q., John J. DiIulio Jr., Meena Bose, and Matthew Levendusky. 2017. *American Government: Institutions and Policies.* 16th ed. Boston: Cengage.

Witko, Christopher. 2011. "Campaign Contributions, Access, and Government Contracting." *Journal of Public Administration Research and Theory* 21 (4): 761–78.

CHAPTER 8

Good Government

Persistent Challenges, Smart Practices, and New Knowledge Needed

Shelley Metzenbaum

We need government. Beyond that, we need it to work well. For that, we need it to be understood, adequately resourced, wisely implemented, and appropriately staffed. For reasons laid out here and in other chapters in this volume, meeting those conditions can prove difficult and set up a vicious cycle that undermines confidence in government and its employees, ultimately impeding government's ability to operate successfully.

This chapter explores ways to manage through the vicious cycle. It begins with a reminder of why we need government and need it to work well, and then discusses seven realities that have challenged and are likely to continue to challenge well-functioning governments. It describes how government can navigate through these challenges by mastering outcomes-emphasizing, goal-focused, data-informed government. It identifies seven practices that high-performing government organizations have begun embracing that help them manage and communicate what they do, why, how, and how well in order to improve performance on multiple dimensions that matter. Happily, evolving technologies make these practices increasingly feasible and affordable. The chapter closes by spotlighting three areas where additional intellectual attention is needed to discover more effective, cost-effective ways to operate: managing across organizational boundaries to achieve better outcomes, successfully developing and promoting rapid uptake of new knowledge, and communicating and using performance information in a timely, multidirectional manner across every aspect and level of government policy making and operations.

We Need Government

Much of what government does can be grouped into two categories: efforts to "slow the bad" and "grow the good." Even government's greatest skeptics tend to look to government when disaster or other harms hit, whether a hurricane, fire, or infectious disease. We turn to government for guidance and information to prevent and prepare before these events, and for assistance responding to and recovering from them. As a former Coast Guard official once described his work to me, "I try to prevent bad things from happening and keep costs as low as possible when they do." All levels of government take various actions to prevent and reduce the frequency and costs of harmful incidents such as transportation fatalities and accidents, fires and crime, morbidity and mortality, discrimination and rights violations, harmful releases to air and water, criminal and cybersecurity attacks, injustice, and unfairness. In addition, they try to prevent and reduce fraud and improper payments.

Governments also try to "grow the good." They offer public education to help young people thrive as adults. They collect and provide information, or otherwise require it, about who we are and what we do in order to provide a sense of patriotic pride (Kelman, 1987). They share or require honest sharing of information to enable individual and organizational choices about where to live, where to invest, and even whether to take an umbrella in the morning. They support discovery efforts to explore, understand, and explain the world within, around, and beyond us—whether the human genome, physics, space, or the ocean—to satisfy our curiosity and desire to understand the world and to enable invention and economic breakthroughs that improve the quality of our lives.

Government alone cannot slow the bad and grow the good. It works with others—private companies, nonprofit organizations, community groups, religious institutions, individuals—to make progress on the problems it tries to tackle and the opportunities it tries to seize. Government also often works with other governments to advance public goals.

We Need Government to Work Well

We do not only need government. We need it to work well. When it does not, it cannot accomplish what we want and need it to. Beyond that, as Paul C. Light lays out in Chapter 1, poorly functioning government undermines people's confidence and trust in government and their willingness to resource it adequately, setting up a vicious cycle of declining trust in and funding for well-performing government. What does *well-performing government* mean? It means government organizations improve continually at a respectable pace on multiple public objectives identified through democratic and other decision-making processes, including but not only mission-linked objectives. It means government carries out its work in honest, fair, just, courteous, understandable, and cost-effective ways with minimal unwanted side effects.

Government Works Well Much of the Time

Government has worked well in many areas over the years. Infant mortality is down in the United States, and life expectancy rose consistently until the opioid surge began in 2016. Smallpox and polio have been nearly wiped out worldwide, while elder poverty in the United States has dramatically declined. U.S. traffic fatalities dropped steadily for five decades, although with upticks in 2012, 2015, and 2016 (National Highway Traffic Safety Administration, 2017). The number of fires, too, fell from 1977 through 2014, rising slightly in 2015 and 2016 (Ahrens, 2017). Air quality continues to improve in most parts of the United States, and water quality in some (U.S. Environmental Protection Agency, n.d.; U.S. Geological Survey, n.d.). Additionally, far more children in the United States are educated than were a century ago (Ryan and Bauman, 2016). Meanwhile, government-supported research continues to contribute to our ability to communicate and calculate; enhances the functional life of our eyes, ears, hips, and hearts; and boosts our understanding of the world beyond our planet.

Despite the numerous problems in government today that are discussed elsewhere in this book, effective government remains alive and well. Public roads and transit systems support the daily travel of hundreds of millions of people. Government standard setting and enforcement give confidence that most of what we buy, whether gasoline or publicly traded investments, is what we expect. Tap water in most of the United States is safe to drink, public parks and other recreational opportunities enrich people's lives, and infectious diseases are prevented or quickly controlled. Almost unnoticed, operational improvements simplify processes, such as driver's license renewals and toll payment systems, and reduce per-unit costs.

In short, government has worked well in the past and continues to do so today in many areas, although few notice when it does.

Some of the time, however, government does not work well.

Governments Do Not Always Work Well

As the contaminated drinking water tragedy in Flint, Michigan, reminded us, government often screws up even in areas of longtime responsibility. Problems also arise when governments face new challenges of unprecedented size, as with Hurricane Katrina in New Orleans and Hurricane Maria in Puerto Rico (U.S. Federal Emergency Management Administration, 2018), and when people make immoral decisions, as with the Tuskegee syphilis study and Japanese American internment during World War II. Some problems that government experiences arise in the private sector as well, such as false claims, fraudulent payments, cybersecurity attacks, and dysfunctional employee responses to poorly structured incentives, such as those underlying the Enron and Wells Fargo scandals.

Less obvious but no less trivial, governments frequently experience problems by failing to gauge and communicate progress on the outcomes they try to improve, focusing instead on proposed and past spending levels. Similarly, governments have problems when they fail to learn from their own and others' experience and from well-designed, measured trials, repeating past failures, wasting money, and missing opportunities to improve.

Good Government Is Hard to Do

Several realities impede government efforts to advance public objectives and win public trust, including the following:

- Government lacks strong drivers that encourage continuous learning and improvement.

- Few notice when government works well, but plenty notice when it does not.
- Recurring debate about government objectives confuses the public and complicates implementation.
- Governments tackle problems that do not align neatly with jurisdictional boundaries.
- Big ships are hard to turn.
- Gut instincts to reward good performers and punish bad ones undermine improvement, accountability, and public trust in government.
- Good government costs money, yet no one likes to pay taxes to cover those costs.

Government Lacks Strong Drivers That Encourage Continuous Learning and Improvement

Competition, the fear of going out of business, and the desire for investor interest continuously motivate much private-sector improvement. Similar motivators are hard to find in government. Some (but not all) parts of governments can compare similar organizational subunits and create a healthy competitive dynamic, but few government organizations worry as private firms do about going out of business for poor comparative performance or implementation ineptitude. They worry more that their budgets will be slashed for political reasons having little to do with delivery competence.

Arguably, elected legislators could function as citizens' investors, identifying and pursuing comparatively better returns on constituents' tax dollars. Legislators have little incentive to play that role, however. They garner far more media attention lambasting government for not working well, attending ribbon cuttings and funding announcements, and celebrating the passage of new laws. Only the most altruistic legislators try to play a constructive oversight role, making sure previously passed laws work well.

The media, too, have little reason to motivate better government in a constructive way. The mainstream media—funded by advertisements, subscriptions, and, increasingly, the sale of readers' personal data—know that negative stories, especially polarizing and sensational ones, get more attention and are remembered longer than positive or bipartisan ones (Soroka, 2015). Negative and sensational stories, unfortunately, tend to discourage, not inspire, government workers, while polarizing stories complicate their lives. The government trade press does play a valuable role by informing willing government change agents of good ideas and emerging risks, but it lacks the political clout needed to motivate continual improvement.

Elected executives have little incentive to encourage better government performance other than their own desire to do good. Few constituents ask about past government accomplishments. Elected executives can grab just as much, and often more, media and voter attention with attacks, events, and funding announcements as they can with analytic updates on progress, problems, and plans. On occasion, some elected executives announce specific, ambitious targets to show their intent to act on issues they and their constituents consider important, perhaps knowing that stretch targets with certain characteristics stimulate discovery and innovation, leading to improved performance. In doing so, however, these government leaders boldly take on the very real risk that political opponents will use their missed targets as ammunition during reelection campaigns.

As with any large organization, mission and personal pride motivate some in government to excel. Many, however, choose to do what they have always done and know how to do rather than trying something new that might fail and attract unwanted attention. Status quo is safer and easier (Moynihan, 2017).

Advocacy groups and government delivery partners that share government's objectives seem logical advocates for better government, but seldom are. Advocacy groups tend to get consumed pressing for new policies and funding rather than for well-framed goals and improved results, while delivery partners, such as grantees, tend to get caught up seeking new grants and satisfying conditions of their existing grants to avoid putting them at risk.

Few Notice When Government Works Well, but Plenty Notice When It Does Not

The harsh reality is that people tend not to pay much attention to government when it works well—when roads are smooth, drivers' licenses easily renewed, and tap water clean. Nor do citizens build up the sort of brand loyalty customers feel toward company products when government delivers highly valued products and services, such as Medicare and public parks, as Donald F. Kettl's vignette in Chapter 6 about the sign-carrier warning government to keep its hands off the government program Medicare so vividly illustrates.

Brand loyalty to government is further challenged by the reality that many, possibly most, people's most salient experience with government comes in the form of obligations, restrictions, and taxes that governments impose on them to protect or help others (Sparrow, 1994), not services and life-enriching opportunities. Even when government imposes obligations through regulations, taxes, and fees in efficient, honest, just, and courteous ways, it seldom wins new admirers.

Government's reputational problems are part of our political culture, dating back to the nation's founding. Francis Fukuyama, in Chapter 5, reminds us that American politicians have long railed against bureaucrats and viewed government as excessively large. Government's reputational problems are further exacerbated by the reality that the media, elected officials, would-be political opponents, and the public pay plenty of attention when government messes up. Indeed, it is in the political or economic interest of some and the natural cognitive inclination of others to do so. Few, however, pay attention when government works well—when planes land safely, advertisements are honest, and drugs are safe and effective.

At the same time, those with opposing political views search for and spotlight failed trials and failed investments in otherwise successful portfolios that, in business, would be considered routine and expected. The resultant negative tilt to government stories undermines its reputation and ability to get the resources needed to work well.

The lack of attention to government when it works well and hyperattention when it does not is exacerbated by the lousy job most governments do communicating their goals and objectives and their performance relative to those objectives. In Chapter 6, Kettl describes government budgets as "the foundation for public policy decisions" and "good road maps of the government's activities," but most budgets and budget debates focus far more on proposed and past spending levels than on what the proposed spending will buy and what past spending accomplished. The sad reality is that government decision makers, both executive branch budget officials and legislators, make massive spending, legislative, and regulatory decisions without insisting on, and using, the kind of past and comparative performance information they would turn to before buying a car or dishwasher.

Progress has been made in recent years in communicating proposed and planned government priorities, strategies, rationales, performance, and next

steps in ways that build understanding of what government does and accelerate progress on objectives within and across governments working on
shared objectives (Metzenbaum, 2016). Far more progress is needed, however,
including but not only progress on making it easier for policymakers, citizens, and consumers of government services to compare performance fairly
on multiple dimensions and relative to cost, as *Consumer Reports* does for
vacuum cleaners and cars, OpenTable does for restaurants, and Amazon does
for the products it makes available through its website (Metzenbaum and
Shea, 2016; Metzenbaum, 2019).

Recurring Debate About Government Objectives Confuses the Public and Complicates Implementation

What gets interpreted, or asserted, as government incompetence is often in
fact the reality of perennially unresolved debates about government objectives. Managing and balancing these seemingly competing objectives, such
as economic development and environmental protection or the needs of current and future generations, can make government seem confused. Yet all
levels of government constantly face this balancing challenge, within and
across agencies. Consider, for example, the U.S. Forest Service, which must
manage forests for multiple objectives: yield, recreation, fire safety, and near-
and long-term ecosystem protection.

Managing this balance becomes even more demanding with elections. Career employees must work to understand and implement the shift
in priorities that newly elected and appointed officials introduce. Both
career and newly appointed officials must also balance new priorities with
existing law, as well as with court-ordered actions and deadlines, some of
which advance priorities that do not synch well with the priorities of the
newly elected government leaders. Newly appointed government executives must also sort out policy priorities with the person who appointed
them—whether a president, governor, local elected executive, or more
senior appointed official.

These sorting-out processes take time and can be misinterpreted as government incompetence when much of it is, in fact, the messiness of democracy and the need to balance competing public-sector objectives. When
transitional messiness occurs, political opponents often use it to make

government look incompetent, while the media may use it for a good story, further undermining government's implementation reputation.

Governments Tackle Problems That Do Not Align Neatly with Jurisdictional Boundaries

Whether dealing with air quality, terrorism, or health issues, few of the problems and opportunities governments tackle fit neatly within the geographic lines of government jurisdictions or the organizational units of government. This is not a problem when government objectives are clearly identified, cross-government goal leaders designated and accepted, goal-focused teams assembled to support progress on each objective, start-up resources and legal authorities secured, and people and resources allowed to flow freely to do what needs to be done on a timely basis (Moynihan and Kroll, 2015). Problems can and do arise, however, when any of those actions do not happen. The formal and informal accountability and personnel management systems of government make the needed personnel and funding fluidity for this kind of work challenging even within a single governmental jurisdiction. When multiple governments are involved, problems arise more frequently, especially if no government steps forward to lead efforts to tackle the problem, as happened with the 2017 government response to Hurricane Maria in Puerto Rico, or when a problem requires action from multiple national governments yet no effective cross-government coordinating mechanism such as the World Health Organization exists.

Big Ships Are Hard to Turn

Bureaucracy, whether of large governments such as the United States and California or large companies such as General Motors, is hard to change. This is not so much a government problem as a size problem, illustrated nicely by the famous case of GM and New United Motor Manufacturing, GM's collaboration with Toyota at one of GM's least productive plants in Fremont, California. GM and Toyota worked together with the existing Fremont workforce to mimic Toyota's advanced production methods, realizing great productivity gains. Nonetheless, despite access to Toyota's methods,

Toyota's competitive pressure, the partnership, and GM's wholly separate, heavily benchmarked startup plant, GM Saturn, GM had great difficulty changing. GM's culture overwhelmed both the New United Motor Manufacturing and Saturn change efforts, explicitly introduced to bring about badly needed change, at least in the short term. According to some accounts, GM took twenty years to integrate the lessons it learned from New United Motor Manufacturing and Saturn into its operations and product quality (Kiley, 2010).

Gut Instincts to Reward Good Performers and Punish Bad Ones Undermine Improvement, Accountability, and Public Trust in Government

Fear of using goals, measurement, and evaluation; misunderstandings regarding why and how to use them; and poorly designed accountability and motivational mechanisms seriously constrain government implementation improvement efforts.

Goals are most valuable when used to communicate government objectives to the people in an organization; the delivery network; clients, consumers, and regulated parties; and the public. Goal setting should encourage needed priority setting. Goal use and communication should focus, motivate, and inspire. Measurement and evaluations are most valuable when used to find ways to improve, inform priorities, and tailor program design.

When goals, measurement, and evaluations are used instead in high-stakes accountability systems, whether for reward or punishment and whether for people or organizations, including contractors and grantees, it can distract from improvement efforts and trigger debilitating, performance-depressing fears in otherwise motivated people and organizations.

Problems can arise in a variety of ways. When rewards or punishments are linked to an incomplete set of measurements, for example, it hyperfocuses attention to what is measured instead of the fuller set of indicators that need to be considered to advance objectives (Blau, 1963). Ill-structured incentive arrangements can also deter adaptation efforts to test and assess to find the mix of activities that work best in different situations. This is especially true when legislation mandates motivational mechanisms, compelling programs to link rewards or punishments prematurely to what can be measured rather than to what matters (Heckman et al., 2011). Problems arise, too, when performance thresholds or relative rank triggers an on/off penalty switch (CLASS Condition of the Head Start Designation Renewal System, 2017). Far more effective is a graduated response that does not penalize low performers willing to apply lessons from others' experience, contribute data to shared learning efforts, and participate in well-designed measured trials, but rather helps them find ways to improve. This is especially true for individuals and mission-focused nonprofits.

Nuanced incentive structures sensitive to context are needed (Austin, 1996; Bohnet and Eaton, 2003), especially but not only for private-sector contractors (Harvard Kennedy School Government Performance Lab, 2017, 2). One particular challenge, for example, is how best to structure incentives when contractors operate without capable competitors. Evidence exists on effective incentives and motivational mechanisms, but far more is needed to appreciate when and how to structure incentives likely to work and how to avoid those likely to backfire, triggering dysfunctional, performance-impairing responses rather than performance-improving ones.

One such ill-structured incentive may be the way some in government execute compliance and oversight activities. Hyperattention paid by program managers and oversight entities, such as auditors and inspectors general, to the completion of mandated activities and other compliance requirements rather than to figuring out how to improve continually on multiple dimensions also creates problems. It reinforces a culture that favors the status quo, rather than continuous improvement.

Good Government Costs Money, Yet No One Likes to Pay Taxes to Cover Those Costs

Alexander Hamilton once observed, "To pay Taxes for the one or the other purpose, which are the only means of avoiding the evil, is always more or less unpopular. . . . Hence it is no uncommon spectacle to see the same men Clamouring for Occasions of expense . . . yet vehement against every plan of taxation which is proposed" (quoted in McCraw, 1997, 346). Hamilton's words of warning are as apt today as when he wrote them.

These seven realities that challenge government are likely to persist ferociously into the future. At the same time, new challenges of the sort Sheila Bair and Ramayya Krishnan discuss in their chapters will continually emerge, further complicating the work of government. Evolving technology will render government's geographic boundaries less meaningful, while introducing new cybersecurity and other online risks. Extreme weather events and armed conflict across the world may accelerate interjurisdictional flows of people. More countries may embrace what seems to be an evolving approach to mercantilism, with country-owned and country-influenced businesses investing heavily in businesses beyond their borders. These changes, and more, will raise new questions about when and how we need government to act. For example, should government regulate social media, artificial intelligence, robotic travel, the monitoring and sharing of personal data, algorithmic bias, and bioengineering? If so, how? Answering these questions will take time that may get interpreted as government incompetence, further undermining government's reputation and resources to operate effectively and efficiently.

Seven Smart Practices to Help Overcome These Challenges

Despite these challenges, we need government and need it to work well. Seven practices can help governments and their delivery partners, including other governments, nonprofits, and for-profit entities, take on these challenges and continually improve in honest, fair, just, courteous, timely, and understandable ways:

- Clearly articulate outcomes-focused goals and other objectives and explain why they were chosen and how they relate to one another.
- Measure and analyze performance to find ways to improve on multiple dimensions by learning from past experience—detecting patterns, outliers, and anomalies that suggest better program and practice design, as well as areas in need of attention—and pair this information with measured trials to find ways to excel beyond past performance.
- Clearly communicate strategies and explain why they were chosen.
- Regularly and broadly discuss progress on goals to learn from experience, brainstorm ways to improve, and decide next steps.
- Sort out responsibilities for making progress on objectives.
- Communicate performance information broadly in timely, readily understandable, and easily accessed and used ways.
- Use effective motivational and accountability mechanisms.

Clearly Articulate Outcomes-Focused Goals and Other Objectives and Explain Why They Were Chosen and How They Relate to One Another

To work well and build citizen understanding, governments and their major organizational units and delivery partners need to be clear about what they are trying to accomplish. The simplest way to do that is by articulating general goals—for example, clean water, healthy people, safe transportation, expanding the space frontier, more accurate claims processing—and specific targets (how much of what, where, and by when) to advance the goals—for example, the Mystic River will be swimmable in ten years, hospital-acquired infections will decline 10 percent in two years, traffic fatalities will drop 5 percent in ten years.

High-performing governments identify a few priority areas among their goals for which they seek breakthrough progress. They adopt stretch targets in those areas because a few specific, ambitious targets that are reasonable relative to available skills and resources focus, energize, encourage persistence, and stimulate discovery, leading to better results (Locke and Latham, 2002). They complement their priority goals with a fuller set of strategic and annual goals and objectives to communicate to the workforce and the public the pace of progress sought across government's portfolio of objectives.

Without clear objectives and indicators communicating areas where progress is being pursued, how can government agencies, their employees, and their delivery partners, including grantees and contractors, execute well? How can the public and their elected representatives know whether they support what their government is trying to accomplish? Clear articulation of government goals and specific targets, not just past and proposed spending, communicates what government is trying to get done. It also implicitly invites those who share the goals to work with government and enables those who disagree with them to engage in public debate to change them.

Setting objectives focused on outcomes rather than on activities used to make progress on the objectives prevents government from getting stuck in the rut of doing what it has always done, hoping, without confirmation, that what it does works. Outcomes-focused objectives have the benefit of being agnostic about means. They encourage and enable continual innovation to find increasingly effective and cost-effective ways to accelerate progress not just on essential, mission-focused objectives but also on complementary objectives for other dimensions of performance that matter to people, such as timeliness, courtesy, fairness, predictability, understandability, and cost.

In addition to articulating clear goals, governments that work well explain why a goal has been chosen. Some government goals are stipulated in legislation; others are promised during an elected executive's campaign or in post-election speeches. Goals can be influenced by a variety of factors. Sometimes, they are a response to emerging problems or burgeoning opportunities. Other times, a goal gets set as a political response to unfavorable comparisons with peer communities, as when Russia launched *Sputnik* in the late 1950s, influencing President John F. Kennedy to set the goal of landing a man on the moon in a decade and returning him safely back home, and again when international educational comparisons embarrassed the United States in the 1970s, eventually leading to more rigorous measurement of progress on educational goals.

Well-run governments also explain how ambitious a target is. The ambitiousness of a target can be informed by a variety of factors, including relative importance compared with competing objectives, past and peer performance, available resources, and relevant knowledge and theories about the best way to make progress. Resource limits constrain government's ability to do everything all the time, of course. The ambitiousness of targets conveys relative priority not just for allocating funds but also and especially for allocating time and organizational intelligence.

Measure and Analyze Performance to Find Ways to Improve on Multiple Dimensions by Learning from Past Experience

Governments must measure progress on their objectives. When they fail to measure progress in meaningful ways and use the data to inform action, announced goals are simply political patter. They stop functioning as a focusing, motivating tool.

Despite widespread assumptions to the contrary, governments that work well do not measure performance primarily to determine the percentage of goals or targets met. They measure, instead, to find ways to improve, frequently examining relevant performance and other data to discover opportunities for gain and identify areas needing attention. They ask questions not only about whether performance is trending in the right direction but also about what government should do next, whether additional data and research are needed, and how government can allocate funds for higher net return on multiple dimensions of performance.

In short, high-performing governments analyze performance and other data primarily to find ways to improve. They look for actions that worked well in the past and ought to be continued and possibly expanded and those that did not work well and need to be adjusted. They look for areas of strength on which to build, as well as areas of weakness needing attention. They complement measurement of past performance with well-designed measured trials that test new approaches to achieve higher or faster performance gains.

In addition to measuring progress on mission-focused goals, such as improved health, and on intermediate outcomes demonstrated to advance those goals, such as reduced smoking, increased exercise, and higher vaccination rates, high-performing governments measure other dimensions of performance as well. For example, they collect, organize, and analyze transaction information, such as the frequency and timeliness of, and satisfaction with, visits to an office or website to make a payment or obtain a benefit, permit, or loan. They similarly characterize and analyze complaint and public inquiry data. In addition, they measure unwanted side effects to detect and prevent them. The best police forces, for example, measure and manage not only crime levels but also police abuse complaints (Southall, 2017). Similarly, they use data to find fraud, as the Centers for Medicare and Medicaid Services at the U.S. Department of Health and Human Services have done to save more than $4 billion, as discussed by Krishnan in Chapter 3.

High-performing government agencies that interact frequently with the public also measure whether people know what to do to complete their interaction successfully, and whether people feel they have been treated in courteous, expeditious ways. Failure to pay attention to public understanding and perceptions increases frustration and distrust. It also undermines government's ability to secure the resources it needs to work well.

Governments that work well use analytics to inform priority setting, causal factor identification, and program and practice design. They understand that analytics work best when data gets characterized, or tagged, at the time of collection to note characteristics such as location, time, demographics, sector, operator and equipment characteristics, and other possible causally linked details. Noting measurement characteristics such as the time of day, day of week, and week of year, for example, reveals performance variations that may suggest more effective treatment design. Because the U.S. Coast Guard notes the timing of violating spills into the navigable waters of the United States, for example, one Coast Guard office was able to see that most violations occurred at night, while all inspectors worked during the day. Shifting inspection schedules to cover when most spills occurred dramatically reduced the number of violations. It similarly helps to note how recently it rained when measuring water quality because rain stirs up contaminated bottom sediments. Segmenting trends for wet and dry weather days helps government discern whether dry weather problems remain or whether government can focus primarily on wet weather situations. Geocoding those water quality data then suggests where to take action. Similarly, noting operator, automobile, and location characteristics for fatal car accidents, plus accident costs, enables traffic safety planners to discern which cars, car features, drivers, and road conditions cause the most problems.

In sum, characterizing what gets counted enables government to look for patterns, relationships, outliers, and anomalies. Positive outliers may point to practices worth trying to replicate and, if successfully replicated, roll out to other places. Negative outliers, in contrast, may point to problem areas warranting a deeper dive to identify root causes. Finding patterns and relationships can contribute to the discovery of causal factors that government can try to influence.

High-performing governments do not just measure past performance. They complement performance data with well-designed measured trials to find and deliver in smarter ways. In the United States, the Cooperative Extension Service and Office of Road Inquiry, both in the U.S. Department of Agriculture, started conducting well-designed measured trials to compare different farming and road-building methods objectively over a century ago. Appreciation for the value of well-designed trials has surged in recent decades, as has sophistication in applying lessons from the design of large-scale randomized control trials and other evaluation methods to more affordable, frequent, feasible, smaller-scale trials, including nudge studies, iterative design approaches, rapid-cycle evaluations, and fast-fail trials. Governments are starting to use these trials not just to find better ways to improve outcomes, such as traffic fatalities and water quality. They are also using them to look for better ways to run programs, such as better ways to communicate goals and data, to engage others in priority setting and problem solving, to make interacting with the government a more pleasant and productive experience, and to make it more fair. One British nudge trial, for example, tested and found that redesigning the wording of an email inviting applicants to participate in a police entry exam significantly reduced ethnically linked differences in exam results (Linos, Reinhard, and Ruda, 2017). Others have found that differences in the wording and design of letters affect recipient compliance levels. Programs can similarly test and assess whether forms prepopulated with previously submitted data will reduce the time for, and frustration with, form completion without compromising data quality.

Perhaps the greatest waste and missed opportunity is when governments measure but do not use data they collect to find ways to improve. This not only wastes resources, it also frustrates the government employees and delivery partners expected to submit data to central data repositories. High-performing governments embrace data and data systems in ways that help people on the front line, in central offices, and in policy-making bodies use data both to improve outcomes and to inform individual and organizational choices.

Clearly Communicate Strategies and Explain Why They Were Chosen

To work most productively, governments that work well communicate how they plan to advance their objectives and why that plan makes sense, providing the evidence and logic behind their strategies. They do this in part to figure out and explain the budget they want, but also to engage the intelligence, efforts, and resources of people across government, delivery partners, and the public. Sharing this information coherently enables those critical to effective delivery, the frontline workers who often make more timely and accurate decisions with local knowledge, as Fukuyama reminds us, to learn from others' experience and speed progress on objectives. Clearly mapping the relationship among goals, objectives, and the strategies being used to advance the objectives help those in the delivery chain, as well as the public, understand government and engage where they can contribute (U.S. Department of Health and Human Services, n.d.). Clearly articulating strategies and why they were chosen also invites others with relevant knowledge and resources, sometimes explicitly and other times implicitly, to share that knowledge and suggest adjustments (Performance.gov, n.d.; Imagine Boston 2030, n.d.; City of Albuquerque, New Mexico, 2018).

Regularly and Broadly Discuss Progress on Goals to Learn
from Experience, Brainstorm Ways to Improve, and Decide Next Steps

High-performing governments regularly run data-rich discussions to review progress and problems in advancing toward a goal, discuss why progress occurred or problems arose, consider whether progress has proceeded at a sufficiently healthy pace, and decide next steps—actions to be taken, new information to be gathered, additional analyses needed, and new approaches to test. They work to understand the causal factors that affect problems and progress so they can tackle the problems and replicate progress, identify barriers to progress, and figure out how to surmount them. They periodically benchmark with best-in-class peers to find ways to improve overall performance and streamline production processes, and they continually look for new knowledge to apply while scanning for existing and emerging threats (Varley, 1992). They identify knowledge gaps, then create learning agendas and fill those gaps, updating the learning agenda as new knowledge gaps are discovered (Nightingale, 2017). They similarly identify skills gaps that are slowing progress on specific objectives and figure out how to fill them. They think about whom they need to inform or engage and how best to do that. At the same time, they continually try to find lower-cost ways to achieve the same level of progress. When appropriated funds and staffing levels change, they decide whether changes are needed to objectives, strategies, and timetables.

These outcomes-focused, data-informed meetings occur regularly and relatively frequently in governments that work well. They not only reinforce the continued importance of previously stated goals but also make it easy to update objectives, actions, and information in a timely manner as new knowledge is gained or events in the world change. Operational meetings of this sort establish an implementation-focused discipline in the organization. They also provide midlevel managers the opportunity to get senior-level attention and feedback on noncrisis issues. Less frequent strategy reviews, perhaps once a year, are used to decide major changes in strategy and knowledge acquisition priorities. Some leaders like to call these meetings "stat" meetings, signaling by the name the importance of looking at statistics. The exact size, shape, frequency, and name of these outcomes-oriented, goal-focused, data-informed discussions can vary by objective and organizational culture (Behn, 2014). What cannot vary is an organization's commitment to holding regular data-informed discussions involving key players on the delivery team. When they do not happen, organizations continue doing activities they have always done without knowing whether they make a difference, or they adopt new activities with the hope but without the discipline to confirm that they work.

Sort Out Responsibilities for Making Progress on Objectives

Outcomes-focused meetings and other data-rich discussions create the setting where those working on the same government objective can decide whether to stay the course or make adjustments. They also afford a convenient venue for sorting out who needs to do what by when. First, though, someone must convene and run these discussions, decide who attends, and make sure that the organization is adequately staffed before, during, and after the meeting to support decision-making and ensure that commitments are fulfilled. These meetings work well when an elected executive or his or her clearly appointed delegate convenes the meetings or otherwise shows continuing interest in progress on specific objectives, which many governors, mayors, and heads of state have done. These meetings can also work well even when an elected executive does not adopt this practice but a leader elsewhere in an organization—the head of a program or regional office, for example—assumes the mantle in his or her area of responsibility (Metzenbaum, 2002).

Just as important as an organization-wide leader convening people to ask questions and decide next steps for future performance gains, someone needs to be assigned responsibility for acting as a goal leader (or assume the role if no one opposes the assumption), leading efforts to make progress on each goal. Each goal leader, in turn, must be assigned or assemble a team—in person, virtually, or both—to search continuously for progress, problems, strengths, opportunities, and threats; decide a course of action; implement it; learn from experience by measuring relevant indicators; test to find better ways to work; and continually improve.

Identifying a goal leader is straightforward when government objectives align neatly within a single organization's purview. Often, however, multiple government organizations contribute to the advancement of a shared objective. When that is the case, designating or otherwise agreeing on a goal leader or leaders and clearly assigning them not only responsibility but also the authority to tap others to get the job done is critical to success.

Communicate Performance Information Broadly in Timely, Readily Understandable, and Easily Accessed and Used Ways

Governments that work well do not just set goals, measure performance, and use performance and other data to figure out how to do better and continually improve on multiple dimensions. They also communicate that information to multiple users for three distinct purposes: to improve performance on multiple dimensions, to build public understanding of what government does, and to inform individual choices among options.

High-performing governments recognize that performance improvement depends on a vast array of people—including employees and others in the field, subject matter experts, those providing mission-support functions, central office planners, contractors, and other governments and nonprofit organizations with shared or similar goals. To support complementary decision-making and action, these government organizations devote significant resources and expertise to communicating goals, relevant performance information, and the results of measured trials. They understand that this kind of communication helps to keep everyone thinking about the objectives, aware of revisions to them, updated on lessons learned, and tuned in to planned next steps to decide whether they want to adjust their actions accordingly. They make it easy for field staff to communicate data and other feedback to government and each other in ways that inform future action. They communicate to enlist those willing to contribute ideas, expertise, and resources to advance the objectives—whether for a mission to Mars, high-speed intercity transit, thriving children, clean water, or faster power restoration to hurricane-hit islands.

Communicating government's goals, strategies, performance trends, and other accomplishments also contributes to public understanding of government: what it wants to accomplish and why, how government tries to make progress on goals and why, how well government actions have worked, and future government plans. In addition, it informs and invites democratic debate about whether government's objectives and proposed means for accomplishing them make sense.

Governments that work well also provide performance information to aid individual decision-making, and sometimes motivate as well. They might provide "league tables," for example, that encourage fair comparisons among government providers in similar situations and enable consumers of government services to make more informed decisions about where to live, which government office to visit, and when. Their comparisons recognize different dimensions of performance, as *Consumer Reports* does when it reviews products such as cars and vacuum cleaners, so consumers can choose the mix of attributes best suited to their wants and needs and producers are able to benchmark accurately.

High-performing governments understand that successful communication requires sorting out who government performance information users are or might be, understanding what they need to know and when they need to know it, and figuring out how to get information to and from them successfully in timely, easily understood, and useful ways. Governments that work well carefully consider the users and uses of performance information and invest to create effective mechanisms to gather and disseminate data so data suppliers and others in the delivery chain, such as social workers and inspectors on the front line, can easily enter and retrieve relevant timely, accurate, and affordable information (Annie E. Casey Foundation, 2015). They appreciate that one key to quality data is returning data to suppliers with value added through analyses and user-focused translations that make the data more relevant, understandable, useful, and readily available.

Use Effective Motivational and Accountability Mechanisms

Perhaps counterintuitively, despite emphasizing targets and trends, governments that work well try, but do not expect, to meet all of their targets all the time. They do not manage the percentage of targets met or report trends for that percentage. They understand that focusing on target attainment rather than performance improvement makes people reluctant to adopt the kinds of specific, challenging targets that stimulate innovation and breakthrough performance gains. At the same time, they know that too much focus on the percentage of targets met can tempt people to adopt timid targets that they know they can meet, add easier targets to a suite of objectives, set targets that are less ambitious than current performance, and manipulate measurements.

Similarly, high-performing governments take great care in the way they run their data-rich discussions. They do not blame goal leaders for missed targets or for progress trending in the wrong direction, provided the leaders know why problems are happening and have a plan to deal with them or, when they do not, have a cogent plan to figure it out. They realize that "gotcha" sessions attacking those who miss their targets create an unhealthy defensiveness that keeps people from bringing valuable information forward and makes them reluctant to test new approaches that might fail in multiple initial trials. At the same time, they hold managers accountable for knowing relevant data and making decisions using that information.

In addition, high-performing governments avoid ineffective motivational mechanisms. They appreciate that fair comparisons can be motivational when done not to "name and shame" but rather to create a healthy pressure to do better and point to opportunities for improvement. They use explicit incentives cautiously, especially financial ones, aware that financial rewards tend to drive out intrinsic inclinations to do well and altruistic instincts motivated by mission. Further, they know that bonuses intended to motivate employees discourage them instead when employees receive a lower bonus than they expect or than that received by a colleague whose work they consider inferior. Governments that work well motivate, instead, with mission-focused goals, information, and constructive feedback offering specific suggestions for improvement. They also prefer team to individual bonuses because they encourage the kind of teamwork essential to progress on outcome-focused goals. (For a lay review of the relevant academic literature, see Metzenbaum, 2006; Pink, 2009.)

Governments that work well are very careful in structuring organizational incentives, especially financial ones. They know that high-stakes rewards or penalties linked to an overly narrow set of goals and indicators can result in worse performance and increased risk. Not infrequently, organizational incentive systems, whether linked to rankings, ratings, or goal attainment, divert resources from improving performance to catalyzing those being measured and implode the measurement system (Gormley and Weimar, 1999).

This does not mean that organizations responsible for making progress on goals are not held to account. What it means is that they are held accountable for making progress on objectives at a respectable pace based on available knowledge, building knowledge about how to do better, and exchanging information about goals, strategies, progress, problems, and planned next steps that informs their own and others' actions and decisions to achieve better performance on multiple dimensions and to enable more informed individual choice.

Governments that work well embrace these seven core practices. Indeed, to appreciate fully why, consider the alternative: a government that is unclear about what it wants to accomplish; that lacks the means to gauge progress objectively; that fails to look for increasingly effective practices and emerging problems; that introduces new programs, practices, and technologies without assessing whether they work better than past ones; that fails to communicate government priorities, strategies, progress, problems, and trade-offs in easy-to-find, easy-to-understand ways; and that rewards and penalizes in ways that provoke dysfunctional, performance-impeding reactions.

Adopting these practices will help governments tackle the seven challenging realities discussed earlier by making it easier for the public to find and understand what government does, why, how, and how well, and by engaging others in solutions to the problems government tackles. The exciting technological developments Krishnan discusses in Chapter 3 that are transforming the variety, volume, and velocity of information being shared, analyzed, and managed make adoption of these seven practices more feasible and affordable than ever before.

In truth, the transition will not be easy. The seven challenging realities discussed here are persistent, strong, and unlikely to change any time soon. Recent history also suggests that many government employees will try to adopt these practices in a compliance-oriented way, filling in the box of required activities rather than appreciating their value and mastering their use. Change will not be easy. Nonetheless, progress has been made. Let us hope that current and future government officials have a healthy appetite for navigating through the inevitable obstacles to high-performing government that they will encounter so that government continues to contribute to improved societal outcomes.

Knowledge Needed in Three Areas

To continue to work toward high-performance government, innovation and knowledge building are needed in three areas:

- Managing across organizational boundaries to achieve better outcomes
- Successfully developing and promoting rapid uptake of new knowledge

- Ensuring timely, multidirectional communication and use of performance information across every aspect and level of government policy making and operations

Managing Across Organizational Boundaries to Achieve
Better Outcomes

The plumbing systems of government—such as budget, finance, personnel, information technology, contracts, grants, and risk management—need to evolve for government to improve continually on multiple dimensions. These systems tend to operate as functional silos, with communities of practice organized around each function, reinforcing the silos. Better mechanisms need to be developed that allow funding and personnel to move quickly and easily across functional silos and program offices to enable progress on goals and process efficiency, without compromising government's ability to assure legislators and the public that appropriated funds have been spent for authorized purposes. Better oversight mechanisms are also needed, so that auditors, inspectors general, legislative committees, and the media do not treat as problems resource and personnel shifts made to advance shared goals.

Successfully Developing and Promoting Rapid Uptake
of New Knowledge

To improve how well government works, it needs to enhance knowledge building and sharing. In the near term, it should approach these two functions as strategic priorities. They are especially critical for continuous, multidimensional improvement in the many government grant programs that so heavily depend on other governments and nonprofits for progress. Knowledge building and sharing across the many similar areas government presides over, such as benefits processing, permit and loan applications, regulatory compliance, case management, payment collection, and contract management, also promise high returns. Sadly, knowledge management responsibilities are often underresourced and unassigned.

Progress requires discovery and mastery of better ways to build and share knowledge, including how to structure knowledge collection (for example, collecting data for the right unit of analysis), characterize collected data (for example, through geocoding, time stamping, and recording demographic detail), organize information for easier and cross-subject retrieval (for example, through application programming interfaces), and frame and answer questions in user-centered ways that successfully convey knowledge to the front line and others in the delivery chain about which practices are likely to work well in which situations. It requires building and sharing knowledge about factors influencing the uptake and persistence of better practices (Pfeffer and Sutton, 2000). It also entails increased use of A/B testing, like that performed by many private-sector websites, to find better ways to exchange information not just with researchers but also with the field-based practitioners whose decisions and actions are key to achieving better outcomes. The growing number of government What Works Clearinghouses, for example, would greatly benefit from this sort of rigorous, user-centered design, testing, and iterative improvement. Knowledge building also requires understanding how to create and staff successful knowledge networks around outcome-focused goals and around similar processes to support coordination and cooperation, lesson sharing across disciplines and functions, and shared investment, for example, in interchangeable information system modules.

Ensuring Timely, Multidirectional Communication and Use of Performance Information Across Every Aspect and Level of Government Policy Making and Operations

Hardware and software technology breakthroughs have drastically cut the cost of collecting, analyzing, sharing, and otherwise communicating information, as Krishnan so elegantly explains in Chapter 3. Governments need to learn how to tap these new technologies to enable wiser decision-making on the front line, in central offices, and by policymakers; better individual and collective action; and more informed individual choices. At the same time, governments need to harvest from multiple disciplines lessons learned about effective and ineffective communication methods, not just what new technologies make available but also lessons about the factors affecting the uptake, accurate interpretation, and appropriate use of less advanced technology communication approaches, including storytelling and graphic interpretation (Moynihan, 2017; Isett and Hicks, 2018; Cialdini, 2001; Kotler,

Roberto, and Lee, 2002; Conzola and Wogalter, 2001; Tufte, 2006). Government must not only evaluate current approaches to communicating but also test and assess to discover better approaches. Are data and research findings reaching key people in a timely way, and are people accurately interpreting and appropriately applying the information (Metzenbaum and Kelman, 2018)? Is shared information helping enlist goal allies and relevant expertise, informing continual improvement and individual choice, and strengthening government accountability? Are those supplying relevant information from the field getting it back with value added through evaluation, analysis, visualization, and anecdote in a form that motivates them to continue supplying high-quality data and participate in well-designed trials? Are people talking, writing about, and visually displaying information in ways that capture people's attention and encourage constructive action?

A Constructive Role for Researchers and Journalists

Progress in these three areas, and adoption of the seven practices, will never eliminate the seven persistent challenges governments face, such as weak drivers pushing for continuous government improvement and the bias of the media and political players toward negative over positive stories. They can, however, enhance efforts to navigate through them to realize higher value for the taxpayer dollar and build public trust in government.

Scholars can help accelerate the pace and increase the magnitude of improvement by developing theories and objective evidence on the seven practices and the three areas, working with government employees and advocates, and building their graduates' mastery of these tools. This is especially likely to happen if, as Angela Evans recommends in Chapter 11, universities and scholarly journals adjust their incentive systems to reward and encourage relevance.

The emerging field of data-savvy, mainstream journalists, too, can play a constructive role by reporting every year and quarter, as financial journalists do, on the what and why of the goals government chooses, whether progress is being made, patterns of problems, and the rationale for the goals set and the strategies being tried. Doing so would introduce a badly needed driver for continuous government improvement.

Bibliography

Ahrens, Marty. 2017. *Trends and Patterns of U.S. Fire Losses.* Quincy, MA: National Fire Protection Association. https://www.nfpa.org/News-and-Research/Fire-statistics-and-reports/Fire-statistics/Fires-in-the-US/Overall-fire-problem/Trends-and-patterns-of-US-fire-losses.

Annie E. Casey Foundation. 2015. "Casebook's Unique Features Garnering Attention and Awards." December 20, 2015. http://www.aecf.org/blog/casebooks-unique-features-garnering-attention-and-awards/.

Austin, Robert. 1996. *Measuring and Managing Performance in Organizations.* New York: Dorset House.

Behn, Robert D. 2014. *The PerformanceStat Potential.* Washington, DC: Brookings Institution with Ash Center for Democratic Governance and Innovation.

Blau, Peter M. 1963. *The Dynamics of Bureaucracy: A Study of Interpersonal Relationships in Two Government Agencies.* Chicago: University of Chicago Press.

Bohnet, Iris, and Susan C. Eaton. 2003. "Does Performance Pay Perform? Conditions for Success in the Public Sector." In *For the People: Can We Fix Public Service?*, edited by John D. Donahue and Joseph S. Nye Jr., 238–54. Washington, DC: Brookings Institution.

Cialdini, Robert B. *Influence.* 2001. Boston: Allyn and Bacon.

City of Albuquerque, New Mexico. 2018. *Albuquerque Progress Report.* http://abqprogress-report.sks.com/home.htm.

CLASS Condition of the Head Start Designation Renewal System: A Proposed Rule by the Children and Families Administration. 82 Fed. Reg. 57,905 (proposed December 8, 2017) (to be codified at 45 C.F.R. pt. 1304). https://www.federalregister.gov/documents/2017/12/08/2017-26483/class-condition-of-the-head-start-designation-renewal-system.

Conzola, Vincent C., and Michael S. Wogalter. 2001. "A Communication–Human Information Processing (C–HIP) Approach to Warning Effectiveness in the Workplace." *Journal of Risk Research* 4 (4): 309–22. http://www.safetyhumanfactors.org/wp-content/uploads/2011/12/201Conzola_Wogalt2001.pdf.

Gormley, William T., Jr., and David L. Weimer. 1999. *Organizational Report Cards.* Cambridge, MA: Harvard University Press.

Harvard Kennedy School Government Performance Lab. 2017. "Active Contract Management: How Governments Can Collaborate More Effectively with Social Service Providers to Achieve Better Results." https://govlab.hks.harvard.edu/files/siblab/files/acm_policy_brief.pdf.

Heckman, James J., Carolyn J. Heinrich, Pascal Courty, Gerald Marschke, and Jeffrey Smith, eds. 2011. *The Performance of Performance Standards.* Kalamazoo, MI: W. E Upjohn Institute for Employment Research.

Imagine Boston 2030. n.d. "Imagine Boston 2030 Metrics Dashboard." Accessed April 29, 2019. https://analytics.boston.gov/app/imagine-boston.

Isett, Kimberley R., and Diana M. Hicks. 2018. "Providing Public Servants What They Need: Revealing the 'Unseen' Through Data Visualization." *Public Administration Review* 78 (3): 479–85.

Kelman, Steven. 1987. "The Political Foundations of American Statistical Policy." In *The Politics of Numbers*, edited by William Alonso and Paul Starr, 275–302. New York: Russell Sage Foundation.

Kiley, David. 2010. "Goodbye, NUMMI: How a Plant Changed the Culture of Car-Making." *Popular Mechanics*, April 2, 2010.

Kotler, Philip, Ned Roberto, and Nancy Lee. 2002. *Social Marketing*. 2nd ed. Thousand Oaks, CA: Sage.

Linos, Elizabeth, Joanne Reinhard, and Simon Ruda. 2017. "Levelling the Playing Field in Police Recruitment: Evidence from a Field Experiment on Test Performance." *Public Administration* 95 (4): 943–56.

Locke, Edwin A., and Gary P. Latham. 2002. "Building a Practically Useful Theory of Goal Setting and Task Motivation: A 5-Year Odyssey." *American Psychologist* 57 (9): 705–17.

McCraw, Thomas K. 1997. "American Capitalism." In *Creating Modern Capitalism*, edited by Thomas K. McCraw, 301–48. Cambridge, MA: Harvard University Press.

Metzenbaum, Shelley. 2002. "Measurement That Matters: Cleaning Up the Charles River." In *Environmental Governance*, edited by Donald F. Kettl, 58–117. Washington, DC: Brookings Institution.

———. 2006. *Performance Accountability Expectations: The Five Building Blocks and Six Essential Practices*. Washington, DC: IBM Center for the Business of Government.

———. 2016. "Higher Performing Government: Progress Made, Problems Encountered, Opportunities & Challenges." Presentation to the Metropolitan Washington Council of Governments Chief Administrative Officers. Washington, DC, April 6, 2016.

———. 2019. "Progress, Problems, and Possibilities: Communicating Government Performance Information." In *Perspectives on the President's Management Agenda*, edited by Alan Balutis, 65–71. Washington, DC: National Academy of Public Administration. https://www.napawash.org/uploads/Academy_Studies/Final_PMA_Book_3.18.2019.pdf.

Metzenbaum, Shelley, and Steve Kelman. 2018. "Doing Evidence Right." *PATimes*, Winter 2018, 15–17.

Metzenbaum, Shelley, and Robert Shea. 2016. "Performance Accountability, Evidence, and Improvement Reflections and Recommendations to the Next Administration." Working paper, National Academy of Public Administration and the Volcker Alliance, October 2016. https://www.napawash.org/uploads/Academy_Studies/MetzenbaumSheaWhitePaper_final.pdf.

Moynihan, Donald. 2017. "Challenges for Goal-Based Learning in Public Investments: A Behavioral Perspective on Performance Information Use." Presented at the Organisation for Economic Co-operation and Development, Paris, March 31, 2017. https://www.oecd.org/cfe/regional-policy/Moynihan-A-behavioural-perspective-on-performance-information-use.pdf.

Moynihan, Donald, and Alexander Kroll. 2015. "Performance Management Routines at Work? An Early Assessment of the GPRA Modernization Act." *Public Administration Review* 76 (2): 314–23.

National Highway Traffic Safety Administration. 2017. "Traffic Safety Facts Crash Stats: Early Estimates of Motor Vehicle Traffic Fatalities in 2016." December 7, 2017. https://crashstats.nhtsa.dot.gov/Api/Public/ViewPublication/812401.

Nightingale, Demetra Smith. 2017. *Making Evidence Relevant to Government: The Role of Evaluators and Researchers*. Washington, DC: Urban Institute.

Performance.gov. n.d. Performance.gov website. Accessed December 11, 2018. https://www.performance.gov.

Pfeffer, Jeffrey, and Robert I. Sutton. 2000. *The Knowing-Doing Gap.* Boston: Harvard Business School Press.

Pink, Daniel. 2009. *Drive.* New York: Riverhead Books.

Ryan, Camille L., and Kurt Bauman. 2016. *Educational Attainment in the United States: 2015.* Washington, DC: U.S. Census Bureau. https://www.census.gov/content/dam/Census /library/publications/2016/demo/p20-578.pdf.

Soroka, Stuart. 2015. "Why Do We Pay More Attention to Negative News than to Positive News?" London School of Economics British Politics and Policy blog, May 25, 2015. http://blogs.lse.ac.uk/politicsandpolicy/why-is-there-no-good-news/.

Southall, Ashley. 2017. "Crime in New York City Plunges to a Level Not Seen Since the 1950s." *New York Times,* December 27, 2017.

Sparrow, Malcolm. 1994. *Imposing Duties: Government's Changing Approach to Compliance* Westport, CT: Praeger.

Tufte, Edward R. 2006. *Beautiful Evidence.* Cheshire, CT: Graphics Press.

U.S. Department of Health and Human Services. n.d. HealthyPeople.gov website. Accessed December 11, 2018. https://www.healthypeople.gov/.

U.S. Environmental Protection Agency. n.d. "Air Quality—National Summary." Accessed April 29, 2019. https://www.epa.gov/air-trends/air-quality-national-summary.

U.S. Federal Emergency Management Administration. 2018. *2017 Hurricane Season FEMA After-Action Report.* https://www.fema.gov/media-library-data/1533643262195-6d13983 39449ca85942538a1249d2ae9/2017FEMAHurricaneAARv20180730.pdf.

U.S. Geological Survey. n.d. "Water-Quality in the Nation's Streams and Rivers—Current Conditions and Long-Term Trends." Accessed December 11, 2018. https://water.usgs.gov /nawqa/swtrends/.

Varley, Pamela. 1992. *Vision and Strategy: Paul H. O'Neill at OMB and Alcoa.* Harvard Kennedy School Case C16-92-1134.0. Cambridge, MA: President and Fellows of Harvard College.

PART III

Public Service and Public Leaders

CHAPTER 9

A Personal Reflection on the Importance
of Public Service

William W. Bradley

This chapter is about public service, including my own. But first I want to reflect on an extraordinary public servant—a man I am proud and fortunate to call a friend—Paul Volcker.

I recently spoke with Jim Collins, who was U.S. ambassador to Russia when Paul was trying to help the country establish a private banking system. Jim said that Paul has a way of getting to the core of a matter. I agree. For example, Paul once said, "The financial services industry has made only one socially redeeming contribution in the last 25 years—the ATM."[1]

Actually, no one has made a bigger contribution to America over the last fifty years than Paul. When the financial system was in crisis, Paul was there. At the Treasury Department in the early 1970s when the world financial system almost broke apart, Paul played a significant role in moving exchange rates to the floating system. At the Federal Reserve in the 1980s, he slayed the dragon of inflation that threatened the livelihood of every person in America. In the mid-1980s at the Fed, he oversaw the Third World debt crisis, which had the potential, in less steady hands, of bankrupting large American banks and putting the global economy into a tailspin. In 2008 his prestige and record gave a young presidential candidate the credentials he needed to assure a nation that he could handle the economic meltdown, and then, serving as chairman of the President's Economic Recovery Advisory Board, his advice shaped how the president and Congress responded to the crisis. The Volcker Rule gives us comfort today that things, at least in one respect, are different from the state of things in 2008. No other American has played such an important role in all four crises.

Paul is the quintessential public servant, blessed with great competence and courage and possessed of an unshakeable integrity. Paul knows that public service is a calling that can change the world for the better. As he quoted Thomas Edison as saying, "Vision without execution is hallucination" (Volcker, 2014). That is why his work at the National Commission on the Public Service and at the Volcker Alliance is intended to bring more talent to public service and to deploy it more wisely. Whether it has been in enhancing preparation for public service, mitigating risk to the financial system, or bringing clarity to the budget process, Paul, by his life and actions, has stated clearly and emphatically that public service is a noble profession.

I have believed the same thing about public service since I was in high school. I grew up in a small town in Missouri. There were ninety-six students in my high school graduating class, and the town had one stoplight. My father was the local banker and my mother was a former fourth-grade teacher who poured all of her energy into her only child—me. In the basement of our home, we had stacks of *Life* magazines going all the way back to the 1930s. They became my window on the larger world. I would read them and dream about faraway places. A few years later, in high school, I decided I wanted to be a diplomat.

Then, in college, I read a book called *To Be a Politician* and another possibility occurred to me. I wrote my senior thesis at Princeton on Harry Truman's reelection to the U.S. Senate in 1940, went to Oxford and studied the origins of the Cold War, and then returned to play basketball for ten years with the New York Knicks. It was during those Knicks years in the three-month off-seasons that I tasted different possible career futures, including federal civil service, and ultimately decided to run for political office—the U.S. Senate right out of the box. With some luck, I won in 1978.

The feeling that underlay that journey was that public service was important—whether I was a diplomat or a federal employee working in the poverty program or serving as a U.S. senator. I guess you can boil down my motivation to one thing—I wanted to do good. I wanted to leave the world a little better than I had found it.

I remember, as a summer intern from Princeton, sitting in the Senate chamber the night the 1964 Civil Rights Act passed. It was the act that desegregated public accommodations such as hotels and restaurants. I watched the roll call vote and thought, "Something happened here tonight that will make America a better place. Maybe someday I can be here and help to make America a better place." The Oxford and Knicks years intervened, but I never forgot that feeling.

The NBA is an unusual training ground for the presidency. In 2000 when I ran, and Paul supported me, I wanted to do an event with NBA players. I asked the NBA to help. The commissioner said the league could not get involved. I said, "Tell anyone who asks that you have a policy: The NBA doesn't get involved in presidential politics—unless a former player is running." He agreed, and the event took place.

The NBA affected my Senate career in at least two ways. When I was a rookie, I was thought to be a transformative player. That, plus the fact that I was white and got what was then a big contract, brought a ton of publicity. In my first game, eighteen thousand fans cheered every time I touched the ball in warm-ups. But it shortly became evident that I was too slow to play guard and the public turned against me—booing me, spitting on me, throwing coins at me, and accosting me in the streets with, "Bradley, you overpaid bum." It hurt, but I just kept moving forward. Nothing that ever happened to me in politics was as visceral or as hostile. I owe my tough skin to the NBA.

The second way was that it influenced my understanding of publicity. As an NBA player, you meet reporters at least three times a week. It is easy to get carried away with the media, when the real thing is what happens on the court. Your team either wins or loses. That is the core of the work.

When I got to the Senate, a veteran senator said I had a choice. I could be a show horse or a workhorse. It was an easy decision for me. I decided to become a workhorse—to know what I was talking about on taxes, trade, health care, and water policy and leave the press attention to others. The same impulse that told me that winning was the purpose in basketball and that one player was just one point of a five-pointed star told me in the Senate that passing laws was what the job was about. The NBA helped me see that what was important was your ability in the arena—not the publicity.

If the result—passing laws—was the most important thing, you could not do that alone. You needed enough votes to win. A Republican vote was as good as a Democratic vote. I realized that like the dynamics that made a championship team, legislating was fundamentally about people. Republicans were not villains to be despised. They were colleagues who shared a common commitment to public service. Today, whenever young politicians who are going into the Senate ask my advice, I tell them, "Make five friends from the opposite party. There will be a moment even in times of extreme partisanship when that friend will help you."

In 1986 there were two major pieces of legislation: one on immigration and the other on tax reform. It was a Republican Senate. The immigration bill was being guided by Al Simpson of Wyoming. I went to see him one day about the substance of the bill. I had twenty-two questions written on a yellow pad. Just he and I sat in his office and I asked my questions. I agreed with sixteen of his answers and disagreed with six, but on balance I thought the bill moved the country forward. So, when I left, I told him I would be voting with him. I did not even know what the Democratic position was.

Tax reform was something I cared about. I ran for the Senate in part to pursue it. I wrote a book about it in my first term on the Senate Committee on Finance and became its major advocate. When Ronald Reagan and his Treasury secretary James Baker endorsed it, I became their partner even though I was a Democrat and they were Republicans. Ultimately, after three detailed proposals over three years and thirty hearings, the bill came down to four Republicans and three Democrats in a group convened by Republican finance chairman Bob Packwood. We wrote the final bill in two weeks. As we made our way through the issues, we voted up or down on each provision. Sometimes three Democrats and one Republican supported a provision; sometimes three Republicans and one Democrat. Whoever prevailed, the group agreed to support that position—unanimously.

How could that happen? Because we respected and trusted each other. We knew where we wanted to go, and together we found a path to get there. The trust dimension was critical.

Paul also helped me with the 1986 tax act, but he probably does not remember. In a casual conversation during that period, he told me that he had raised interest rates but still could not prevent dangerous real estate speculation, given the tax treatment of the industry, which allowed for noneconomic real estate development and phony tax shelters. His words gave me great determination to redouble my tax reform efforts.

During those years, Paul, who lived in New York, and I, who lived in New Jersey, would often take the Friday-night shuttle between DC and New York. One night virtually all seats were taken on the plane so there we were—two Princeton basketball players, one six foot eight and the other six foot five—squeezed into the center and window seats of row 21 with our knees at our chins. We thought nothing of it. It was just the luck of the draw that night.

Later I came to see that picture of us sitting folded up in those seats as a reflection of what public service is all about: public devotion and private sacrifice.

In America the honor was not in the perks. It was in the service—the chance to help your neighbor have a slightly better opportunity to succeed; the chance to give with no expectation of return. Public service at its best requires integrity, commitment to the law, perseverance in the face of obstacles, and, yes, professional courage. That is true not just for senators or for the chairman of the Fed but also for judges on the federal bench, civil servants turning policy into action, and soldiers prepared to die for our country.

Public service creates the foundation of a more just and prosperous world. In a way, the private sector depends on the public sector. Public resources— higher education, roads, health care—make freedom possible. Business depends on decisions of the Federal Aviation Administration, the Federal Trade Commission, the Federal Communications Commission, the National Labor Relations Board, and many other governmental agencies to set the rules for playing the economic game. The American people depend on the government to ensure that their food is safe and pharmaceutical drugs will not harm them. The work of competent and respected elected and appointed officials can also send an unambiguous message to our best and most enthusiastic young people that government service is the way to make their marks.

But we should be under no illusion about where we are today in this country. Government is under siege. It began in 1980 when Ronald Reagan said government was "the problem," and it reached a turning point in 1994 when Bill Clinton declared that "the era of big government was over." These statements were followed by eight years of George W. Bush and eight years of Barack Obama playing a ping-pong match of executive orders, unable to get their agendas through Congress.

Today the whole enterprise of government has been endangered by the political movement financed by Charles and David Koch. Over the last twenty years, the brothers have spent billions promoting their libertarian political views, and in the last decade they have built a juggernaut. They operate in every state. In 2015 they employed more political workers than all the Republican committees in the country combined. The core libertarian view, as expressed by Nobel Prize–winning economist James Buchanan, who established public choice theory, is that the prime purpose of democracy is to protect economic liberty, which means that things that would restrict economic

liberty—such as labor unions, efforts to contain global warming, or the taxing of citizens to pay for public education, infrastructure, and Medicare—
must be ended, along with virtually any government program beyond the
police and the military. This movement considers government and the public servants it requires as the enemy.

The libertarian movement's ideological effort takes on more ominous implications for our democracy when it promotes voter suppression, justified
by the conviction that broadening participation in voting has led to bigger
government and higher taxes. Instead of seeing government as a means to
promote social justice, they see it as an impingement on liberty. Therefore,
by suppressing the vote, they will reduce pressures for government expenditures, with their attendant taxes. Indeed, from 2012 to 2014, Koch state legislators in forty-one states introduced 180 bills that curtail who and how
people can vote. Such bills shrink participation and harm our democracy.

If government survives the Koch libertarian assault, which is an open
question, and if the pendulum swings back to a more activist government, it
is essential that government work better than it does now. When modifying
a bridge in New Jersey takes forty-seven permits from nineteen different government entities, it delays for years what the public desperately needs. When
it takes twenty years to tear down a federal dam in Washington State and fifteen years to establish a coastal heritage trail along the Jersey shore, and
when mind-numbing rules hobble nursing homes and schools, people wonder what government does other than raise taxes. As a friend of mine says,
"Failures of implementation become failures of policy."

Then there is the basic competence of government employees and the
work rules that govern them. The 2003 report by Paul's National Commission on the Public Service observed that effective government workers resent
"the protections provided to those poor performers among them who impede
their work and drag down the reputation of all government workers" (24).
Indeed, we need more accountability of government workers. There has to
be a process to terminate unproductive deadwood so that government employees have more flexibility to act and are measured by results, not by se-
niority, endless grievance procedures, or how many bureaucratic boxes they
have checked.

Given rulings of the Supreme Court and laws passed by Congress, civil
service, in the words of author Philip Howard, "has become a property right
of the employees themselves. . . . Public employees answer to no one." If that is
the world we live in, it is particularly dangerous because it plays into the hands

of the growing libertarian movement that wants to eliminate government. After all, government was established to do things, solve problems, make life better for people, and provide clear rules of the road. If public employee unions do not see the value of making a more accountable system, designed by them to achieve results, I fear the whole system itself will be in danger.

When President John F. Kennedy said, "Ask not what your country can do for you, but what you can do for the country," he called the best and brightest of a generation of Americans to public service. Today many of our talented young people go into finance or business consulting. But at the end of the day, everyone has to go home at night and tell their kids what they do. What purpose do they serve? What role model do they offer? What moral choices have they made? How do they make the world a better place?

It is at those moments that those citizens who have opted for public service can be proud. We have had the privilege of experiencing how meaningful public service can be. The choice of public devotion that brings private sacrifices ignores the self-fulfillment of seeing that what you did gave the elderly financial security, taught the young the value of math, rendered a just verdict, cleaned up the environment, led to the medical breakthrough that saved lives, invented processes that reshaped an economy, and, yes, averted war. These important acts cannot possibly be performed by an individual acting alone. They will take government—and government requires public servants like Paul Volcker. That is just the way it is.

Note

1. "Paul Volcker: Think More Boldly," *Wall Street Journal*, December 14, 2009, https://www.wsj.com/articles/SB10001424052748704825504574586330960597134.

Bibliography

Howard, Philip K. 2017. "Civil Service Reform: Reassert the President's Constitutional Authority." American Interest, January 28, 2017. https://www.the-american-interest.com/2017/01/28/civil-service-reform-reassert-the-presidents-constitutional-authority/.

National Commission on the Public Service. 2003. *Urgent Business for America: Revitalizing the Federal Government for the 21st Century*. Washington, D.C.: The Brookings Institution.

Volcker, Paul A. 2014. "Vision Without Execution is Hallucination." *Public Administration Review* 74 (4): 439–41.

CHAPTER 10

Competencies of the Public Service in Challenging Regulatory Times

Paul R. Verkuil

As the authors of the previous chapters have shown, the public-sector workforce is under siege at all levels of government. The civil service virtues of merit appointment and objective management, long thought settled, are now contested. As a result, James L. Perry, in his introduction to this volume, highlights "the decline of administrative capacity."[1]

The public seems conflicted about the role of the civil service and career employees. Twenty-eight states have adopted some form of at-will public employment, which challenges the permanency and independence of the bureaucracy (Verkuil, 2017). At the federal level, at-will has been considered by bills such as H.R. 6278, the Promote Accountability and Government Efficiency Act, and while legislative action has yet to win a floor vote, there are other undermining forces. Unlike their military counterparts, civil servants face unprecedented demands to their authority, competency, and purpose, even though more than 26 percent of them are retired or separated military. Perhaps the nature of the jobs bureaucrats do masks their fundamental qualifications and achievements.

When the Trump administration attacks public employees' value and very existence and hollows out the career staff at key agencies like the Department of State and the Environmental Protection Agency, it is hard to be optimistic about the future of government management of the regulatory state. *Valuing Bureaucracy* makes the case for professional government based on lessons learned in my five years of federal service as chairman of the Administrative Conference of the United States (Verkuil, 2017). This assignment taught me that there are many professionals in government agencies doing excellent work for the right reasons—to serve the public interest as defined by Congress and directed by the executive. Too few are being recognized for their service, which is as important to our country as that provided by their military counterparts.

In discussing the subject of this essay—the critical capabilities and knowledge that public servants will need in the future—I was inspired by the National Academy of Public Administration report *No Time to Wait, Part 2*, which urges the government to move "toward a system based on occupational standards and individual competencies" (National Academy of Public Administration, 2018, 2). To learn about these competencies, I turned to those who know best—the professionals themselves. Human resources specialists led me to the realm of "knowledge, skills, and abilities," the standard format for describing what talents are required for civil servants. "KSAs" is the bureaucratic term used in hiring federal employees, and dozens of DC firms exist purely to coach prospective applicants in maximizing their presence on a résumé. Federal agencies, guided by the MOSAIC program of the U.S. Office of Personnel Management (OPM), provide competency descriptions that applicants respond to (U.S. Office of Personnel Management, 2013). The future competencies required for the federal service are probably best described by those who must write and review them. A top-notch government human resources director agreed to anonymously offer his views of the top competencies needed for the future federal workforce. In honor of Paul Volcker's ninetieth birthday, we made the competencies come out to ninety: the "Ninety for Ninety" list, Table 10.1. While overly comprehensive, the list offers insights into what government officials themselves believe are the needed capacities for future success. No individual candidate could encompass them all, of course, and many are job specific. But most of them are essential for government and its workforce to succeed.

Macro and Micro Competency Concerns

Understanding the critical knowledge, skills, and abilities federal agencies will need in the future requires two different inquiries: What are the forces outside the civil service system that will affect it, and what are the inside requirements to make the system work in light of these forces? Numerous

Table 10.1. Ninety for Ninety: Top Competencies Needed for the Future Federal Workforce

Rank	Competency	Definition
1	Integrity/ honesty	Contributes to maintaining the integrity of the organization; displays high standards of ethical conduct and understands the impact of violating these standards on an organization, self, and others; is trustworthy
2	Accountability	Holds self and others accountable for measurable high-quality, timely, and cost-effective results; determines objectives, sets priorities, and delegates work; accepts responsibility for mistakes; complies with established control systems and rules
3	Teamwork	Encourages and facilitates cooperation, pride, trust, and group identity; fosters commitment and team spirit; works with others to achieve goals
4	Interpersonal skills	Shows understanding, friendliness, courtesy, tact, empathy, concern, and politeness to others; develops and maintains effective relationships with others, which may include effectively dealing with individuals who are difficult, hostile, or distressed; relates well to people from varied backgrounds and different situations; is sensitive to cultural diversity, race, gender, disabilities, and other individual differences
5	Customer service	Works with clients and customers (that is, any individuals who use or receive the services or products that the work unit produces, including the general public and individuals who work in the agency, other agencies, or organizations outside the government) to assess their needs, provide information or assistance, resolve their problems, or satisfy their expectations; knows about available products and services; is committed to providing quality products and services
6	Writing	Recognizes or uses correct English grammar, punctuation, and spelling; communicates information (for example, facts, ideas, or messages) in a succinct and organized manner; produces written information, which may include technical material, that is appropriate for the intended audience
7	Oral communication	Expresses information (for example, ideas or facts) to individuals or groups effectively, taking into account the audience and nature of the information (for example, technical, sensitive, controversial); makes clear and convincing oral presentations; listens to others, attends to nonverbal cues, and responds appropriately

Rank	Competency	Definition
8	Flexibility	Is open to change and new information; adapts behavior or work methods in response to new information, changing conditions, or unexpected obstacles; effectively deals with ambiguity
9	Creative thinking	Uses imagination to develop new insights into situations and applies innovative solutions to problems; designs new methods where established methods and procedures are inapplicable or are unavailable
10	Change management	Has knowledge of change management principles, strategies, and techniques required for effectively planning, implementing, and evaluating change in the organization
11	Leadership	Influences, motivates, and challenges others; adapts leadership styles to a variety of situations
12	Problem solving	Identifies problems; determines accuracy and relevance of information; uses sound judgment to generate and evaluate alternatives and to make recommendations
13	Attention to detail	Is thorough when performing work and conscientious about attending to detail
14	Conflict management	Manages and resolves conflicts, grievances, confrontations, or disagreements in a constructive manner to minimize negative personal impact
15	Decision-making	Makes sound, well-informed, and objective decisions; perceives the impact and implications of decisions; commits to action, even in uncertain situations, to accomplish organizational goals; causes change
16	Decision support	Has knowledge of decision support theories, methods, and tools for identifying, synthesizing, representing, and evaluating the important aspects of a decision situation and prescribing the recommended course for decision makers and other stakeholders
17	Knowledge management	Has knowledge of the value of collected information and the methods of sharing that information throughout an organization
18	Resilience	Deals effectively with pressure; remains optimistic and persistent, even under adversity; recovers quickly from setbacks
19	Organizational awareness	Knows the organization's mission and functions, and how its social, political, and technological systems work and operates effectively within them; this includes the programs, policies, procedures, rules, and regulations of the organization

(Continued)

Table 10.1. (*Continued*)

Rank	Competency	Definition
20	Public service motivation	Shows a commitment to serve the public; ensures that actions meet public needs; aligns organizational objectives and practices with public interests
21	Human capital management	Builds and manages workforce based on organizational goals, budget considerations, and staffing needs; ensures that employees are appropriately recruited, selected, appraised, and rewarded; takes action to address performance problems; manages a multisector workforce and a variety of work situations
22	Self-management	Sets well-defined and realistic personal goals; displays a high level of initiative, effort, and commitment toward completing assignments in a timely manner; works with minimal supervision; is motivated to achieve; demonstrates responsible behavior
23	Strategic thinking	Formulates effective strategies consistent with the business and competitive strategy of the organization in a global economy; examines policy issues and strategic planning with a long-term perspective; determines objectives and sets priorities; anticipates potential threats or opportunities
24	Computer network defense	Has knowledge of defensive measures to detect, respond, and protect information, information systems, and networks from threats
25	Listening	Receives, attends to, interprets, and responds to verbal messages and other cues, such as body language, in ways that are appropriate to listeners and situations
26	Reasoning	Identifies rules, principles, or relationships that explain facts, data, or other information; analyzes information and makes correct inferences or draws accurate conclusions
27	Planning and evaluating	Organizes work, sets priorities, and determines resource requirements; determines short- or long-term goals and strategies to achieve them; coordinates with other organizations or parts of the organization to accomplish goals; monitors progress and evaluates outcomes
28	Stakeholder management	Has knowledge of the concepts, practices, and techniques used to identify, engage, influence, and monitor relationships with individuals and groups connected to a work effort, including those actively involved, those who exert influence over the process and its results, and those who have a vested interest in the outcome (positive or negative)

Rank	Competency	Definition
29	Partnering	Develops networks and builds alliances; collaborates across boundaries to build strategic relationships and achieve common goals
30	Learning	Uses efficient learning techniques to acquire and apply new knowledge and skills; uses training, feedback, or other opportunities for self-learning and development
31	External awareness	Identifies and understands economic, political, and social trends that affect the organization
32	Data interpretation	Has skill in collecting, analyzing, and interpreting data and policies in order to determine actions and develop and propose guidance
33	Leveraging diversity	Fosters an inclusive workplace where diversity and individual differences are valued and leveraged to achieve the vision and mission of the organization
34	Vision	Understands where the organization is headed and how to make a contribution; takes a long-term view and recognizes opportunities to help the organization accomplish its objectives or move toward the vision
35	Risk management	Has knowledge of the principles, methods, and tools used for risk assessment and mitigation, including assessment of failures and their consequences
36	Technology management	Keeps up-to-date on technological developments; makes effective use of technology to achieve results; ensures access to and security of technology systems
37	Influencing/ negotiating	Persuades others to accept recommendations, cooperate, or change their behavior; works with others toward an agreement; negotiates to find mutually acceptable solutions
38	Communications and media	Has knowledge of the production, communication, and dissemination of information and ideas to inform and entertain via written, oral, and visual media
39	Developing others	Develops the ability of others to perform and contribute to the organization by providing ongoing feedback and by providing opportunities to learn through formal and informal methods
40	Employee development	Has knowledge of employee development concepts, principles, and practices related to planning, evaluating, and administering training, organizational development, and career development initiatives
41	Project management	Has knowledge of the principles, methods, or tools for developing, scheduling, coordinating, and managing projects and resources, including monitoring and inspecting costs, work, and contractor performance

(*Continued*)

Table 10.1. (*Continued*)

Rank	Competency	Definition
42	Information management	Identifies a need for and knows where or how to gather information; organizes and maintains information or information management systems
43	Legal, government, and jurisprudence	Has knowledge of laws, legal codes, court procedures, precedents, legal practices and documents, government regulations, executive orders, agency rules, government organization and functions, and the democratic political process
44	Political savvy	Identifies the internal and external politics that affect the work of the organization; perceives organizational and political reality and acts accordingly
45	Workforce planning	Has knowledge of human resource concepts, principles, and practices related to determining workload projections and current and future competency gaps to align human capital with organizational goals
46	Entrepreneurship	Positions the organization for future success by identifying new opportunities; builds the organization by developing or improving products or services; takes calculated risks to accomplish organizational objectives
47	Business process reengineering	Has knowledge of methods, metrics, tools, and techniques of business process reengineering
48	Administration and management	Has knowledge of planning, coordination, and execution of business functions, resource allocation, and production
49	Data management	Has knowledge of the principles, procedures, and tools of data management, such as modeling techniques, data backup, data recovery, data dictionaries, data warehousing, data mining, data archiving, data disposal, and data standardization processes
50	Communications security management	Has knowledge of the principles, policies, and procedures involved in ensuring the security of communications services and data, and in maintaining the communications environment on which it resides
51	Design	Has knowledge of conceptualizing, developing, producing, understanding, and using plans, models, blueprints, and maps, including the use of tools and instruments to produce precision technical drawings, working prototypes, components, or systems

Rank	Competency	Definition
52	Budget administration	Has knowledge of the principles and practices of budget administration and analysis, including preparing, justifying, reporting on, and executing the budget, and the relationships among program, budget, accounting, and reporting systems
53	Contracting/ procurement	Has knowledge of various types of contracts, techniques, or requirements (for example, the Federal Acquisition Regulation) for contracting or procurement, and contract negotiation and administration
54	Research and statistics	Has knowledge of scientific principles, methods, and tools of basic and applied research (for example, statistics and data analysis) used to conduct a systematic inquiry into a subject matter area
55	Organizational development	Has knowledge of the principles of organizational development and change management theories and their applications
56	Organizational performance analysis	Has knowledge of the methods, techniques, and tools used to analyze program, organizational, and mission performance, including methods that deliver key performance information (for example, comparative, trend, diagnostic, root cause, predictive) used to inform decisions, actions, communications, and accountability systems
57	Information technology program management	Has knowledge of the principles, methods, and tools for the coordinated management of an IT program, to include providing oversight of multiple IT projects, integrating dependent schedules and deliverables, and related activities (for example, benefits management, life-cycle management, program governance)
58	Information assurance	Has knowledge of methods and procedures to protect information systems and data by ensuring their availability, authentication, confidentiality, and integrity
59	Identity management	Has knowledge of methods and controls to validate the identity of individuals to verify access approval and level and to monitor activity to ensure that only authorized access is taking place
60	Computer forensics	Has knowledge of tools and techniques used in data recovery and preservation of electronic evidence
61	Vulnerabilities assessment	Has knowledge of the principles, methods, and tools for assessing vulnerabilities and developing or recommending appropriate mitigation countermeasures

(*Continued*)

Table 10.1. (*Continued*)

Rank	Competency	Definition
62	Cost-benefit analysis	Has knowledge of the principles and methods of cost-benefit analysis, including the time value of money, present value concepts, and quantifying tangible and intangible benefits
63	Computer skills	Uses computers, software applications, databases, and automated systems to accomplish work
64	Financial management	Prepares, justifies, or administers the budget for program areas; plans, administers, and monitors expenditures to ensure cost-effective support of programs and policies; assesses financial condition of an organization
65	Acquisition strategy	Has knowledge of the principles and methods for developing an integrated acquisition management plan that describes the business, technical, and support strategies, including the relationship between the acquisition phases, work efforts, and key program events (for example, decision points, contract awards, test activities)
66	Capital planning and investment assessment	Has knowledge of the principles and methods of capital investment analysis or business case analysis, including return-on-investment analysis
67	Technology awareness	Has knowledge of developments and new applications of information technology (hardware, software, telecommunications), emerging technologies and their applications to business processes, and applications and implementation of information systems to meet organizational requirements
68	Systems engineering	Has knowledge of the practice of integrating multiple disciplines into a team as part of a structured development process throughout a system's life cycle
69	Reading	Understands and interprets written material, including technical material, rules, regulations, instructions, reports, charts, graphs, or tables; applies what is learned from written material to specific situations
70	Quality assurance	Has knowledge of the principles, methods, and tools of quality assurance and quality control used to ensure a product fulfills functional requirements and standards
71	Sales and marketing	Has knowledge of showing, promoting, and selling products and services
72	Operating systems	Has knowledge of computer network, desktop, and mainframe operating systems and their applications

Rank	Competency	Definition
73	Requirements analysis	Has knowledge of the principles and methods to identify, analyze, specify, design, and manage functional and infrastructure requirements, including translating functional requirements into technical requirements used for logical design or presenting alternative technologies or approaches
74	Human factors	Has knowledge of the principles, methods, and tools used to identify and apply information about human behavior, abilities, limitations, and other characteristics to the design of tools, machines, systems, tasks, jobs, and environments for effective human use
75	Mathematical reasoning	Solves practical problems by choosing appropriately from a variety of mathematical and statistical techniques
76	Arithmetic/ mathematical reasoning	Performs computations such as addition, subtraction, multiplication, and division correctly; solves practical problems by choosing appropriately from a variety of mathematical concepts such as formulas and percentages
77	Auditing	Has knowledge of generally accepted auditing standards and procedures for conducting financial and compliance, economy and efficiency, and program audits
78	Computer languages	Has knowledge of computer languages and their applications to enable a system to perform specific functions
79	Configuration management	Has knowledge of the principles and methods for planning or managing the implementation, update, or integration of information system components
80	Financial analysis	Has knowledge of the principles, methods, and techniques of financial analysis, forecasting, and modeling to interpret quantitative and qualitative data, including data modeling, earned value management, and evaluating key financial indicators, trends, and historical data
81	Artificial intelligence	Has knowledge of the principles, methods, and tools used to design systems that perform human intelligence functions
82	Information technology performance assessment	Has knowledge of the principles, methods, and tools (for example, surveys, system performance measures) to assess the effectiveness and practicality of information technology systems

(Continued)

Table 10.1. (*Continued*)

Rank	Competency	Definition
83	Information technology architecture	Has knowledge of architectural methodologies used in the design and development of information systems, including the physical structure of a system's internal operations and interactions with other systems
84	Classification	Has knowledge of classification concepts, principles, and practices related to structuring organizations and positions and determining the appropriate pay system, occupational grouping, title, and pay level of positions
85	Grants management	Has knowledge of requirements, practices, and procedures for soliciting, receiving, reviewing, and processing proposals and awarding and administering grants and agreements
86	Criminal investigation	Has knowledge of the guidelines, regulations, and procedures associated with criminal investigation, including evidence detection and handling and drawing appropriate factual inferences and conclusions
87	Accounting	Has knowledge of traditional accounting practices, including accrual, obligations, and costs methods
88	Accessibility	Has knowledge of tools, equipment, and technologies used to help individuals with disabilities use computer equipment and software
89	Civil engineering	Has knowledge of the concepts, principles, theories, and methods required to plan, design, construct, operate, and maintain facilities such as buildings, transportation systems, water and sanitary systems, and other public works systems
90	Foreign language	Has knowledge of sign language or of the structure and content of a foreign (non-English) language, including the meaning and spelling of words, rules of composition, and grammar

Work is constantly evolving. Whether in the private sector, nonprofit, or government, jobs can and do change over time, as do the skills needed for those jobs. This is a list of the top ninety competencies that will be needed across the federal workforce moving into the future. Source: Author.

outside forces are well documented in this volume, including those referred to in Part I (for example, Ramayya Krishnan's chapter on algorithms and Sheila Bair's chapter on financial-technical regulation) and Part II (for example, Donald F. Kettl's and John J. DiIulio Jr.'s chapters on structural issues). The outside force emphasized here is the use of contractors and the reality of blended government. Working with these "outsiders" shapes federal employees' working environments and can cause confusion over who is in charge. I have called this the "Who's on First" problem in honor of the hilarious baseball joke told by Abbott and Costello (Verkuil, 2017). Often, contractors and federal employees will be working next to each other and doing the same jobs. Competencies such as flexibility (item 8 in Table 10.1), change management (item 10), and organizational awareness (item 19) are necessary skills in this environment. A big determinant of civil service competency is going to be what the role of contractors will be in the future. As Paul C. Light has shown in this volume, the blended workforce of civil service, contractor, and grant employees has been part of government since the beginning, although in recent decades the number of contract and grant employees has grown much larger, surpassing that of federal employees, which is at two million (Light, 2017). This brings to light a sobering statistic: governments now employ a smaller share of the U.S. workforce than at any time since 1957 (Fox, 2018).

The Blended Workforce

Despite legal authority in the civil service, some agencies are effectively contractor driven, with 90 percent of their workforce under contract. *Valuing Bureaucracy* studies the Department of Energy and United States Agency for International Development, which fall into this category (Verkuil, 2017). It is harder to lead and inspire contractors who, by definition, have specific and limited assignments and are paid by third parties. Management challenges are heightened when the federal workforce is in the minority, and this has consequences. The Government Accountability Office (GAO) has yet to take a contractor-dominated agency off its high-risk list (Verkuil, 2017). The contractor–civil servant relationship becomes even more complex when the jobs performed are the "intrinsic functions of government" that Francis Fukuyama discusses.

These "delegations" to nongovernment actors deeply affect the kind of work federal employees do and the qualifications needed to succeed. Federal employees are increasingly managing a set of actors who are providing much of the services the public expects. Despite good arguments to the contrary by scholars like DiIulio in *Bring Back the Bureaucrats* (2014), this situation is not likely to change in the short term. The blended workforce has become entrenched partially because the civil service system is so cumbersome. There are so many difficulties in terms of hiring and firing that agency leadership turns to contractors since they can be hired with relative ease and removed just as easily.

The skills needed to lead this diversified workforce are more complex when the people being led are not bound by the same rules. For one thing, unlike civil servants, who have broad responsibilities defined by statutes, rules, and practices, contractors have specific duties created by agreement, and the civil servants who manage these workers have to understand the scope and limits of this employment relationship. When it comes to grant employees, many of whom work for state or local governments, the management challenges may be even greater. The need to motivate and direct workers who are away from Washington, often in remote locations, creates major span-of-control problems. The Social Security Disability Insurance program, for example, utilizes state employees to operate the critical initial application and reconsideration stages for over two million applicants annually, in addition to sixty thousand Social Security Administration employees spread across roughly 1,230 field offices (Social Security Administration, n.d.). There are few decision systems of greater size and complexity in the Western world, and decision consistency, accuracy, and productivity are major challenges (Verkuil, 2017).

The civil service system is becoming more one that manages others than one that does the work directly. While the number of federal employees has remained the same for many decades, there has been an upward move in grades under the General Schedule system that reflects the increasing number of managers. The average employee grade has undergone an "upward creep" from 6.7 to over 12 today on a 15-level General Schedule ranking (Kettl, 2016). A focus on the development of management skills, often associated with business schools and MBA programs, can be found in the curricula of public administration schools at all levels. The Ninety for Ninety, Table 10.1, lists several key components for managers in its top ten competencies: integrity/honesty, accountability, teamwork, interpersonal skills, customer service, writing, oral communication, flexibility, creative thinking, and change management.

Given the realities of the blended workforce, the competencies most needed for civil servants may be teamwork, customer service, and change management. While the listed competencies do not directly refer to supervision of contract or grant employees, customer service and teamwork are key skills for a diverse employee base with differing motivations.

The Digitization of Everything

Another macro concern for the civil service is the entire information technology (IT) environment. The Brookings Institution surveyed 545 occupations covering 90 percent of the U.S. workforce and found that virtually all fields required at least some, and often a high, degree of digital skills (Muro et al., 2017). The federal government's occupational needs certainly mirror the digitalized needs of the workforce as a whole and may be at the higher end of the digital competency scale. Government is inseparable from technology, and its investment in technology is over $80 billion annually. However, as GAO has shown, about 75 percent of that amount is spent on maintaining legacy systems, including the Internal Revenue Service's taxpayer information, which is stored on fifty-seven-year-old IBM mainframes in an archaic assembly language, and the U.S. nuclear operations, which are stored on fifty-four-year-old eight-inch floppy disks (GAO, 2016). The effectiveness of federal employees is often dependent on their agency IT acquisition practices. How can they even know what systems to learn if the systems are outmoded but seemingly perpetual? The Social Security Administration reported rehiring retired employees to maintain its systems that use COBOL, a programming language from the 1970s that today is included in less than a third of university computer science curriculums (Micro Focus, 2013). In IT training and systems development, the need for flexibility is paramount, and the competencies required, such as operating systems and IT architecture, appear throughout the Ninety for Ninety chart. The use of new versus legacy technologies has an impact on aspects of nearly every federal job, especially on the acquisition skills listed in the table (competencies 53, 57, and 65) that must show awareness of that impact.

As a result, the government's IT challenges are close to overwhelming. GAO (2016) shows that 5,233 of 7,000 IT investments go entirely to operations and maintenance, leaving modest resources for modernizing investments in software and hardware upgrades, cloud computing, or shared services. Federal employees are pedaling as fast as they can on stationary bicycles while sleek new road bikes zip by. Moreover, the investments can be doubly deleterious, as they reduce the incentive to make new investments that might improve services and be less costly. This is why IT is a constant presence on GAO's High Risk List (GAO, 2015).

The Obama administration tried to address the IT skills gap with the short-term employment of Silicon Valley technocrats who were located in the General Services Administration's 18F operation, so named for its location at the intersection of Eighteenth and F Streets NW, in Washington, DC (18F, n.d.). Called Presidential Innovation Fellows, these IT specialists were assigned to agencies to solve endemic problems on an agency cost-recovery basis. Envisioned as the hub for digital innovation, 18F faced several obstacles, including opposition from traditional IT contractors and GSA's inspector general (Miller, 2017). While its future is far from secure, the operation's recent focus has been on IT acquisition problems under GSA's Federal Acquisition Service (Rockwell, 2017).

It is difficult to appoint a small group of even talented outsiders with the mission of helping to drive agency IT policy. While resentments from the career staff are to be expected, of course, the real need is for more IT and cyber talent across government, through both job expansion and upgrading existing employees. Innovation fellows are still outsiders who are viewed much like contractors. The hope would be that some of these fellows might transition into the federal service. This would integrate them better and reduce strains that 18F reimbursements place on the human capital system and agency budgets during a time of retrenchment. Still, the effort to create tech mentors and advisors to those on the career side are well intentioned and remain one of the IT ideas that show promise.

Skill Sets and Personnel Realities

GAO has identified six skill areas that are "mission critical": cybersecurity, acquisition, human resources, auditing, economics, and STEM (science, technology, engineering, and mathematics). But the talent gaps in these areas are hard to fix because of compensation limits and restrictions on hiring. As Kettl has shown in *Escaping Jurassic Government* (2016), these gaps require government employees of increasingly higher education and experience than in earlier years (see Figure 10.1).

In fact, the Office of Management and Budget (OMB) has shown that government demands greater numbers of workers in higher-paid professions

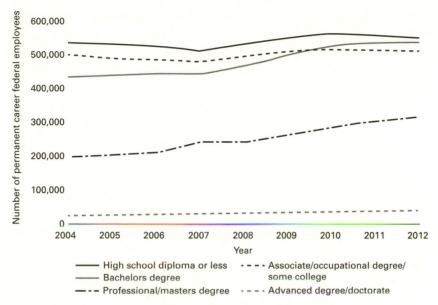

Figure 10.1. Change in Composition of Federal Civilian Workforce by Education, 2004–2012
Source: GAO, 2014.

than does the private sector (Mulvaney, 2017). This recognition of the need for highly educated talent in government only makes it harder to achieve success. The burdens placed on the human resources departments at most agencies in light of these hiring realities need greater recognition, and Congress and the executive branch must be committed to addressing them. These are the jobs with the most competition from the private sector, where compensation and benefits are often far superior.

Cyber Vulnerabilities

Cyber vulnerabilities increase the need for a public service that can accomplish the goals of twenty-first-century government. There have been serious breaches of security at the National Security Agency, where contractors like Edward Snowden have leaked to a group known as the Shadow Brokers vital hacking tools and software, which can be used to breach or hijack virtually any device connected to the internet. In effect, the National Security Agency's own cyberweapons are being used against them (Shane, Perlroth, and Sanger, 2017). In addition, millions of personnel files and social security numbers were leaked from OPM and the Internal Revenue Service. Our security system has been totally compromised. This is not, of course, a problem unique to government: consider the 146 million compromised files at Equifax. Government, however, has a limited ability to respond given its aforementioned problems. Until high-quality public servants, including contractors, have been trained and retained, these vulnerabilities will continue. The search for new talent takes on an unprecedented degree of urgency, yet there are few signs of progress.

One place the government might find qualified cyber specialists is in the military. The Department of Defense reacted to the need for cyber expertise by designating that field as a new branch of service in 2017. The army has established an enlisted 17C Cyber Operations Specialist military occupational specialty with a five-year service requirement after training is completed. The applicants must qualify through tests and be eligible for top-secret clearance. The program is oversubscribed. The RAND Corporation was recently asked to evaluate the likelihood that these new cyber experts will be wooed away by the private sector once their service obligations are completed (Wenger, O'Connell, and Lytell, 2017). But suppose the wooing was done within government, and cyber specialists transferred to the civil service after their commitments were completed.

RAND was not asked to study the prospect that these cyber experts would be attracted to the civil service, but that is an obvious career path that is in the national interest. Many in the federal workforce are veterans, and veterans' preference is a powerful recruiting tool. For the military, federal employment is a standard career option with attractive retirement and other benefits. Perhaps we can fill some needed positions more efficiently in this manner. Moreover, within the military, federal employment is a matter of public service. Many joined with altruistic motivations, much like those Senator William W. Bradley described in Chapter 9. There is no reason those motivations should not attract talented individuals to the civil service as well.

Civil Service Reform—Big and Small Steps

Fulfilling the need for more skilled personnel in government requires many fixes and initiatives. For one thing, the civil service has to be made more employment friendly. But wholesale reform of the civil service is a confound-ingly complicated proposition (Light, 2017). Leading observers have long proclaimed that "government is broken," and powerful voices, like that of Paul Volcker, have called for its reform. But the pressures against reform are intense, entrenched, and seemingly intransigent. The political consensus is lacking in both parties. On the Republican side, conservative voices of those who do not believe in government (or who, like Grover Norquist, want to "drown it in a bathtub") keep more pragmatic members of the party from moving forward. On the Democratic side, the will to reform exists, but it is often stymied by those working in government and the public-sector unions who represent them.

Unions like the American Federation of Government Employees see civil service reform as a zero-sum game since much of the reform effort depends on bringing new talent into government (or promoting existing employees to managers). This "grade inflation" has produced employees who may not fit into existing bargaining units (Romero, 2014). By viewing their white-collar members' jobs as at risk, public-sector unions are on the defensive and stymie reforms. Democratic legislators rarely move on civil service is-sues without union support.

Civil service reform at the state level faces some of the same obstacles. Red states continue to unwind civil service protections, and blue states face unions that often oppose efforts to streamline the hiring process. To date, the main efforts have come in those states where at-will public employees have replaced many career employees. This usually occurs in states where public-sector unions are not powerful, except in Wisconsin, where they were overridden. In *Valuing Bureaucracy*, I discuss the Wisconsin situa-tion and the North Carolina and Texas situations, where the displacement of career officials has led to dysfunctional public actions (Verkuil, 2017). The need at the state level to address professionalism is particularly acute since states do not have the equivalent of OMB Circular A-76 (discussed by Fuku-yama in Chapter 5), which identifies and protects jobs that are "inherently governmental." In effect, states have an "unbounded" workforce to privatize.

But even without major reforms, there are incremental changes that are worth noting. For example, a continuing difficulty for agencies is the time the hiring process eats up. And when agencies get several good finalists to choose among, they are not permitted to share the runners-up with other agencies even though they may be entirely suitable for government service. In the Competitive Service Act of 2015 (enacted 2016; 114th Cong., S. 1580),

Congress provided that agencies could share vetted lists of the best-qualified finalists. That this seemingly innocuous reform took legislation shows how difficult it is to fix government hiring. At the federal level, OPM is the agency that can make the human resources system work better. OPM staff would do well to follow up on former acting director Beth Cobert's many helpful ideas set out during the Obama years. For example, she developed a "myth busters" program that was designed to show how OPM could and would facilitate agency personnel actions without legislation or even new regulations. A can-do OPM administrator will do much to solve hiring problems.

Finally, some members of Congress are showing interest in key human capital issues by engaging in a broad-based inquiry into civil service reform. By calling on a wide range of experts, Senators James Lankford and Heidi Heitkamp of the Senate Subcommittee on Regulatory Affairs and Federal Management are learning how to make the hiring process work better (Ogrysko, 2017). They have charged GAO with developing a detailed set of proposals for consideration that may well lead to bigger reform efforts. Heitkamp, in addressing the Senior Executives Association during Public Service Recognition Week, stated, "We are not anywhere near coming up with the big rolling package, but as time goes on, this will be the focus in this Congress" (Ogrysko, 2017). One has to admire these senators for pursuing civil service reform as a matter of good government. It just may be that Heitkamp's "big rolling package"—that is, comprehensive civil service reform—could emerge from these smaller efforts. In addition, the National Academy of Public Administration has issued a report on creating a public service for the twenty-first century (National Academy of Public Administration, 2017), and OMB has issued a "comprehensive plan for Executive Branch reorganization" (Mulvaney, 2017). These efforts could lead to broader congressional efforts in the next Congress.

Concluding Thoughts

The government knows the KSAs needed to qualify the next generation of federal workers, as Table 10.1 shows. But this is not just about qualifications. It is more about the will to deliver. Agencies like GAO understand the age of digitization and the implications for technology improvement and cybersecurity protection. Unfortunately, there is a big gap between knowing what to do and making that a hiring reality. This is why system reforms are so important for building the quality workforce we need. How to find talent, what to pay for it, and how to mix career with contractor personnel are the overarching questions that agencies grapple with. The federal government is, in effect, a collection of agencies that need help system-wide. A civil service system for the twenty-first century needs to be launched. This takes enlightened leadership both inside and outside the career service.

The Lankford-Heitkamp partnership shows that this need not be a partisan issue, but rather is an essential structural matter that will affect the quality of all other actions involving government. There is no shortage of ideas or groups to assist. Institutions like the Volcker Alliance, the Partnership for Public Service, and the National Academy of Public Administration are ready to be of service. Our nation needs to call on them. Civil service preparedness is no less important than military preparedness.

Note

1. I would like to thank Kevin H. Bell for his careful and creative assistance on this chapter.

Bibliography

Bertrand, Natasha. 2017. "'Dumbfounded' Diplomats Say Trump's Comments About Embassy Cuts 'Make Him Putin's Patsy.'" *Business Insider*, August 12, 2017. http://www.businessinsider.com/dumbfounded-diplomats-say-trumps-comments-about-embassy-cuts-make-him-putins-patsy-2017-8.

DiIulio, John J., Jr. 2014. *Bring Back the Bureaucrats: Why More Federal Workers Will Lead to Better (and Cheaper!) Government*. West Conshohocken, PA: Templeton.

18F. n.d. "About." Accessed April 30, 2019. https://18f.gsa.gov/about.

Fox, Justin. 2018. "Government Work Has Been Going Out of Style." Bloomberg, September 7, 2018. https://www.bloomberg.com/view/articles/2018-09-07/jobs-report-government-work-has-been-going-out-of-style.

GAO (U.S. Government Accountability Office). 2014. *Federal Workforce: Recent Trends in Federal Civilian Employment and Compensation*. GAO-14-215. Washington, DC: U.S. Government Accountability Office. https://www.gao.gov/assets/670/660449.pdf.

———. 2015. *High Risk Series: An Update*. GAO-15-290. Washington, DC: U.S. Government Accountability Office.

———. 2016. *Federal Agencies Need to Address Aging Legacy Systems*. GAO-16-696T. Washington, DC: U.S. Government Accountability Office.

Kettl, Donald F. 2016. *Escaping Jurassic Government: How to Recover America's Lost Commitment to Competence*. Washington, DC: Brookings Institution.

Light, Paul. 2017. "The True Size of Government: Tracking Washington's Blended Workforce, 1984–2015." October 2017. https://www.volckeralliance.org/sites/default/files/attachments/Issue%20Paper_True%20Size%20of%20Government.pdf.

Micro Focus. 2013. "Academia Needs More Support to Tackle the IT Skills Gap." March 7, 2013. https://www.microfocus.com/about/press-room/article/2013/academia-needs-more-support-to-tackle-the-it-skills-gap/.

Miller, Jason. 2017. "GSA IG Uncovers Further Misdeeds by 18F Executives." Federal News Radio, February 21, 2017. https://federalnewsradio.com/agency-oversight/2017/02/gsa-ig-uncovers-18f-misdeeds-executives/.

Mulvaney, Mick. 2017. "Comprehensive Plan for Reforming the Federal Government and Reducing the Federal Civilian Workforce." Memo M-17-22, April 12, 2017. https://www.whitehouse.gov/sites/whitehouse.gov/files/omb/memoranda/2017/M-17-22.pdf.

Muro, Mark, Sifan Liu, Jacob Whiton, and Siddharth Kulkarni. 2017. "Digitalization and the American Workforce." Brookings Institution, November 2017. https://www.brookings.edu/research/digitalization-and-the-american-workforce/.

National Academy of Public Administration. 2017. *No Time to Wait: Building a Public Service for the 21st Century*. Washington, DC: National Academy of Public Administration, July 2017.

———. 2018. *No Time to Wait, Part 2: Building a Public Service for the 21st Century*. Washington, DC: National Academy of Public Administration, September 2018.

Ogrysko, Nicole. 2017. "Senate Subcommittee Asking Hard Questions on Civil Service Reform This Year." Federal News Radio, May 11, 2017. https://federalnewsradio.com/workforce/2017/05/senate-subcommittee-asking-hard-questions-on-civil-service-reform-this-year/.

Rockwell, Mark. 2017. "GSA Elevates Davie, Makes Changes at 18F." *FCW*, September 18, 2017. https://fcw.com/articles/2017/09/18/gsa-fas-18f-changes-rockwell.aspx.

Romero, Henry. 2014. "Grade Inflation: Does It Matter?" *Government Executive*, September 5, 2014. http://www.govexec.com/excellence/promising-practices/2014/09/grade-inflation-does-it-matter/93218/.

Shane, Scott, Nicole Perlroth, and David E. Sanger. 2017. "Security Breach and Spilled Secrets Have Shaken the N.S.A. to Its Core." *New York Times*, November 12, 2017.

Social Security Administration. n.d. "Organizational Structure of the Social Security Administration." Accessed December 11, 2018. https://www.ssa.gov/org/.

U.S. Office of Personnel Management. 2013. *Multipurpose Occupational Systems Analysis Inventory—Close Ended (MOSAIC) Competencies*. Washington, DC: U.S. Office of Personnel Management. https://www.opm.gov/policy-data-oversight/assessment-and-selection/competencies/mosaic-studies-competencies.pdf.

Verkuil, Paul. 2017. *Valuing Bureaucracy: The Case for Professional Government*. Cambridge: Cambridge University Press.

Wenger, Jennie W., Caolionn O'Connell, and Maria C. Lytell. 2017. *Retaining the Army's Cyber Expertise*. RR-1978-A. Santa Monica, CA: RAND.

CHAPTER 11

Upending Public Policy Education

Angela Evans

Public policy schools[1] play an indispensable role in bridging the divides among policymakers, public servants, and scholars. These schools have been valued for housing scholarship relevant to societal challenges, for serving as the training ground for emerging public servants, and for using data and information to offer common ground as the basis for well-informed policy debates.

Public policy schools are more important today than ever. The environments in which policy is formulated, debated, and executed have fundamentally shifted to accommodate the domination of political ideologies, the plethora of information resources, the addiction to finding immediate solutions, and the willingness to accept unsubstantiated facts as likely truths. To succeed in accomplishing their historic mission amid these challenges, public policy schools must change (Evans, 2015). They must rethink their curricula, experiment with new kinds of partnerships on university campuses and beyond, and make research more accessible to those who make and implement public policy.

Emerging Challenges to the Public Policy School

While policy analysts and public managers have achieved a bona fide identity and presence in the policy community, it has become increasingly difficult for academics to remain at the cutting edge of issues. Public policy is far more complex today than in the past, for reasons including the influence of international policy making, the complexity of policy made at different levels of government in our federal system, and the growing importance of public and private partnerships and the nonprofit sector. The velocity of emerging policy issues, coupled with the growing complexity of these issues, demands nimbleness and agility, two attributes difficult to find in academia.

Another challenge is the decline of the influence of traditional agenda setters, including political parties, experts, and journalists. The converse of this is the proliferation of entities like think tanks, consulting firms, and lobbies that claim to be nonpartisan, objective sources of policy information and analysis and threaten to crowd out academic participation in the policy process.

Adding to the challenges faced by today's public policy schools is how media are used to influence deliberations. The multiplication of media is in itself daunting. Half a century ago, when the political parties shared a broad consensus, there were three television networks and a few influential magazines, and the public showed high levels of deference to institutional leaders. Fast-forward: now information is cherry-picked, brought to users through customized feeds of news outlets (see Chapter 3 for discussion about newsfeed algorithms and their implications), prized for its immediacy, and riddled with unsubstantiated narratives.

The confluence of these factors creates the need for broad capacity to keep up with the knowledge generated by the emergence of these issues, fluency in tackling unchartered public policy challenges, a discerning eye to select trustworthy information sources, the ability to thrive in a fast-paced environment, and, not least, the skill to demonstrate that one's own perspective adds value to the policy discussion. These factors also require management skills that foster alliances among nontraditional partners, enable the forecasting and execution of budgets in uncertain and delayed funding cycles, and convey quantifiable measures of high overall performance.

Given these conditions, schools of public policy must freshly determine whether they have a unique role in advancing sound public policy and, if so, what that role is. They need to assess the curricula they deliver, the partners with whom they collaborate, and the ways they communicate with policymakers and public servants. Reluctance to engage in a fundamental shift in the way policy schools teach, build constructive partnerships, and seek collaboration outside academia can prevent these schools from achieving their vital educational and social missions.

Rejuvenating the Curricula

In considering how to make policy research more relevant to policymakers, public policy schools need to adapt their curricula to the demands of our changing society (U.S. Government Accountability Office, 2018).

The education programs and degree requirements shared by public policy schools have been aimed at preparing students to enter a variety of public policy professions, including management, legislative and policy design, policy research, and policy advocacy. These programs came of age and thrived for nearly fifty years, in large part because of the relevance of the training students received, which allowed them to excel in a wide range of positions, policy sectors (public, private, and nonprofit), and policy transformations. Public management, policy analysis, microeconomics, quantitative methods and research design, and public finance formed the foundational core of the curricula in most public affairs programs. Today a similar set of selected courses continues to make up core offerings at policy schools. These include policy analysis, public administration, public financial management, quantitative methodologies, microeconomics, and research design. Collectively, these are foundational to the policy school experience. They allow for a rigorous treatment of issues that rests on the ability to discover and identify problems; to secure the information, data, and research to authenticate the problems; to formulate feasible approaches and options to address the problems; and to offer potential implications for the adoption of options.

If one were to look at these core offerings across schools and time, one would see consistency and longevity. But this evidence of their quality and relevance can create a false sense of assurance that traditional curricula are in no danger of crowding out innovation. Unfortunately, while the content and format of curricula are key to the early and continued success of public policy graduates, all too often faculty and administrators are hesitant to reform curricula to adjust to the changing demands of current policy and management environments. Neglecting to consistently review and change courses, to adjust the manner in which they are delivered, and to assess faculty who offer them could result in a steady deterioration of the ultimate worth of a public policy education.

Today as in the past, public policy and management programs at their best can add value to policy deliberations, execution, and innovations. These programs present excellent turf on which to convey the essence of decision-making, which is the application of practical reason to policy choices. Sound analysis does not guarantee informed choices, but it does help decision makers define and appraise choices.

Analysis essentially goes through three stages. The first is the hard thinking that accompanies the identification of a problem, since problem definition is the most important step in analysis. Is a problem real, can it be solved as framed, or must it be reframed? Also, it is important to discuss the tensions that are always present in any analysis, since the elevation of a policy issue up the policy food chain usually conveys that the problem could not be solved at lower levels. There is never a perfect solution that will eliminate the tension or present a perfect solution.

Second is the framing and forecasting of options for addressing the problem. This is the side of analysis that makes the most use of research and rigorous methods. In addition, this stage will identify sources for options outside traditional academic research—for example, past attempts at change, reasons for recurring stalemates in policy development, and lessons from one-off problems.

Third is the consideration of political and practical constraints. This is an art more than a science, although it does make use of scientific methods. The essence of this stage of analysis cannot be reduced to a single technique. It is a habit of mind that seeks to solve public problems rationally, but with due regard to political and practical pressures. One must determine how to solve a problem "on the merits" but also pay attention to the political and institutional constraints. Squaring that circle is the essence of statecraft, and also the challenge that analysts face. Policy argument is really a high-level systems analysis where one reasons back and forth among various problem definitions, sources of evidence, and solutions until the problem and the solutions are consistent and also politic.

Public policy analysis is what might be called "firing line analysis," done by those aiming to craft policy options immediately for the decision makers. Understanding the connection between the two and delivering sound analysis to build that connection is a goal of policy schools. In this realm, one considers how to create and convey the results of critical thinking and problem solving applied to real-life issues within relevant time frames.

For the most part, this training has been successful in imparting the skills needed in public policy positions primarily because of the relative predictability of the content of policy debates and stability of both policy-making environments and management settings. However, recent studies of public policy school graduates and their employers in different sectors conclude that while important shifts have occurred in the ways policies are formulated and executed, curricular innovations tend to be slow and iterative. Some of this can be explained by how policy formulation has developed and how the execution and oversight of those policies have evolved and matured over the last decades.

Policy making in the era of the Great Society led to two important transformations in public policy education. The sheer volume and accelerated timing of enacting and implementing over two hundred new policies across a vast array of issues revealed the challenges facing policymakers seeking the expertise of the academy when developing policy options. On-demand development of relevant and feasible policies to address a wide array of societal challenges created an immediate opportunity for policy researchers to contribute to policy debates. Methods for translating research findings for use by nonacademics were limited. One consequence of this was the refinement of policy analysis as a viable method for informing policy formulation. Another consequence was the founding of schools of public affairs that institutionalized this approach through core educational programming.

The spike in policy creation led to another transformation in policy education, this one more incremental. The implementation of these new policies required adjustments in the oversight, management, and evaluation of programs. Both traditional public administration and the relatively new public affairs schools identified additional administrative skills needed by those administering programs. Over the years, microeconomics, quantitative analysis, and program evaluations assumed larger roles in the policy community and thus in our schools. An unintended consequence of the adjustments made to policy education has been adherence to modalities that modify and adjust existing policies (focusing on the viability of existing policies or solutions aimed at mitigating past policy problems) rather than examining the roots of problems and creating never-before-enacted policies.

For example, some would say that policies are needed to regulate payday lenders because they exploit the poor by charging high interest rates. If policy deliberations and management focus on payday lenders, the root problem is overlooked—namely, that the poor and near poor do not have access to short-term loans. As this example shows, the conventional definition of the problem that public policy is expected to address may need to be reconsidered.

The traditional content and objectives of some core courses fall short of providing the skills and expertise necessary for working in today's policy arenas, given the complexity of decision-making in policy settings rife with major management, political, and fiscal challenges. For this reason, traditional policy analysis as the basis of public policy school curricula needs to be supplemented by two other kinds of approaches: iterative and transformative.

The iterative approach is based on improvements to the format and content of the current curricula in public policy schools. It generally reflects the traditional way policy and management schools have approached curricular reform—through adjustments to existing core courses. Several studies, including ones sponsored by the Volcker Alliance, identified skills that could be built into current programs. These include public leadership and ethics, the ability to build and sustain coalitions and partnerships, team management–building agendas, facilitation and measurement of results, project and contract management, and managing a diverse workforce (broadly defined as multigenerational, off-site, and multidisciplinary, as well as including the more traditional diversity categories).

At a recent summit of deans of public policy schools,[2] several adjustments were discussed. These included teaching new technical courses about data science and geographic information systems; adopting new learning technologies, such as data visualization, augmented reality, and advanced simulation; emphasizing written communication skills that reflect balance, objectivity, and accessibility of content; social entrepreneurship; and ethical decision-making and behavior. The deans also emphasized that graduates of policy schools must master basic analytic skills in areas such as logic and reason, the collection and assessment of authoritative evidence, and identification of the implications of the foundational roles of the Constitution, the rule of law, and due process in the development and execution of public policies.

In addition to incremental reforms, public policy schools should consider more radical transformations of the curricula. These would involve moving away from a more technical, deep disciplinary approach to policy education and toward an approach that prepares students to understand complex public policy frameworks and the concepts behind them. Students are exposed to the recurring tensions that exist within these frameworks, the issues that remain unresolved despite attempts to address them, the data and research associated with these frameworks, and the multidisciplinary expertise that can enlighten the policy debates that take place within these frameworks.

A framework approach also allows for a modular structure to course delivery. Instead of being confined by semester length and required contact hours per week, these courses could be offered in time frames that vary from several hours to several weeks. Some of the modules also could be delivered in work settings, thus offering critical experiential learning blended with traditional course work. The involvement of practitioners in educational programming is critical since they could bring new skills to students and could create new strategies for developing continuing education opportunities.

This approach may better prepare students to engage in deliberations by providing them with the agility to be comfortable in a variety of settings with a variety of professionals in a variety of disciplines. It may also help students to identify new ideas and explore them. And finally, students who have navigated through policy frameworks may be better skilled at gathering information from a broad range of resources and disciplines and better able to assemble a robust set of experts to work on a policy problem.

Policy frameworks would be relatively consistent since these learning experiences would be organized around major, ongoing issues that will persist in a society that is balancing the needs of a capitalistic economic system with government programs and regulations. Several examples of this approach are offered shortly. The structure of the frameworks and the questions posed within are illustrative. They offer opportunities to ground courses and learning experiences on core tensions and questions inherent in persistent societal problems and on aspirational goals of societies. The nature of the questions within each framework forces recognition of the role of multiple disciplines in arriving at policy options. Relying on traditional disciplines of policy analysis, public administration, public finance, microeconomics, and qualitative methods as the organizing structure for policy programs not only limits the scope of knowledge conveyed but also ignores the foundational purpose of policy education: to prepare students for unknown policy challenges. Even currently emerging policy challenges cannot be met by the expertise resident within singular, traditional disciplines. Providing students with a starting point on how to think about societal challenges, what questions to ask, and which disciplines to consult equips them to play a critical role in the development and execution of solutions.

Income Security

What is a "fair" distribution of income? What is an "efficient" distribution of income? What is the role and what are the limits of the market in providing outcomes that are fair and efficient? What are the major policy approaches— minimum wage, labor rights, social security, health insurance, public education, welfare, basic income grants—and how have they worked in practice? What are the legislative and regulatory tools that will be the vehicles for their implementation (grants, revenue forgone)? How does this issue play out across the life cycle and across international frontiers?

Climate Change

What is the present scientific consensus on anthropogenic climate change? What are the impending environmental, economic, and social costs? What are the most and least promising steps to mitigate and to adapt? How can one best assess the nature and the scale of investments that should be made? What are the advantages and disadvantages of specific technical choices, including the use of shale gas, industrial wind, and solar power?

War and Peace

Why do countries and peoples fight? What are the roles of resources, capabilities, and deterrence? When is war justified, and when is it not justified? What can we learn from specific cases in American and world history, including the two world wars, Vietnam, Afghanistan, and Iraq—as well as the Cuban missile crisis and other classic situations—about decisions that led to war or that helped to avoid it? What role do nonstate players have in conflicts, and what socioeconomic, political conditions empower them?

Social Justice

What does the history of the United States teach us about the struggle for human, civil, social, and economic rights? Discussions might explore the Civil War, populism, Jim Crow, the New Deal, the civil rights movement, voting rights, school desegregation, immigration, farmworkers' struggles, prisons, and the battle for women's rights and access to reproductive services.

E Pluribus Unum

What are the political tensions that can serve as barriers to bridging differences (for example, regionalism, isolationism, globalism, political homogeneity)? What role do institutions play in blending peoples and cultures, bringing peoples together, and preserving cultural identity? What role could or should government policy play in fostering cultural harmony and preserving cultural heritage? How much of a disconnect is there between policy output and outcome along racial, ethnic, and regional dimensions? Under what circumstances is it appropriate to give up aspects of cultural identity? When is it not? What role does technology (for example, media) play in preserving cultural landscapes, as well as homogenizing peoples? How can we assess the nature and scale of investments, as well as the acceptability of government, private-sector, and nonprofit interventions?

New Alliances for Public Policy Schools

In addition to rethinking curricula, it is necessary to rethink the settings for public policy education. Contemporary education in public policy and public administration is generally offered in a university setting. This model of the public policy school, which emerged in the 1970s, continues to predominate. Alternative opportunities to deliver education, training, and experiential learning exist for policy schools: some within existing programs, others requiring significant shifts in approaches to curricula, learning settings, and control over programs.

Within Existing University Constructs

Policy schools currently participate in hybrid programs supported by university rules and procedures. These programs tend to operate based on affiliation rather than true integration of the curricula. In some of these arrangements, policy schools pollinate their faculty from other departments, and in others these programs are taught by jointly appointed faculty.

These programs have played a key role in attracting and retaining policy school students in large part because they allow the exploration of specific disciplines to complement core knowledge and skills received through policy education.

The association of public policy schools with universities presents opportunities for collaboration. Along with these benefits comes the potential for tension between the needs of the public policy school and university-wide academic norms with respect to standards for tenure and promotion.[3] The contemporary public policy school occupies the space between academic disciplines like economics and political science, which are focused on research, and professional schools like schools of law, business, and medicine, which emphasize both research and the training of the next generation of nonacademic practitioners.

The policy school can lose the advantage of its unique position and function if it leans too much to one side or the other—sacrificing scholarly rigor to the tradecraft of policy making and public management, or, what is arguably a more striking danger, too closely imitating disciplinary departments and turning, in practice, into a conventional economics department or political science department under another name.

This is meant as a cautionary note and not as a criticism of academic departments elsewhere in the university. On the contrary—the potential for constructive partnership between disciplinary departments and the public policy school is greatest if each provides different and unique contributions. Some examples of these programs are briefly described next.

CONGLOMERATE DEPARTMENTS

Some public policy schools are administratively placed within a multidisciplinary department. For example, at Arizona State University, public affairs is imbedded in the College of Public Service and Community Solutions along with criminology, social work, and community resources and development.

JOINT DEGREES

Many public policy schools offer joint degrees with law, business, and health. Students apply specifically for the joint degree program. These programs generally require students to meet core requirements for each program, and they provide flexibility to enroll in either cross-listed or native school electives.

DUAL DEGREES

These programs differ from joint degree programs in that students apply to, and are accepted into, each individual degree program, and they must meet all of the requirements for each program. Partner schools may make exceptions to requirements depending on individual student credentials.

SPECIALIZATION, PORTFOLIO PROGRAMS, AND CERTIFICATES

These programs are a variation of the dual degree program model. Policy students can receive formal recognition for taking a series of preordained, limited courses on a specific theme—for example, nonprofit, philanthropy, data computation, and specific regional studies. These are not separate degree programs but simply an attempt to allow students to show that they have received endorsed training within a specific study area.

Emerging Models

While the hybrids just discussed are well established and growing in some areas, there are other models that offer policy schools significant opportunities to affect policy immediately and to increase the visibility and relevance of programs in the broader policy community. Some emerging models involve partnering with entities external to the university, others operate within the university setting, and others are in nascent stages of consideration.

To create these programs, policy schools would have to adjust traditional governance and funding practices. Despite these challenges, the salient features of these models are worth exploring.

INTERNAL PARTNER PROGRAMS

It is clear from the popularity of joint and dual degrees that students want the benefit of understanding public policy while attaining more in-depth knowledge in specific disciplines. One model may be to better integrate the curricula required in each program by establishing joint responsibility for creating course requirements that more directly blend the knowledge and skills instilled in policy education with those assigned to the study of specific disciplines.

In contrast to the approach of adjusting requirements for dual and joint degree programs, another approach may be to establish courses that are specifically tailored as stand-alone electives for graduate students enrolled in other departments. These courses would offer foundational concepts in policy analysis, policy deliberations, and political influences. Students could receive a certificate or some other credential for having successfully completed the program.

EXTERNAL PARTNER PROGRAMS

Policy schools have begun to design public policy graduate degree programs that are offered in full partnership with think tanks, nonprofits, for-profits, and governmental entities. These emerging models could be studied and shared to determine the feasibility of more widespread adoption. Schools also should consider delivering their programs primarily in the partner entity's physical location. These partnerships could extend to international, global entities. These models differ from online degree-granting programs since students would be in locations where policy work is actually being conducted. Partner leadership and staff and policy school faculty would develop the program, teach courses, and determine and oversee experiential components of the program.

Students would benefit from acquiring a tacit understanding of a variety of policy environments and be exposed to practitioners and their challenges. Partners would benefit by exposure to faculty and their expertise.

COMBINATION

The discussion of emerging models thus far has attempted to stay within current university protocols, but there may be other models for policy schools to consider. The ones offered here would provide the opportunity for policy schools to mix academic learning with experiential lessons that take place in a policy or administrative setting.

- Breakup: Students enroll in policy school for one year, followed by one to two years of work, during which they receive credit along with counsel by faculty and mentors. They return for one more year of study. The last year of undergrad could serve as the first year of the graduate program.
- Pulse: Students enroll in a policy school where courses are taught on a wide range of timetables outside of the traditional structure of once a week for fifteen weeks or courses are offered during semester breaks. The design of these courses would include intervals when students are in academic settings and intervals in which students are

in policy communities. This differs from the traditional internship or clinical placement in that students would be placed in several settings throughout their studies and these settings would be closely aligned with course content.

- Apprenticeship: Students would enroll in policy school for one year, after which they would work within a policy community relevant to their career objectives and continue their studies online in areas that are relevant to their jobs, with cohorts pursuing similar careers.

While innovations in the way curricula are constructed, the settings in which they are offered, and the timing and sequencing of core courses are critical, the ability to achieve these transformations is predominantly determined by the agility and talent of faculty in designing and offering research that is relevant to policymakers and public administrators. The next section of this chapter identifies potential obstacles to this alignment.

Research That Matters: The Perilous Gap Between Academia and Policy Making

The challenges of today's society mean that it is more important than ever that policymakers benefit from our universities in two ways. First, decision makers need to be informed by the best evidence and analysis, and second, they need to be advised and supported by public servants who are skilled at moving between the worlds of scholarship and public policy. In the process of meeting these needs, extraordinary forces come into play. Unfortunately, at a time when the expertise gained by research could and should be center stage in policy debates, too often it has been in the wings.

Many have bemoaned the fact that knowledge and discoveries originating in academia are not making their way to policymakers and public managers, while, conversely, policymakers and managers are not considering the data and information needs of researchers (Pollitt, 2017). Often, the problems pursued by policy researchers are not the ones for which policymakers need answers. And the research that is produced is not conveyed in a language and format intelligible to policymakers.

This discontinuity can be attributed in part to an important shift in research from public policy analysis to specialized, discipline-specific research (economics, sociology, political science, education, engineering, and so on).

This shift has had several unintended consequences. Reducing the production of sound policy analysis has diminished the skills and expertise resident in academia needed to teach it. Also, graduates of public policy and management programs may not learn how to engage with policymakers and public administrators in high-stakes, contentious policy deliberations that require common understandings among diverse stakeholders.

These distinctions are important to understand. They may serve as indicators for how we might overcome barriers between policymakers and academics while preserving the unique defining values of each. There remains a lack of breakthrough research that can be applied directly to broad and enduring public policy and public management problems. Even with the current research, there are barriers in applying that research to immediate policy and management problems. Many of the barriers arise from the norms and culture of the university itself, as well as through the incentives that drive them and the expected outcomes they generate.

Norms and Culture
SPECIALIZATION

Specialization makes it more challenging to seek commonalities across research findings originating from multiple disciplines. This narrows the applicability of the research. It also can result in neglecting important questions, instilling overconfidence in results, ignoring contrary results, restricting the range of insights emerging from research, and finding commonalities among research findings. These are all critical mistakes that graduates of policy schools should avoid.

Research specialization does not fully account for the gaps that exist between policy and management schools and those that practice policy. Few would deny that the environments in which academic scholarship, policy management, and policy making take place are distinct. They differ along a broad array of factors ranging from their core values to the incentives that govern their behavior.

CORE VALUES

Academia values objectivity above all. Concerns arise about blurring the line between research and advocacy; policy making in a democratic system takes place in an inherently political environment. What makes knowledge valuable to policymakers is ultimately its ability to enable them to make better decisions and to act based on knowledge, not opinion. If knowledge does not improve decision-making, then what is the point?

EXPRESSION

Academics are trained to present their work in technical language, which often is not easily understood by policymakers, who seek the "short and sweet" "in plain English." For their work to be accessible to policymakers, researchers have to be skilled in translating complicated, technical, and methodologically saturated articles into clear, concise, and direct language.

SCALE OF PROBLEMS ADDRESSED

Progress in academic research tends to be made in small increments within specialized niches. Many policy issues, however, such as health-care reform, financial-sector reform, environmental protections, immigration, and transportation policy, are considered in larger and interconnected pieces as comprehensive proposals. Add to this the implications of global features of policy and the scale expands.

DEGREE OF DOCUMENTATION

Academia tends to value longer, coherent studies based on well-designed, well-documented, and well-maintained databases. While policymakers use longer research studies, they also rely on individual pieces of information, which are neither collected on a consistent basis nor standardized across sources.

STARTING POINTS

Academic research tends to take the state of knowledge in the field as the starting point and then work to extend the frontiers of knowledge from that starting point. Policy making tends to start with the state of affairs in the world as its starting point and try to make changes to existing policy to address a problem with the status quo.

METHODS

A significant volume of research conducted in the policy and public management arenas focuses on program evaluation, randomized control trials, evidence-based research, cost-benefit analysis, and return on investment. While these methods are important, they mainly serve as inputs to actual deliberations taking place closer to the government. The elevation of these methods as superior to those focused on experiential learning and problem solving makes it difficult to create a narrative that communicates the relevance of these research endeavors outside academia. Indeed, when research along these lines does migrate from the academy to practice, it may do so by a process that is somewhat random or, in the worst case, selective and partisan. In addition, the nature of methods used tends to define the nature of the problems worth investigating and the data sets needed to answer them. As a result of the combination of these two issues, it is increasingly the case that the methods of the field cause a disconnect with policy relevance.

INCENTIVES

Incentives governing the academic community may discourage necessary activities that support the diffusion of relevant research to the policy communities. For example, requirements for earning tenure place nearly exclusive weight on publications that appear in scholarly, peer-reviewed journals, while little to no credit is given for research that is disseminated in popular press and media or through public agency venues (for example, news articles, congressional testimony, executive agency reports, and so on). Standards for publication often require significant discussion of research design and methodology, the contents of which are not easily understood by policymakers. External funding for research often uses publication in scholarly journals, counts the number of times research products are cited by other researchers, and assesses past research awards to award new research funding proposals. And finally, while cross-disciplinary research is often most useful to policymakers, universities often do not provide incentives for departments to collaborate better and integrate their research more fully.

Together, schools of public affairs could do much more to shift tenure standards. The real problem is that no school wants to stand out from the crowd and allow itself to be beaten by schools that hire scholars whose work is deemed superior.

Expected Outcomes

THE IMPACT OF RESEARCH ON POLICY

The scholarly community focuses on the direct impact of specific pieces of research, but policymakers may be less concerned about the latest research findings and more in need of the collective wisdom and judgment that come with years of research. Also, and importantly, there is no agreed-on systematic way of demonstrating or measuring the impact research has on practice.

TIMING

Publication of academic output has its own time cycles based on journal review timelines and book publication timelines. These timelines are not always synchronized with the timing of legislative policy development and action. If one is a minute late in the policy-making arena, one is not relevant. Adding to this problem is the fact that much of public affairs research is based on data sets that define the problem and are often years old before the research begins. That creates both tunnel vision on questions and a backward-looking focus.

RELEVANCE

Early efforts among researchers and policymakers to better define the data and information needs of both sectors have not been conducted on a regular and consistent basis, thus leading to a misalignment between research and its use in policy-making deliberations. Policymakers believe that research can benefit them but do not regard many research topics as focusing on immediate, key issues of relevance.

FOCUS OF INTEREST

Academics work on problems of their own choice that interest them, seeking fundamental discoveries about how people and things work. In comparison, policymakers often have to solve problems not of their own choosing but out of necessity. They have to work toward solutions that permit pragmatic muddling through. Policymakers are forced to choose among competing values, like efficiency, effectiveness, fairness, and equity, and to navigate the tensions between who wins and who loses. The upshot here is that academics complain that policymakers do not pay attention to them and their work, but they do not take cues from policymakers about the issues where they most need answers.

COMMUNITIES AND RELATIONSHIPS

The academic community tends to be oriented locally around campuses and departments and nationally around disciplines and subdisciplines. State and national policymakers have an entirely different ecosystem of policymakers, think tanks, and trade associations. Thus, it is not necessarily easy for academics to come to be trusted members of the broader national communities.

EXPECTATIONS ESTABLISHED BY 24/7 AND
PARTISAN NEWS OUTLETS

The growth of the 24/7 news cycle and the proliferation of partisan news sources have placed pressure on policymakers to know and have a learned opinion on nearly every current event and active policy issue. This often leads to them seeking information from those who can offer it quickly.

The academic community is not generally sensitive to news cycles, does not have immediate access to policymakers, and is not skilled in marketing expertise directly to policymaking communities.

In sum, finding ways to overcome practices and cultures that separate the scholars from the practitioners of public policy is necessary if public policy schools are to flourish in the twenty-first century.

Conclusion

The public policy school has been a historic success. But resting on past successes is not an option. To earn a critical role in securing the capacity of this nation to design and implement sound policy and to execute that policy in an efficient, effective, and equitable way, schools have to understand their role and to meet challenges to that role in the current policy environment. These challenges in part require adapting to the new and growing complexity of public policy, the explosion and reach of new media, the rise of rival policy experts and advisors, and the new and changing landscape of political powers. To secure future success, schools should focus on their core, foundational mission and how to advance that mission by rethinking curricula, experimenting with and developing new alliances on and off campus, and advancing research that is useful and accessible to policymakers.

Curricula are the keystone of policy schools. Determining the most appropriate course content and inventory will lay the foundation not only for early success of graduates but also for their continued career development. Engaging in continuous curricular review and redesign is essential to ensuring that students are exposed to new ways of thinking about policy problems, new methodologies to study them, and new approaches to learning. While stable, foundational curricula are the result of regular adjustments, the enduring relevance of the curricula depends on schools' willingness to step back and consider transformational change. The changes in the current policy environments and the demands placed on those operating in those environments offer an opportune moment for schools of public policy to consider transformational reforms that involve not only the curricula but also who designs it and where it is delivered.

Exploring opportunities to form alliances with partners within and outside the university further enriches the expertise and experience to which policy school faculty and students are exposed. While policy schools have been pioneers in undertaking interdisciplinary collaborative research, they must also be open to developing alliances with partners beyond the academic setting and for reasons beyond research. To provide students with knowledge and to offer them experience in "real-life" situations, policy schools traditionally have used internships. Perhaps they should consider developing alliances in which their partners are full participants in the development of the curricula, help teach the courses, and provide the actual physical setting in which courses take place. Ways to exploit the full potential of what some may see as uncommon instructional alliances (with private companies, nonprofits, and public-sector agents) are worth exploring.

Additionally, at a time when we need more collaboration, more mutual understanding, and a diverse base of knowledge to apply to policy challenges, the research generated by scholars in policy schools often reflects narrow, singular policy niches. This focus may not be intentional but rather a natural outcome of tenure protocols, which reward selected research that is published in selected journals that are themselves governed by the very researchers who have successfully published in those journals.

Research that is used by policymakers because it is relevant to their immediate needs is often not recognized by the university when making promotion decisions. Research outcomes that result from tensions that policy school faculty must navigate to be awarded tenure and promotion may lose their relevance to ongoing policy deliberations. The barriers to the advancement and support of relevant policy research are inherent in university tenure and promotion rules that are driven by an academic culture that diminishes the value of communication to policymakers. Reconciling these differences is crucial to the role research plays in policy formulation.

Policy schools have a strong and noteworthy history. Their legacy lives in the contributions of their alumni, who lead in all sectors of society here in the United States and around the globe; in the relevance, standing, and rigor of the research produced by their faculty; in the engagement they promote with their academic colleagues; and in the alliances they form with diverse stake-holders. These schools have endured over half a century because they have been relevant, because they have attracted smart and passionate faculty and students, and because they have a mission that is fundamental to the health of our society—supporting the needs of maintaining an informed citizenry.

Celebrating a school's legacy comes with the responsibility of ensuring its endurance. Public policy schools face no lack of innovative ideas for how to transform the way they think and work. What is lacking is a sufficient commitment to recognizing these new ideas, establishing ways to vet them, and sustaining efforts to implement them.

Policy schools are uniquely positioned to lead the transformation of public policy education, enabling researchers, practitioners, and policymakers to join together to advance knowledge, to share discoveries, and to generate ideas for improving public policy.

The German poet Goethe wrote, "Whatever you can do, or dream you can, begin it. Boldness has genius, power and magic in it." Now is the moment for boldness in rethinking and reinventing the public policy school.

Notes

1. This chapter uses the term *public policy school* to refer to schools of public affairs, public administration, public service, and public policy. The distinctions among these programs do not affect the basic premises on which this chapter is based.

2. In October 2017, the Lyndon Baines Johnson School of Public Affairs hosted a summit of deans of public policy schools to discuss challenges and opportunities faced by the schools. This section and the next contain some of the ideas generated at that summit.

3. For a review of tenure standards, see Volcker Alliance (2017).

Bibliography

Evans, Angela M. 2015. "Reflections of an Accidental Analyst." *Journal of Policy Analysis and Management* 34 (2): 256–66.

Pollitt, Christopher. 2017. "Public Administration Research Since 1980: Slipping Away from the Real World?" *Journal of Public Sector Management* 30 (6/7): 555–65.

U.S. Government Accountability Office. 2018. *Trends Affecting Government and Society*. GAO-18-396SP. Washington, DC: U.S. Government Accountability Office, February 22, 2018. https://www.gao.gov/products/GAO-18-396SP.

Volcker Alliance. 2017. "Tenure and Promotion at Schools of Public Affairs." Working paper, Volcker Alliance, New York.

CHAPTER 12

The Emerging Public Leader

Characteristics, Opportunities, and Challenges

Norma M. Riccucci

In 1995, I wrote a book, *Unsung Heroes* (Riccucci, 1995), that profiled six high-level career bureaucrats in the federal government. In addition to the six senior executives, I interviewed a multitude of elected and nonelected officials who had experience working with those six bureaucrats. I asked these officials—among them Vice President Al Gore, Secretary of State George P. Shultz, Surgeon General of the United States C. Everett Koop, and South African antiapartheid activist Albertina Sisulu—to identify one of the main characteristics that contributed to their success as public servants. The consistent response was effective leadership. Today, the best-selling books on what drives successful organizations continue to designate leadership as a key element. Most of these blockbusters cover private firms or corporations, or generic leadership.[1]

While some of the elements of effective leadership cross sectors, the institutions and environment of government create differences among public leadership styles and behaviors. The public focus makes the unique challenges of leading in a constitutional democracy a primary driver. Moreover, politics plays a pivotal role; not the personal or office politics that every organization experiences and endures but rather partisan politics, which is endemic to public organizations and affects the efficacy of public leaders. And it is this political context, as we will see, that creates obstacles and opportunities for public servants to successfully lead in government during turbulent technological, social, and economic times.

Effective leadership is perhaps a key ingredient in rebuilding trust in government. Former chair of the Federal Reserve Board Paul Volcker dedicated his career to improving the work and image of the public service as a means to promote trust in government. Thus, the significance of effective leadership in the public sphere cannot be overstated. Indeed, the field's accrediting body, the Network of Schools of Public Policy, Affairs, and Administration, lists the ability "to lead and manage in public governance" as the number one universally required core competency for master's degrees in public administration and policy programs (Haupt, Kapucu, and Hu, 2017; Network of Schools of Public Policy, Affairs, and Administration, Commission on Peer Review and Accreditation, 2014).

In the Beginning

Public leadership has historically captured the interest of academics and practitioners. Early representations of effective leadership include Luther Gulick's (1937) PODSCORB, or efficacy in planning, organizing, directing, staffing, coordinating, reporting, and budgeting, as well as the work of Mary Parker Follett (1941). Since these early treatises, leadership, whether public or private, has perhaps been overanalyzed and oversold. Simply punching the term *effective leadership* into Google's book search returns almost one million hits. But interestingly enough, these many treatments on leadership have overlapping qualities, in that no matter how it is sliced, certain elements of effective leadership continue to rise to the top even today, and some of those elements reflect the influence of the early voices just mentioned. Moreover, despite patterns of disruptive technological, social, or economic change over time, certain leadership characteristics have endured. Teddy Roosevelt, for example, faced such upheavals with the rise of the Industrial Revolution in the early twentieth century, but tried-and-true leadership styles worked for him, just as they work today as environmental forces continue to upend American society.

Influential, forward-thinking experts of effective leadership such as John M. Bryson, Barbara C. Crosby, Barbara Kellerman, and Daniel Goleman point to such critical factors as long- and short-term planning, the coordination of leadership tasks and work groups, effective communication and connectivity, navigation through budgets and personnel regulations, and the successful management of competing interests. But these experts further identify contemporary issues and concerns that reflect the complexities, uncertainties, and challenges of leading in the twenty-first century. As they recognize, the world has evolved dramatically since early writings on leadership began to appear, as has government's response to those changes. Today, our populations and workforces have become increasingly socially diverse. Emerging leaders, the current experts maintain, must share power and leadership responsibilities, successfully manage diverse groups and collaborate across sectors and global boundaries, adapt according to environmental demands, exhibit integrity and emotional intelligence, and manage during national as well as international crises. The political, cultural, economic, and technological environment within which public servants lead calls for such skills, tools, and actions (Goldstein, 2016). Given the dramatic changes over time, I next address the context within which public leaders of today and tomorrow must navigate to lead successfully in government.

The Context

The U.S. government was founded on the principles of a constitutional democracy. James Madison's *Federalist Papers* Nos. 47 and 51 provided the core framework of American politics (Madison, 1788a, 1788b). He set forth the basic tenets of American constitutionalism: separated institutions and checks and balances. The separation of powers ensured that power would be shared by the three branches of government—the executive, legislative, and judicial branches—and that the powers would be checked by each to ensure that no single branch dominated. The accumulation of powers in any single branch would constitute a threat to liberty, justice, and democratic rule. A further check-and-balance force can be seen in the operation of federalism in the United States. Our system of government has been seen globally as the very foundation of liberal democracy. Its historical and political significance has endured, and it has become a symbol of constancy and accountability. It is the sine qua non of how laws and policies are made in the United States and serves as a blueprint for how leaders must lead and promote democratic governance.

The very structure of our federal system makes managing and leading more complex and complicated. For example, an inordinate amount of planning, collaboration, negotiation, and compromising ultimately led to passage of President Barack Obama's Affordable Care Act in 2010. But no sooner had it passed than the National Federation of Independent Business filed suit against the government, claiming that the individual mandate to buy health insurance was unconstitutional. The U.S. Supreme Court in *National Federation of Independent Business v. Sebelius* (2012), in a slim majority, upheld that provision of the act as a constitutional exercise of Congress's taxing power. But, the individual mandate was then repealed in late 2017 with the passage of a tax bill by a GOP majority in Congress. There have been additional challenges (for example, *King v. Burwell* [2015]), but the ultimate downfall of the entire Affordable Care Act may come as a result of the quintessential emblem of our constitutional democracy: the election of a new president, one whose party affiliation differs from President Obama's. Indeed, an early effort by the Trump administration to gut the entire act failed, but it is conceivable that renewed efforts will result in it being dismantled even if only incrementally. For example, the Justice Department filed a legal brief in a recent lawsuit filed by twenty states supporting the states' position that the protections for people with preexisting conditions are unconstitutional (for example, see *Texas v. U.S.* [2018]). If the act is ultimately repealed, it must be credited not to poor leadership and management of specific individuals charged with developing and "faithfully" administering and executing the law but rather to a function of our system of government.

Perhaps the greatest challenge emerging public leaders face today is what Donald F. Kettl (2015) has called "hyperpartisanship," which is the massive gridlock between presidents and Congress. In particular, during the Obama administration and now under the Trump administration, an intransigent Congress has forced presidents into taking executive action. When majority leaders in Congress are unable or unwilling to muster the support for passage of a law, notwithstanding the party in office, a strong president will issue executive orders and other administrative actions to get the job done. President Obama moved ahead on his Clean Power Plan, aimed at reducing global climate change, in the face of Congress's reluctance or inability to address the matter. President Trump, frustrated with congressional failure to fulfill his campaign promise to dismantle the entire Affordable Care Act, has begun to chip away at the act via executive order. So what is the significance of hyperpartisanship and political polarization for the emerging public leader? It will push more of the decision- and policy making into executive agencies, necessitating strong leadership at this level of government. This is not to say that executive orders cannot be neutralized by Congress or the courts, but it will be the work of strong leaders going forward in agencies charged with developing and administering executive actions to get the job done.

Again, leading successfully in our constitutional democracy does not ensure that outcomes will endure. Nonetheless, there are unique sets of skills and qualities of leaders who operate successfully in the complex environment of governments at every level. And importantly, effective leadership requires a diverse set of skills to lead government across political jurisdictions, as well as within the organization or agency, at the workforce level.

The Significance of Effective Leadership

As noted, there are several elements of effective public leadership that have been identified by leading experts, as well as through my own observations, research, and decades of interaction with mid- to upper-level public servants. These elements include demonstrating the ability to share power and leadership responsibilities, collaborating across sectors and global boundaries, embracing inclusiveness and diversity, adapting to extant environmental demands, exhibiting integrity and emotional intelligence, managing during crisis, managing for results, and investing in public employees at every level (see Chapter 10, where Paul R. Verkuil addresses the knowledge, skills, and abilities that federal employees will require in the future). These are some of the key characteristics of the emerging leader that have been recognized by government officials at every level, and by the researchers who have studied them. These key features are important at the broader, governmental level, as well as within the organization or workplace.

Sharing Power and Leadership Responsibilities

Past and current leaders consistently argue that fostering teamwork and collaboration is critical for success. Public leadership is not a singular, isolated enterprise. It takes building effective teams to successfully govern. Leadership experts Barbara C. Crosby and John M. Bryson (2005, 14) point out that "singular models of leadership don't match the needs of the twenty-first century. Shared and widespread leadership is required for dealing with the effects of global complexity and interdependence, from economic shifts to climate change to terrorism."

Examples abound here, but one can be seen in Leon Panetta's experience as director of the Central Intelligence Agency. Panetta enjoyed a long career in public service, having served in Congress and in both the Clinton and Obama administrations. Focusing mostly on budgetary issues in Congress (for example, he chaired the U.S. House Committee on the Budget), President Clinton appointed Panetta to serve as director of the Office of Management and Budget and later as his White House chief of staff to help negotiate the budget. In 2009, he was nominated by President Obama and confirmed by the Senate for the post of CIA director. The appointment raised a host of concerns in the Washington establishment because of his lack of experience in intelligence. In his memoir, *Worthy Fights*, Panetta (2014) acknowledges that he had no prior experience in covert action or intelligence gathering and, thus, his various responsibilities posed a number of hurdles. But, based on his previous experience, a good understanding of and ability to adapt to his environment allowed for the transferability of his leadership skills. He enjoyed a good deal of success in leading the CIA, the agency most directly responsible for hunting leaders of al-Qaeda around the world, because he assembled a senior team to share in leadership responsibilities. His ability to manage conflict between political appointees and professional career staff was vital. This greatly improved communication within and among the various components of the agency. It allowed for a diverse set of voices to be heard, created greater commitment among the players toward strategies and goals, allowed for greater creativity, and reduced stress levels of those involved. In his own words, Panetta (2014, 466) views shared leadership responsibilities as critical to guaranteeing that America's "enduring values—integrity, hard work, respect for others, courage—be preserved and honored. The next generation of Americans needs them just as much as mine did."

Collaborating Across Sectors and Boundaries

Crosby and Bryson (2010) have long argued that the ability to effectively tackle such intractable problems as the HIV/AIDS crisis, global climate change, homelessness, and poverty requires collaboration across boundaries and sectors. We continue to learn every day that many of America's major challenges and threats no longer stop at jurisdictional or national borders. Emerging public leaders will be increasingly asked to work across boundaries and to develop coalitions and partnerships. These partnerships, whether cultural, economic, or political, will be fundamental to addressing and meeting America's challenges.

An example of effective leadership in collaborating across boundaries can be seen in the work of Bill Gibson, executive director of the Southwestern Commission, a regional council of governments in North Carolina. Such councils are multiservice entities with local and state-defined boundaries that deliver planning and technical assistance to their member local governments. They also partner with state and federal governments to deliver a variety of programs, including, for example, caregiver services to older adults and people with disabilities (for example, meals and transportation). An important benefit of regional councils is that responsibility is devolved to lower levels of government, where public leaders are able to develop closer and stronger relationships with their constituents. Moreover, regional councils create economic opportunities for smaller, rural communities. The Southwestern Commission was created in 1965 by a joint resolution of seven western counties in North Carolina and includes their constituent towns. The region is predominantly rural, with a population of around 175,000 (Morse, 2012).

Through partnership, engagement, and collaboration across boundaries, Gibson was responsible for initiating and developing a number of critical programs for the rural communities forming this regional council. In addition to creating invaluable educational networks and housing opportunities, Gibson and relevant stakeholders were successful in creating a sewer treatment facility that benefited a number of rural residents, particularly members of Cherokee Indian communities. Sanitary sewer facilities are a public service often taken for granted. But many rural areas lack such services; the collaborative efforts of Gibson and other public, private, and nonprofit sector leaders led to sustainable grants from a variety of outlets that resulted in the creation of a sanitary district to service thousands of community residents. Key to their success was transparency and clear communication, in particular by deliberately engaging citizens face to face. In short, Gibson's boundary-spanning leadership efforts have created significant public value to the often-forgotten rural populations in western North Carolina (Morse, 2012).

Embracing Inclusiveness and Managing Diversity

Leading across sectors and boundaries also calls for an appreciation of inclusiveness and diversity. Race, gender, ethnicity, and religion play prominent roles in American life. And leading outward or externally compels leaders to embrace diversity and inclusiveness. Emerging public leaders will need to develop skills that will be effective in schismatic national and international environments. The experience of the Sheriff's Department in Los Angeles County, California, illustrates the importance of embracing inclusiveness. Sheriff Leroy D. Baca exercised extraordinary leadership skills in his efforts to build trust within the Muslim community in order to reduce tension and fear of law enforcement among members of that community. The relationship had reached a low point as a result of increased surveillance and investigations of Muslims by the federal government after the 9/11 attacks, a systematic practice occurring nationwide. Sheriff Baca had a multifold strategy. First, he organized meetings with imams and Muslim organizations across the county to create an open dialogue. This led to the creation of the Muslim American Homeland Security Congress, comprising the leaders of those organizations who would work with Muslim communities at the grassroots level (Abdeen, 2013).

In addition, Sheriff Baca was successful in creating the position of a Muslim community liaison officer to help restore community trust, build bridges, and develop educational programs for Muslims. He assigned a Muslim Arab American sergeant from his department to serve in this capacity on a full-time basis. The liaison officer also worked with youth groups, which eventually led to the creation of the Young Muslim American Leaders Advisory Council (Y-MALAC). *Malac* is the Arabic word for "angel." The leadership of Sheriff Baca led to greater cooperation and trust between the Muslim community and law enforcement. Police officers began attending many social and religious events within the community, as well as family celebrations. Islamic centers and mosques in Los Angeles were also kept open. All members of the community were, in effect, active allies in efforts to enhance the safety and quality of neighborhoods. Under Sheriff Baca's leadership, the outlook on crime control and prevention has been expanded by making members of the community active participants in the process of problem solving (Abdeen, 2013). In the coming years, building ties and bridges with Muslim communities will continue to require strong leadership at the local as well as state and national levels, given the resurgence of violence against Muslims in the United States (Pew Research Center, 2016).

Embracing inclusiveness also requires managing diversity at the workforce level. Over the past several decades, every level of government has become more diverse, reflecting the increased diversity in American society.

Much has been written about diversity in the workplace and how leaders can harness this power to promote government decisions that better represent the interest of the nation's diverse populations. A policy statement by the U.S. Office of Personnel Management (OPM), which works with agencies to create a more diverse, high-performing workforce, reads, "We strongly believe that a diverse workforce in an inclusive environment will improve individual and organizational performance and result in better value to customers, clients, taxpayers, and other stakeholders" (OPM, n.d.). People are the key resource for government organizations, during stable as well as disruptive times, to meet their missions and achieve their outcomes.

Cultivating an organizational culture that supports flexibility is necessary for leading effectively in a diverse environment. Key here is the ability of leaders to develop ways to address such challenges as the communication breakdowns and misunderstandings that invariably result from working in an environment with people from highly diverse backgrounds, from different age cohorts, and with different lifestyles. But the opportunities are abundant, and the efficacy with which they are seized by public leaders will determine the ability of governments to successfully serve the needs and interests of the American populace. Effective public leaders will also recognize the impact that diverse clients have on whether an organization succeeds or fails in satisfying the needs and interests of its clients.

One of the key challenges public leaders will face in the coming years is creating opportunities for women and people of color to move to the upper, policy-making echelons of government. At every level of government, data show that higher decision-making levels lack racial, ethnic, and gender diversity. The OPM (2016), for example, has shown that the workforce of the Senior Executive Service level is only 35 percent women; 79 percent of service posts are held by white males, 3 percent are Latino, 3.6 percent are Asian, and close to 11 percent are African American. And, at the General Schedule 15 level, only 4.2 percent of employees are Latino, 6.6 percent Asian, and 10 percent African American. About 50 percent are women, predominantly white (OPM, n.d.). It is time that the voices of various groups are heard at the higher-ranking levels of government. Moreover, diversity contributes to the richness of discussions, deliberations, and, ultimately, outcomes. It also promotes economic security for those who have been bereft of opportunities to move upward in organizational hierarchies. As we move further into the twenty-first century, it would be momentous for public leaders to work toward promoting women and people of color to the senior levels of government bureaucracies. To do otherwise may affect the overall morale of public servants and hinder the ability of leaders to maintain or increase the productivity of their workforces.

Adapting to Extant Environmental Demands

A major focus of Barbara Kellerman's (2015) *Hard Times: Leadership in America* is the environment within which leaders operate, the ideological, political, cultural, economic, and technological milieu that they must gain a perspective of and adapt to in order to be effective. Kellerman calls this "contextual expertise," and it can sometimes present a dilemma, especially in the public sector around party politics. She states that context is not proximate and should be thought of as "a series of concentric circles. The inner ones are your own immediate, proximate, context. The outer ones . . . speak to questions such as, What are the larger forces that impinge on us all? And what are the . . . circumstances with which leaders across the board—American leaders—need be familiar if they are to be effective?" (4). She argues that understanding this more expansive contextual environment is critical for effective leadership.

Paul O'Neill, the Treasury secretary during the first term of George W. Bush's presidency, demonstrated contextual expertise in addressing the serious predicament he faced when President Bush sought to institute tax cuts. O'Neill stated,

> In my stint as secretary of the treasury, I disagreed with the president and his other economic advisors that we ought to do endless tax cuts. I believed then and still believe that we need fundamental tax reform; basically, the tax system we have is a disgrace. At the time, I didn't think we could keep cutting taxes and still have an intelligent fiscal policy—that is to say, one that had a chance from time to time of producing a balanced budget. Standing up for what I believed then and still believe was right was pretty unpopular, especially with the president. (Perry, 2017, 132)

Secretary O'Neill demonstrated a remarkable degree of integrity and courage by saying and doing what he believed was right, given the political and ideological pressures created by the environment within which he operated.

Exhibiting Integrity and Emotional Intelligence

Emotional intelligence, according to leadership expert Daniel Goleman (2012), is understanding one's own emotions and those of others in order to manage and guide thought processes and ultimately behaviors. *Emotional intelligence* refers to such democratic leadership qualities as good listening, collaboration, and the ability to empathize. David Gergen (2000), who served as a White House advisor to four presidents, both Democratic and Republican, suggests that the relevance of emotional intelligence cannot be overstated. Gergen writes, for example, that Richard Nixon never experienced the type of personal hardship that other presidents had endured. He observes that had Nixon experienced personal struggles like those encountered by Franklin D. Roosevelt, he might have reached a level of emotional maturity and "Watergate might have never happened" (38).

Emotional intelligence is a quality that Eli Rosenbaum has exhibited throughout his career as director of the Office of Special Investigations (OSI) in the U.S. Department of Justice. The OSI has focused in part on investigating and bringing suit to denaturalize and deport people from the United States who took part in Nazi acts of persecution and atrocity. Rosenbaum's success was based on his cognitive and emotional leadership and management skills. Dr. Jerome Legge Jr. (2012, 180) writes,

> In working for the OSI, emotion can be both an energizing (wishing to attain justice for Holocaust victims in the first place) and a draining force on the individual worker as the details of genocidal crimes are encountered in everyday experiences. . . . On a daily basis, [Rosenbaum and his staff were] exposed to documents that do not elevate the human spirit; simultaneously, the director and staff must maintain a level of detachment so that they can make objective judgments about whom to investigate or prosecute.

Even in more recent cases of human rights violations, the need for emotional management and leadership was greatly intensified as Rosenbaum met face to face with victims of and witnesses to deplorable human rights violations across the globe. Although often overlooked, emotional intelligence is a key skill for the emerging public leader as it represents the human ability to connect with others on an emotional, more compassionate level.

Managing During Crisis

Perhaps one of the major challenges for emerging public leaders in the coming years is foreign policy, particularly in terms of containing and ultimately defeating the Islamic State in Iraq and Syria (ISIS). The global terrorist attacks sponsored or committed by ISIS have kept the world in a perpetual state of crisis. Major cities all over the world have fallen victim to acts of terrorism by ISIS. In 2016, a truck drove into crowds assembled to watch Bastille Day fireworks in Nice. The attack, for which ISIS claimed responsibility, killed 86 people and wounded 433. In recent years, terrorists radicalized by ISIS have claimed more than a hundred lives in the United States from San Bernardino to New York City. Containing ISIS requires both short- and long-term responses, but because it is so ubiquitous, even the most effective counterterrorism strategies may not ensure defeat. Even if vanquished from Iraq and Syria, ISIS will not disappear. It is an extremist movement that continues to attract followers from all over the world, and it will continue to terrorize populations globally.

Strategies to combat ISIS require courage, grit, and reliance on trusted advisors. In consultation with their top officials, Presidents Obama and Trump have both launched airstrikes against ISIS in Iraq and Syria, relying on a steady stream of bombings from remote-controlled aircraft, drones, and missiles fired from warships. At the same time, U.S. forces have been mindful of the need to mitigate the risk to civilians. In addition, President Obama, with the backing of senior officials such as Hillary Clinton, Leon Panetta, and General David Petraeus, provided arms and supplies to Syrian rebel groups; President Trump ended this covert arms and supplies program, as his administration determined that the effort was failing. America currently has around two thousand troops in Syria, and Trump has committed to maintaining this military presence indefinitely. Polls have consistently shown that Americans oppose sending U.S. ground troops to fight ISIS in Iraq and Syria, but they continue to support U.S.-led airstrikes. Listening to the voices of the American people is critical since the battle against ISIS may never be completely won. Nonetheless, as Gergen (2000, 207) has stated, "Sometimes a leader doesn't solve a crisis; he helps followers get through a crisis."

The situation is incredibly complex and involves numerous governments, along with various rebel and militant groups. But going forward, emerging public leaders must not thwart the values enshrined in our democracy. There are democratic norms and time-honored notions of the common good that must be preserved. This is particularly the case for emerging leaders and their treatment of Muslims in our nation, as terrorist attacks have led to a wholesale backlash against them as a result of their being misguidedly equated with violent extremist groups. Similarly, the rule of law, both constitutional and statutory, must guide the actions and strategies pursued by our government. The untethered reliance on airstrikes by our military, for example, has resulted in a spike of civilian deaths in Iraq and Syria. Human rights groups continue to urge the United States and its coalition forces to change the command climate in order to protect innocent civilians. In short, emerging public leaders will need to be vigilant about the ramifications of the strategies employed in the fight against ISIS.

Public Service Motivation and Managing for Results

The prominent public management scholar James L. Perry has advanced the concept of public service motivation (PSM), which tells us that individuals are drawn to professions in which they can work for the broader common or public good. Effective public leaders are able to leverage employees' motivational dispositions and properly channel them to the programs and policies that will benefit the public (Perry, 1996, 2017). Achieving government's goals depends on leaders' ability to guide, motivate, and manage employee performance. Moreover, citizens' trust and confidence in government depends greatly on its ability to achieve desired results. Sound performance management practices are the key to achieving policy outcomes and ultimately promoting greater accountability to the American people. Because Chapter 8 provides a thorough examination of government performance and its implications for reaching results, the present chapter examines how to manage for results in the context of PSM.

Success in managing performance for results requires leaders to effectively motivate their employees. But the traditional tools relied on by government to motivate public-sector employees have largely been unsuccessful because they have been adapted from the private sector. For example, pay-or-performance plans have failed because money has not proved to be an effective motivator for public employees (Perry, 1986; Pearce and Perry, 1983). Unlike traditional motivational systems, PSM places emphasis on values and intrinsic rewards rather than extrinsic incentives. As such, in motivating their employees, successful leaders will focus on and reinforce the value that their employees' efforts and accomplishments bring to others. That is, they will need to stress the fact that their work is contributing to the improvement or betterment of the lives of the people they serve. This ensures that workers perceive their jobs as relevant, and it will further indicate exactly how their work connects to others (Paarlberg, Perry, and Hondeghem, 2008; Christensen, Paarlberg, and Perry, 2017).

Leaders also need to create pathways for employees to reach organizational goals. This can be accomplished by aligning the goals and values of PSM with employees' attraction to the organization's mission. Engaging workers' existing values is key, and many experts point to transformation leadership as the means of doing so. As Bradley E. Wright, Donald P. Moynihan, and Sanjay K. Pandey (2012, 207) point out, "Transformational leaders direct and inspire employee effort by raising their awareness of the importance of organizational values and outcomes. In doing so, such leaders activate the higher-order needs of their employees and encourage them to transcend their own self-interest for the sake of the organization and its clientele." Transformational leaders are able to generate an appealing vision of the organization's mission for their employees and are further able to ensure that their employees will work toward that vision. As Wright, Moynihan, and Pandey further suggest, "Individuals with higher levels of PSM should be stimulated and moved to action by the salience of public sector missions" (207).

Some research indicates that employees with high levels of PSM are more apt to exhibit innovative behaviors, which in turn leads to a greater desire to achieve organizational goals. Qing Miao et al. (2018), for example, point to the role of leaders here (also see Kroll and Vogel, 2014). They find that leaders can drive innovative behaviors among their employees by tapping into their PSMs. Innovative employees are obviously important resources for an organization because of their ability to generate, promote, and implement new ideas for service delivery, organizational performance, and goal attainment. Miao and colleagues find that innovative workers have a better understanding of how their work corresponds with their values, ideals, and beliefs. This in turn can bolster workers' self-confidence and self-efficacy, which leads to a greater sense of competency on the part of the employees. Ultimately, the propensity to achieve organizational goals is enhanced.

In sum, a number of studies point to the positive effects of PSM on employee performance and work outcomes. By relying on PSM, leaders can encourage workers' innovation, personal growth, and self-esteem to the mutual benefit of employees and organizations.

Invest in Public Employees

A recent e-book published by *Government Executive* (2017) has reported, based on an analysis of OPM employee survey data, that "effective leadership has continuously been one of the lowest-rated workplace categories, and 2016 followed this trend with a score that was lower than all but rewards and advancement" (2). Leading government workforces is extremely difficult, particularly when leaders have little to no control over disruptive sources of change and uncertainty, such as government shutdowns, hiring freezes, and attempts to cut federal employee retirement programs and employment protections. Such conditions call for creativity and innovativeness.

The results of a recent OPM Federal Work-Life Survey suggest two meaningful ways to invest in workers: the use of workplace flexibilities (for example, flextime, leave for childbirth) and participation in work-life programs, which include worksite health and wellness programs, telework, and dependent care (Brill, 2018). The acting director of the OPM, Margaret Weichert, points out that these practices can improve employee morale and sustains high individual and organizational performance. Weichert notes, "Organizations across all sectors of work are consistently challenged by continual changes in the availability of resources, the demand of their mission, and the needs of their workforce. Federal agency and employee values are equally important to the success of Government. These values must be recognized at every level to ensure the Federal workforce is engaged and empowered to best serve the American people" (OPM, 2018).

Leaders can also invest in their workers by successfully managing different skill sets. In particular, governments at every level are challenged to harness the disruptive forces of technology, which has significant implications for human capital systems. President Obama is credited with opening up the federal government to modern technologies. Investments in information technology in particular rose substantially under the Obama administration, including in federal workers' information technology skills. Leaders will need to grasp digital transformations and their potential to transform services, engage customers, and empower employees (see Chapter 3, where Ramayya Krishnan explores whether algorithmic systems will preserve our values and promote trust and accountability in government). Leaders can help keep employees engaged in their work as it relates to technology by introducing them to advanced technologies and making a strong commitment to innovation. And most importantly, because technology constantly evolves, leaders must ensure that their employees' skill sets keep up with the rapid changes. Thus, leaders must be vigorous advocates for training.

Investments in education and professional development are key drivers for enhancing quality and productivity and, importantly, ensuring their sustainability. Investing in workers includes involving workers and key stakeholders in strategic and workforce planning efforts; it also includes providing workers with the critical skills and competencies needed to achieve current and future agency goals. The benefits of investing in workers are numerous, including improvements in job satisfaction and employee morale, worker productivity, organizational communication, employee retention, overall culture of the organization, worker-citizen engagement, and goal attainment. In short, investments in public employees are an investment in the clients and citizens served by government organizations.

Summary: Lessons of Effective Leadership

In the decades ahead, government will continue to face technological, economic, political, and social disruptions, which call for sustained, sound leadership styles and strategies (see Chapters 2, 3, and 4 for a fuller discussion of these issues). These disruptions have occurred in the past, and it was effective leadership that brought successful, positive change. Franklin D. Roosevelt faced one of the worst social and economic crises during his presidency, with millions of Americans out of work and the populace on the left seeking to move this country toward socialism. Managing and leading during turbulent change is not new; but it calls for strong leadership and grit, qualities discussed in this chapter. The key lessons for responsible and effective leadership include the following.

Sharing Power and Leadership Responsibilities

Despite a large amount of research on the benefits of shared power and leadership, organizations remain stubbornly hierarchical. A challenge for the emerging public leader is recognizing these benefits, such as improved organizational performance and outcomes. Shared leadership is particularly valuable when it comes to solving difficult, complex problems, which are pervasive in government. Allowing for input from a diverse set of voices promotes creativity and innovativeness.

Collaborating Across Sectors and Global Boundaries

Collaboration helps build knowledge and, in turn, improves leaders' ability to create public policies for complex issues and problems. Public management experts Rosemary O'Leary and Catherine Gerard (2012) argue that collaboration across boundaries can foster capacity building and lead to better service delivery and more sustainable solutions. It can broaden options, build alliances, and build credibility with others. Collaboration remains a key, functional skill for effective leaders both nationally and globally.

Embracing Inclusiveness and Diversity

America is facing turbulent times ahead, particularly in terms of our ability to engage with the rest of the world. Emerging leaders are challenged to embrace inclusiveness and diversity abroad as they maneuver the tangled web of global politics. Leaders will need to counteract the perception that Washington cares only about its own interests. Emerging leaders at the local and state levels in the United States will also need to address the problem of Islamophobia and increased hate crimes against Muslims. Leaders are also responsible for managing diversity within organizations. Successful leadership requires leveraging the diverse pool of human talent to ensure that organizations are running at their full capacity and striving to meet the shifting demands of the citizenry of this nation.

Adapting to Extant Environmental Demands

Contextual expertise is necessary for the emerging public leader. Ideological, political, cultural, economic, and technological factors can impede leaders if they are unable to adapt to the changes in those realms. Leaders have historically faced these challenges, and falling back on inner leadership skills such as integrity, courage, confidence in one's abilities, and moral probity has served them well, as modeled by exemplars like Paul Volcker.

Exhibiting Integrity and Emotional Intelligence

Essential for public leaders' success is the ability to fully understand and manage their own emotions and recognize those of the people around them. Given the complexities and uncertainties leaders face in the turbulent world of government, a high premium is placed on self-control. Reacting without filtering emotions can create mistrust among colleagues, staff, and clients, seriously disrupting good working relationships. Public leaders must be able to recognize situations that require emotional intelligence, and then exhibit appropriate responses (for example, empathy).

Managing During Crisis

The years ahead will likely bring crises at the national as well as international levels. In particular, ISIS and other jihadist groups will continue to be a threat in terms of terrorist attacks. And even though ISIS has been losing ground in Libya, Iraq, and Syria, it continues to develop transnational networks and sleeper cells across and beyond the Middle East. It also continues its urban guerrilla warfare and terrorism across the globe. As a number of experts have pointed out, the caliphate model will inspire the next wave of jihadist combatants and terrorists (Gerges, 2016). Emerging public leaders will need to exercise the leadership qualities and characteristics discussed here.

PSM and Managing for Results

Responsible, effective leadership hinges on managing public servants and directing them toward achieving organizational goals. Reliance on the values or ideals associated with PSM to manage for results promises to improve the quality of life of the American people, because the attributes of PSM hinge on the inherent drive of workers to serve the public interest. Managing for results is significant for public organizations. Research by the U.S. General Accounting Office (2000) points to a number of benefits, including encouraging leaders "to work across traditional organizational boundaries or 'silos' by focusing on the achievement of results-oriented goals" (6), providing a "results-oriented basis for individual accountability," and maintaining "continuity of program goals during leadership transitions."

Invest in Public Employees

Investing in public servants by fully engaging them will help to build morale and loyalty and lead to better-performing teams. By engaging workers and their teams, leaders are better able to acknowledge their value, foster their growth, and show appreciation for all public servants. Investing in employees can also create pools of capable workers who are ready for promotion, which will also boost morale.

The emerging public leader is faced with both opportunities and challenges. A number of leadership lessons, based on experience and research, have been offered as guiding principles, which are meant to be built on. While there are many characteristics, behaviors, and styles, leadership experts maintain that those addressed here are fundamental for significant, positive, and lasting effects. In the challenging government environment, strong, effective leadership holds out the promise that this nation will remain a paramount, formidable player in the national and international public policy arenas. Strong leaders will help solve national and international problems, making life better for the American people, which can also increase trust in government.

As Paul Volcker stated in a speech to the Excellence in Government conference several years ago, "Trust in our leaders and our officials to instinctively do the right thing has eroded for decades. . . . We have a rare opportunity to get attention, to achieve something of a broad consensus, and to be a catalyst for meaningful change" (Brookings Institution, 2002). Government's success in doing the right thing and rebuilding the public's trust depends on strong leadership, capacity, and incentives for performance, as Volcker advocated and demonstrated during his professional career.

Note

1. I would like to thank Jim Perry, Frank Thompson, and Beryl Radin for their valuable feedback on this chapter.

Bibliography

Abdeen, Mike. 2013. "Lessons Learned and Best Practices: The Outreach Efforts of the Los Angeles County Sheriff's Department Community Policing Method with Emphasis on the Muslim Community." In *Preventing Ideological Violence: Communities, Police and Case Studies of "Success,"* edited by P. Daniel Silk, Basia Spalek, and Mary O'Rawe, 166–77. New York: Palgrave Macmillan.

Brill, Julie. 2018. "OPM Federal Work-Life Survey Results Available." *OPM Director's Blog*, April 3, 2018. https://www.opm.gov/blogs/Director/2018/4/3/OPM-Federal-Work-Life -Survey-Results-Available/.

Brookings Institution. 2002. "Paul Volcker: 'The Time Is Right for Reshaping Government for the Twenty-First Century.'" News release, July 17, 2002. https://www.brookings.edu /news-releases/paul-volcker-the-time-is-right-for-reshaping-government-for-the -twenty-first-century/.

Christensen, Robert K., Laurie Paarlberg, and James L. Perry. 2017. "Public Service Motivation Research: Lessons for Practice." *Public Administration Review* 77 (4): 529–42.

Crosby, Barbara C., and John M. Bryson. 2005. *Leadership for the Common Good: Tackling Public Problems in a Shared-Power World.* 2nd ed. San Francisco: Jossey-Bass.

———. 2010. "Special Issue on Public Integrative Leadership: Multiple Turns of the Kaleidoscope." *Leadership Quarterly* 21 (2): 205–38.

Follett, Mary Parker. 1941. *Dynamic Administration: The Collected Papers of Mary Parker Follett.* Edited by C. Henry Metcalf and Lyndall Urwick. New York: Harper.

Gergen, David. 2000. *Eyewitness to Power: The Essence of Leadership, Nixon to Clinton.* New York: Simon and Schuster.

Gerges, Fawaz A. 2016. *ISIS: A History.* Princeton, NJ: Princeton University Press.

Goldstein, Ira. 2016. *The Federal Management Playbook: Leading and Succeeding in the Public Sector.* Washington, DC: Georgetown University Press.

Goleman, Daniel. 2012. *Emotional Intelligence: Why It Can Matter More Than IQ.* New York: Bantam Books.

Government Executive. 2017. *How to Be a Better Manager.* Washington, DC: Government Executive.

Gulick, Luther. 1937. "Notes on the Theory of Organization." In *Papers on the Science of Administration,* edited by Luther Gulick and Lyndall Urwick, 3–45. New York: Institute of Public Administration, Columbia University.

Haupt, Brittany, Naim Kapucu, and Qian Hu. 2017. "Core Competencies in Master of Public Administration Programs: Perspectives from Local Government Managers." *Journal of Public Affairs Education* 23 (1): 611–24.

Kellerman, Barbara. 2015. *Hard Times: Leadership in America.* Stanford, CA: Stanford University Press.

Kettl, Donald F. 2015. *The Transformation of Governance: Public Administration for the Twenty-First Century.* Updated ed. Baltimore: Johns Hopkins University Press.

King v. Burwell, 576 U.S. ___ (2015).

Kroll, Alexander, and Dominik Vogel. 2014. "The PSM-Leadership Fit: A Model of Performance Information Use." *Public Administration* 92 (4): 974–91.

Legge, Jerome S., Jr. 2012. "Prosecuting Nazi Collaborators and Terrorists: Eli Rosenbaum and Managing the Office of Special Investigations." In *Serving the Public Interest: Profiles of Successful and Innovative Public Servants*, edited by Norma M. Riccucci, 173–86. Armonk, NY: M. E. Sharpe.

Madison, James. 1788a. "*The Federalist* No. 47: The Particular Structure of the New Government and the Distribution of Power Among Its Different Parts." February 1, 1788. http://www.let.rug.nl/usa/documents/1786-1800/the-federalist-papers/the-federalist-47.php.

——. 1788b. "*The Federalist* No. 51: The Structure of the Government Must Furnish the Proper Checks and Balances Between the Different Departments." February 6, 1788. http://www.constitution.org/fed/federa51.htm.

Miao, Qing, Alexander Newman, Gary Schwarz, and Brian Cooper. 2018. "How Leadership and Public Service Motivation Enhance Innovative Behavior." *Public Administration Review* 78 (1): 71–81.

Morse, Ricardo S. 2012. "Bill Gibson and the Art of Leading Across Boundaries." In *Serving the Public Interest: Profiles of Successful and Innovative Public Servants*, edited by Norma M. Riccucci, 160–72. Armonk, NY: M. E. Sharpe.

National Federation of Independent Business v. Sebelius, 567 U.S. 519 (2012).

Network of Schools of Public Policy, Affairs, and Administration, Commission on Peer Review and Accreditation. 2014. *Accreditation Standards for Master's Degree Programs.* https://naspaaaccreditation.files.wordpress.com/2015/02/naspaa-accreditation-standards.pdf.

O'Leary, Rosemary, and Catherine Gerard. 2012. *Collaboration Across Boundaries: Insights and Tips from Federal Senior Executives.* Washington, DC: IBM Center for the Business of Government. http://www.businessofgovernment.org/sites/default/files/Collaboration%20Across%20Boundaries.pdf.

OPM (U.S. Office of Personnel Management). 2016. *2016 Senior Executive Service Report.* Washington, DC: U.S. Office of Personnel Management. https://www.opm.gov/policy-data-oversight/data-analysis-documentation/federal-employment-reports/reports-publications/ses-summary-2016.pdf.

——. 2018. *Federal Work-Life Survey Governmentwide Report.* Washington, DC: U.S. Office of Personnel Management. https://www.opm.gov/policy-data-oversight/worklife/federal-work-life-survey/2018-federal-work-life-survey-report.pdf.

——. n.d. "Federal Workforce Data." FedScope. Accessed May 1, 2019. https://www.fedscope.opm.gov/.

——. n.d. "Diversity and Inclusion." Accessed May 23, 2019. https://www.opm.gov/policy-data-oversight/diversity-and-inclusion/.

Paarlberg, Laurie E., James L. Perry, and Annie Hondeghem. 2008. "From Theory to Practice: Strategies for Applying Public Service Motivation." In *Motivation in Public Management: The Call of Public Service*, edited by James L. Perry and Annie Hondeghem, 268–93. Oxford: Oxford University Press.

Panetta, Leon. 2014. *Worthy Fights: A Memoir of Leadership in War and Peace*. New York: Penguin Books.

Pearce, Jone L., and James L. Perry. 1983. "Federal Merit Pay: A Longitudinal Analysis." *Public Administration Review* 43 (4): 315–25.

Perry, James L. 1986. "Merit Pay in the Public Sector: the Case for a Failure of Theory." *Review of Public Personnel Administration* 7 (1): 57–69.

———. 1996. "Measuring Public Service Motivation: An Assessment of Construct Reliability and Validity." *Journal of Public Administration Research and Theory* 6 (1): 5–22.

———. 2017. "Know Your Values and Be Prepared: An Interview with Paul H. O'Neill." *Public Administration Review* 77 (1): 131–34.

Pew Research Center. 2016. "Anti-Muslim Assaults at Highest Level Since 2001." November 21, 2016. http://www.pewresearch.org/fact-tank/2016/11/21/anti-muslim-assaults-reach-911-era-levels-fbi-data-show/ft_16-11-21_muslimhatecrimes/.

Riccucci, Norma M. 1995. *Unsung Heroes: Federal Execucrats Making a Difference*. Washington, DC: Georgetown University Press.

Texas v. U.S., Case 4:18-cv-00167-O, February 26, 2018. https://www.courtlistener.com/docket/6321938/texas-v-united-states-of-america/.

U.S. General Accounting Office. 2000. *Managing for Results: Emerging Benefits from Selected Agencies' Use of Performance Agreements*. GAO-01-115. Washington, DC: U.S. General Accounting Office. https://www.gpo.gov/fdsys/pkg/GAOREPORTS-GAO-01-115/pdf/GAOREPORTS-GAO-01-115.pdf.

Wright, Bradley E., Donald P. Moynihan, and Sanjay K. Pandey. 2012. "Pulling the Levers: Transformational Leadership, Public Service Motivation, and Mission Valence." *Public Administration Review* 72 (2): 206–15.

CONTRIBUTORS

Sheila Bair has had a long and distinguished career in government, academia, and finance. Twice named by *Forbes* magazine as the second most powerful woman in the world, she is perhaps best known for having served as chair of the Federal Deposit Insurance Corporation from 2006 to 2011, when she steered the agency through the worst financial crisis since the Great Depression. She is a frequent commentator and op-ed contributor on financial regulation and system stability, as well as author of the *New York Times* best seller *Bull by the Horns*, her 2012 memoir of the financial crisis. She currently serves on a number of corporate and fintech boards and is a founding board member of the Volcker Alliance.

William W. Bradley is a managing director of Allen and Company. He served in the U.S. Senate from 1979 to 1997, representing New Jersey. In 2000, he was a candidate for the Democratic nomination for president of the United States. Before serving in the Senate, he was a 1964 Olympic gold medalist and from 1967 to 1977 he played professional basketball for the New York Knicks, winning two NBA Championships. In 1982, he was elected to the Basketball Hall of Fame. He holds a bachelor's degree in American history from Princeton University and a master's degree from Oxford University, where he was a Rhodes Scholar. He has authored seven books on American politics, culture, and economy, including his latest book, *We Can All Do Better*. Currently, Senator Bradley hosts *American Voices*, a weekly show on Sirius XM Satellite Radio that highlights the remarkable accomplishments of Americans, both famous and unknown.

John J. DiIulio Jr. is Frederic Fox Leadership Professor at the University of Pennsylvania and formerly professor of politics and public affairs at Princeton. His awards include the Association for Public Policy Analysis and Management's David N. Kershaw Award and the American Political Science Association's Leonard D. White Award in Public Administration. He has directed research centers at the Brookings Institution, the Manhattan Institute, Public/Private Ventures, Princeton, and the University of Pennsylvania. He has developed programs for low-income children, youths, and families, and he served as founding director of the White House Office of Faith-Based and Community Initiatives. His dozen books include *Bring Back the Bureaucrats* (2014) and *American Government* with J. Q. Wilson, M. Bose, and M. Levendusky (2016).

Angela Evans is dean at the Lyndon B. Johnson School of Public Affairs, University of Texas at Austin. Evans joined the LBJ School in 2009 as clinical professor after forty years in public service to the U.S. Congress, including thirteen years as the deputy director of the Congressional Research Service. She recently served as president of the Association for Public Policy Analysis and Management and on the governing board of the Network of Schools of Public Affairs and Administration. Evans earned a bachelor's degree in sociology and psychology from Canisius College, summa cum laude, and master's degree in experimental psychology with honors from the University of Wisconsin at Madison.

Francis Fukuyama is Olivier Nomellini Senior Fellow at Stanford University's Freeman Spogli Institute for International Studies and the Mosbacher Director of the institute's Center on Democracy, Development, and the Rule of Law. Fukuyama received his bachelor's degree from Cornell University and his doctorate from Harvard in political science. He was a member of the Political Science Department of the RAND Corporation, and of the Policy Planning Staff of the U.S. Department of State. Before coming to Stanford, he taught at the School of Public Policy, George Mason University, and at the Paul H. Nitze School of Advanced International Studies, Johns Hopkins University.

Donald F. Kettl is professor at the Lyndon B. Johnson School of Public Affairs and former dean of the School of Public Policy at the University of Maryland. He is also a nonresident senior fellow at the Partnership for Public Service, the Volcker Alliance, and the Brookings Institution. Kettl is the author or editor of many books and monographs, including *Little Bites of Big Data for Public Policy* (2017), *Can Governments Earn Our Trust?* (2017), *The Politics of the Administrative Process* (7th edition, 2017), and *Escaping Jurassic Government: Restoring America's Lost Commitment to Competence* (2016). He has twice won the National Academy of Public Administration's Louis Brownlow Book Award for the best book published in public administration.

Ramayya Krishnan is dean of the H. John Heinz III College of Information Systems and Public Policy at Carnegie Mellon University. He is the W. W. Cooper and Ruth F. Cooper Professor of Management Science and Information Systems at the university. Krishnan's research interests focus on consumer and social behavior in digitally instrumented environments. His recent government service includes his work on technology policy at the IT and Services Advisory Board chaired by Governor Tom Wolf of the state of Pennsylvania. More information is available at http://goo.gl/PZ9KKy.

Paul C. Light is the Paulette Goddard Professor of Public Service at New York University's Wagner School of Public Service and nonresident senior fellow at the Volcker Alliance. He joined NYU after serving as vice president and director of governmental studies at the Brookings Institution. He also designed new initiatives for civic engagement as the director of the public policy program at the Pew Charitable Trusts, educated future public servants as professor and associate dean of the University of Minnesota's Hubert H. Humphrey School of Public Affairs, strengthened public management as a senior advisor to Senator John Glenn and the Senate Governmental Affairs Committee, and oversaw the research agenda at the National Academy of Public Administration. Light was also a special consultant to the 1989 National Commission on the Public Service, which was chaired by Paul Volcker, and has advised Volcker on public service issues ever since.

Shelley Metzenbaum is a nonresident senior fellow at the Volcker Alliance and a good government catalyst. She led federal efforts to improve government outcomes, cost effectiveness, and accountability as the Office of Management and Budget's associate director for performance and personnel management in the first term of the Obama administration, subsequently serving as founding president of the Volcker Alliance. Before that, she was the U.S. Environmental Protection Agency's associate administrator for regional operations and state/local relations; undersecretary of environmental affairs and capital budget director in Massachusetts; founding director of University of Massachusetts–Boston's Collins Center for Public Management; and director of the Kennedy School Executive Session on Public Sector Performance Management.

Norman J. Ornstein is a longtime observer of Congress and politics. He is a contributing editor and columnist for *National Journal* and the *Atlantic* and an election eve analyst for BBC News. He served as codirector of the American Enterprise Institute–Brookings Election Reform Project and participates in the American Enterprise Institute's Election Watch series. He also served as a senior counselor to the Continuity of Government Commission. Ornstein led a working group of scholars and practitioners that helped shape the McCain-Feingold campaign finance reform act. He was elected as a fellow of the American Academy of Arts and Sciences in 2004. His many books include *The Permanent Campaign and Its Future*; *The Broken Branch: How Congress Is Failing America and How to Get It Back on Track*, with Thomas E. Mann (named by the *Washington Post* one of the best books of 2006 and called "a classic" by the *Economist*); and the *New York Times* best seller *It's Even Worse Than It Looks: How the American Constitutional System Collided with the New Politics of Extremism*, also with Mann. The last was named one of 2012's best books on politics by the *New Yorker* and one of the best books of the year by the *Washington Post*.

James L. Perry is distinguished professor emeritus, Paul H. O'Neill School of Public and Environmental Affairs, Indiana University, Bloomington. He was editor in chief of *Public Administration Review* from 2012 to 2017. Perry pioneered research on public pay for performance, civic service, and public service motivation. His leadership in the field has been recognized with scholarly and professional awards, including the Yoder-Heneman Award for innovative personnel research, the Charles H. Levine Memorial Award for Excellence in Public Administration, the American Society for Public Administration/Network of Schools of Public Affairs and Administration Distinguished Research Award, the Dwight Waldo Award, the H. George Frederickson Award, and the John Gaus Award. He is a fellow of the National Academy of Public Administration.

Norma M. Riccucci is Board of Governors Distinguished Professor at the School of Public Affairs and Administration at Rutgers University, Newark, New Jersey. She is author of several books in the area of public management, including *Policy Drift: Shared Powers and the Making of U.S. Law and Policy*. She has received a number of national awards, including the American Society for Public Administration's Dwight Waldo Award for career contributions to public administration and the John Gaus Award. She is a fellow of the National Academy of Public Administration.

Paul R. Verkuil served from 2010 to 2015 as chairman of the Administrative Conference of the United States, a federal agency whose mission is to improve the performance of all agencies. He is president emeritus of the College of William and Mary, and he served as dean of Tulane University Law School and the Benjamin N. Cardozo School of Law. After practicing law at two leading New York law firms, Verkuil began his academic career at the University of North Carolina School of Law. He has focused his scholarship on administrative law and government regulation, publishing over sixty-five articles and several books, including *Valuing Bureaucracy* (2017) and *Outsourcing Sovereignty* (2007). He is a graduate of the College of William and Mary and the University of Virginia School of Law, and he holds a doctor of juristic science from the New York University School of Law. Among his career highlights is serving as special master in *New Jersey v. New York*, an original jurisdiction case in the U.S. Supreme Court that determined the sovereignty of Ellis Island. He is senior fellow at the Center for American Progress and a fellow of the National Academy of Public Administration.

Paul A. Volcker is chairman of the Volcker Alliance. He served in the U.S. federal government for almost thirty years, culminating in two terms as chairman of the Board of Governors of the Federal Reserve System from 1979 to 1987, a critical period in bringing a high level of inflation to an end. In earlier stages of his career, Volcker served as undersecretary of the Treasury for Monetary Affairs during the early 1970s, a period of historic change in international monetary arrangements. He was subsequently president of the Federal Reserve Bank of New York and in earlier years was an official of the Chase Manhattan Bank.

Volcker retired as chairman of Wolfensohn & Company upon the merger of that firm with Bankers Trust. From 1996 to 1999, he headed the Independent Committee of Eminent Persons, formed by Swiss and Jewish organizations to investigate deposit accounts and other assets in Swiss banks of victims of Nazi persecution and to arrange for their disposition. From 2000 to 2005, he served as chairman of the Board of Trustees of the newly formed International Accounting Standards Committee, overseeing a renewed effort to develop consistent, high-quality accounting standards acceptable in all countries. Upon leaving public service in 1987, and again in 2003, he headed private, nonpartisan commissions on the public service, each recommending a sweeping overhaul of the organization and personnel practices of the U.S. government.

In 2004, Volcker was asked by UN secretary general Kofi Annan to chair the Independent Inquiry into the UN Oil-for-Food Program, resulting in identification of substantial corruption and malfeasance. In 2007, Volcker was asked by the president of the World Bank to chair a panel of experts to review the operations of the Department of Institutional Integrity. That effort has culminated in broad reform of the bank's anticorruption effort. In November 2008, President-Elect Barack Obama chose Volcker to head the President's Economic Recovery Advisory Board, whose term expired in February 2011.

Pursuing his many continuing interests in public policy, Volcker has previously served as chairman of the Trilateral Commission and former chairman of the trustees of the Group of Thirty.

Educated at Princeton, Harvard, and the London School of Economics, Volcker is a recipient of honorary doctorates from each of his alma maters, as well as a number of other American and foreign universities.

INDEX

ACKNOWLEDGMENTS

As I observe in my introduction, this book examines two big ideas—America's broken governance system and the promise of reform ingrained in our political culture. Leading public affairs thinkers have come together to offer readers their insights on key governance challenges faced by the nation and how public institutions and public servants might respond.

The book owes a debt to the many who contributed during the year it took to complete the project. My thanks to the authors, who generously stepped forward to share their expertise, passion, and wisdom. They received my many emails during the course of the book's development with good humor. They responded diligently and carefully to my editorial suggestions during multiple rounds of revisions to their chapters. The contents demonstrate that these contributors are among the best minds in public administration and policy. I developed great respect for them as the book became a reality. Their analysis and ideas deserve to be taken seriously.

My thanks, too, to the staff at the Volcker Alliance. I appreciate Tom Ross, president of the Volcker Alliance, for trusting me to serve as the book's editor. Two staff members from the alliance, Peter Morrissey and Maggie Mello, were my partners in this project from day one. An editor's work can often be a solitary undertaking, but Peter and Maggie were ever present for support, perspective, and advice. Their energy and commitment throughout the project helped to sustain my own. In the home stretch, when we were reviewing editorial style, Henry Owens, another Volcker Alliance staff member, stepped forward to contribute important time and expertise.

I am grateful to the University of Pennsylvania Press's editor in chief, Peter Agree. Peter was instrumental in improving the book as a whole and my introduction specifically. His recruitment of two thoughtful reviewers for the draft manuscript had a demonstrable influence on the book. I also thank the staff of the University of Pennsylvania Press for their professionalism throughout the production process. My thanks, too, to Erin Davis, production editor, and the team at Westchester Publishing Services for excellent copyediting and quality control. The contributors and I were impressed with the attention to detail and committed craftsmanship they exhibited throughout the process.

Finally, I would like to thank Paul Volcker, who has inspired me since I first became familiar with his work as Federal Reserve chair. Paul cares deeply about effective government, twice leading national commissions on public service. He acted decisively as a public servant for many decades, and for that our nation owes him a deep debt of gratitude. His founding of the Volcker Alliance reflects his dedication to securing a strong government and public service for American democracy well into the future. I hope this book adds to his lifelong quest for good government.